Migration, Transnationalism and Development in South-East Europe and the Black Sea Region

The South-East Europe and Black Sea region presents fertile terrain for examining recent international migration trends. The contributions to this book cover a range of examples, from Ukraine and Moldova in the north, to Greece and Albania in the south. By intersecting the three key concepts of migration, transnationalism and development, they offer new insights based on original empirical research.

A wide range of types of migration can be observed in this region: large-scale emigration in many countries, recent mass immigration in the case of Greece, return migration, internal migration, internal and external forced migration, irregular migration, brain drain etc. These migratory phenomena occur within the context of EU migration policies and EU accession for some countries. Yet within this shifting migration landscape of migrant stocks and flows, the fundamental economic geography of different wealth levels and work opportunities is what drives most migration, now as in the past.

This book was previously published as a special issue of *Southeast European and Black Sea Studies*.

Russell King is Professor of Geography in the School of Global Studies, University of Sussex, UK and Visiting Professor in Migration Studies at Malmö University, Sweden. His research interests range widely across the general field of Migration Studies, and include special interest in and research projects on return migration, social integration, remittances, gender, international retirement migration and international student migration. In terms of regions, the main focus has been on Europe, the Mediterranean and the Balkan areas.

Maja Povrzanović Frykman is Professor of Ethnology at the Department of Global Political Studies at Malmö University, Sweden, affiliated to the Malmö Institute for Studies of Migration, Diversity and Welfare. Her migration-related research focuses on concepts and practices in the domains of diaspora and transnationalism, highly skilled migrants and material practices.

Julie Vullnetari is Lecturer in Human Geography at the University of Southampton, UK. She holds a DPhil in Migration Studies from the University of Sussex where she also worked as a Postdoctoral Research Fellow for several years. Her research interests span a range of migration-related areas such as the dynamics of development, intersectionality, ageing and care.

Migration, Transnationalism and Development in South-East Europe and the Black Sea Region

Edited by
Russell King, Maja Povrzanović Frykman and Julie Vullnetari

LONDON AND NEW YORK

First published 2017
by Routledge
2 Park Square, Milton Park, Abingdon, Oxon, OX14 4RN, UK

and by Routledge
711 Third Avenue, New York, NY 10017, USA

Routledge is an imprint of the Taylor & Francis Group, an informa business

Chapters 1-2 and 4-10 © 2017 Taylor & Francis
Chapter 3 © Gabriela Tejada, Vitalie Varzari and Sergiu Porcescu

All rights reserved. No part of this book may be reprinted or reproduced or utilised in any form or by any electronic, mechanical, or other means, now known or hereafter invented, including photocopying and recording, or in any information storage or retrieval system, without permission in writing from the publishers.

Trademark notice: Product or corporate names may be trademarks or registered trademarks, and are used only for identification and explanation without intent to infringe.

British Library Cataloguing in Publication Data
A catalogue record for this book is available from the British Library

ISBN 13: 978-1-138-69572-6

Typeset in Times New Roman
by RefineCatch Limited, Bungay, Suffolk

Publisher's Note
The publisher accepts responsibility for any inconsistencies that may have arisen during the conversion of this book from journal articles to book chapters, namely the possible inclusion of journal terminology.

Disclaimer
Every effort has been made to contact copyright holders for their permission to reprint material in this book. The publishers would be grateful to hear from any copyright holder who is not here acknowledged and will undertake to rectify any errors or omissions in future editions of this book.

Contents

Citation Information	vii
Notes on Contributors	ix

1. Migration, transnationalism and development on the Southeastern flank
   of Europe 1
   Russell King, Maja Povrzanović Frykman and Julie Vullnetari

2. Hierarchies and categorical power in cross-border science: analysing
   scientists' transnational mobility between Ukraine and Germany 17
   Anna Amelina

3. Scientific diasporas, transnationalism and home-country development:
   evidence from a study of skilled Moldovans abroad 33
   Gabriela Tejada, Vitalie Varzari and Sergiu Porcescu

4. Welfare through migrant work: what if the Romanian 'safety valve' closes? 51
   Bruno Meeus

5. Variation in transnationalism among Eastern European migrants in Italy:
   the role of duration of residence and integration 71
   Eralba Cela, Tineke Fokkema and Elena Ambrosetti

6. The migration–development nexus in Bosnia and Herzegovina: Center
   for Local Development and Diaspora seen 'from below' 87
   Bojana Babić

7. Albanian-speaking transnational populations in Switzerland: continuities
   and shifts 103
   Bashkim Iseni

8. Migration, remittances and socio-cultural dynamics: the case of Albanians
   from the Republic of Macedonia 121
   Ivaylo Markov

9. Social development and transnational households: resilience and
   motivation for Albanian immigrants in Greece in the era of economic crisis 141
   Domna Michail

10. Transnational actors in national contexts: migrant organizations in
    Greece in comparative perspective 157
    Jennifer Clarke

Index	179

Citation Information

The chapters in this book were originally published in *Southeast European and Black Sea Studies,* volume 13, issue 2 (June 2013). When citing this material, please use the original page numbering for each article, as follows:

Chapter 1
Migration, transnationalism and development on the Southeastern flank of Europe
Russell King, Maja Povrzanović Frykman and Julie Vullnetari
Southeast European and Black Sea Studies, volume 13, issue 2 (June 2013)
pp. 125–140

Chapter 2
*Hierarchies and categorical power in cross-border science: analysing scientists'
transnational mobility between Ukraine and Germany*
Anna Amelina
Southeast European and Black Sea Studies, volume 13, issue 2 (June 2013)
pp. 141–155

Chapter 3
*Scientific diasporas, transnationalism and home-country development: evidence from
a study of skilled Moldovans abroad*
Gabriela Tejada, Vitalie Varzari and Sergiu Porcescu
Southeast European and Black Sea Studies, volume 13, issue 2 (June 2013)
pp. 157–173

Chapter 4
Welfare through migrant work: what if the Romanian 'safety valve' closes?
Bruno Meeus
Southeast European and Black Sea Studies, volume 13, issue 2 (June 2013)
pp. 175–194

Chapter 5
*Variation in transnationalism among Eastern European migrants in Italy: the role of
duration of residence and integration*
Eralba Cela, Tineke Fokkema and Elena Ambrosetti
Southeast European and Black Sea Studies, volume 13, issue 2 (June 2013)
pp. 195–209

CITATION INFORMATION

Chapter 6
The migration–development nexus in Bosnia and Herzegovina: Center for Local Development and Diaspora seen 'from below'
Bojana Babić
Southeast European and Black Sea Studies, volume 13, issue 2 (June 2013)
pp. 211–225

Chapter 7
Albanian-speaking transnational populations in Switzerland: continuities and shifts
Bashkim Iseni
Southeast European and Black Sea Studies, volume 13, issue 2 (June 2013)
pp. 227–243

Chapter 8
Migration, remittances and socio-cultural dynamics: the case of Albanians from the Republic of Macedonia
Ivaylo Markov
Southeast European and Black Sea Studies, volume 13, issue 2 (June 2013)
pp. 245–264

Chapter 9
Social development and transnational households: resilience and motivation for Albanian immigrants in Greece in the era of economic crisis
Domna Michail
Southeast European and Black Sea Studies, volume 13, issue 2 (June 2013)
pp. 265–279

Chapter 10
Transnational actors in national contexts: migrant organizations in Greece in comparative perspective
Jennifer Clarke
Southeast European and Black Sea Studies, volume 13, issue 2 (June 2013)
pp. 281–301

For any permission-related enquiries please visit:
http://www.tandfonline.com/page/help/permissions

Notes on Contributors

Elena Ambrosetti is an Assistant Professor in Demography at the Department of Methods and Models for Economics, Territory and Finance, Faculty of Economics, La Sapienza University of Rome, Italy. Her main fields of interest are the demography of the Mediterranean countries, population ageing, fertility and transition, gender issues and migration in the Mediterranean area.

Anna Amelina is Professor of Sociology of Migration at Goethe University, Frankfurt am Main, Germany. Her research interests include migration and mobility within the enlarged Europe, transnationalization of social inequalities and intersectional approaches. She is co-editor of a special issue of *Ethnic and Racial Studies*, 'Methodologies on the Move: Transnational turn in empirical migration research'.

Bojana Babić holds a European Master's in Migration and Intercultural Relations coordinated by the Working Group Migration-Gender-Politics at the Faculty of Linguistics and Cultural Studies, the University of Oldenburg, Germany. She also holds an MA in Public Policies of the Euro-Mediterranean from the University of Catania, Italy. Her research interests focus on the broader theme of migration and development as well as return migration, including topics such as the interaction between development policies and migration/return, return migration and social transformations, and how return affects gender relations.

Eralba Cela is a Postdoctoral Researcher at the Department of Economics and Social Sciences, Polytechnic University of Marche (Ancona), Italy. Her main fields of interest are: determinants of remittances and immigrant integration, links between integration, transnationalism and return migration, gender and generational dynamics of migration.

Jennifer Clarke is a doctoral candidate in Migration Studies at the University of Kent, UK, and was previously a Research Associate in the Department of Social Anthropology at Panteion University, Athens, Greece. She also has 15 years' experience working on migration-related themes within the third sector.

Tineke Fokkema is a Senior Researcher at the Netherlands Interdisciplinary Demographic Institute in Hague. Her research interests in the field of migration include the determinants of remittances and immigrant integration, gender and generational dynamics of migration, the contested links between integration and transnationalism, return migration and the reintegration of returnees into society and their extended families.

Bashkim Iseni is a Researcher at the Swiss Forum for Migration and Population Studies (SFM), University of Neuchâtel, Switzerland. He earned his PhD in Political Science at

NOTES ON CONTRIBUTORS

the University of Lausanne in 2005. He is also a director of a Swiss Albanian-speaking news agency and a producer of TV programmes related to immigration and integration in Switzerland ('In & Out', with Radio Television of Kosovo and 'Diversité' with the Swiss TV 'La Télé').

Russell King is Professor of Geography in the School of Global Studies, University of Sussex, UK, and Visiting Professor in Migration Studies at Malmö University, Sweden. His research interests range widely across the general field of Migration Studies, and include special interest in and research projects on return migration, social integration, remittances, gender, international retirement migration and international student migration. In terms of regions, the main focus has been on Europe, the Mediterranean and the Balkan areas.

Ivaylo Markov was born in Sofia, Bulgaria. He has a Bachelor's degree in Ethnology and History and a Master's degree in Cultural Anthropology, from Sofia University, Bulgaria. Between 2008 and 2011 he worked on his PhD thesis ('Contemporary Labour Migrations of Albanians from Macedonia') at the Institute of Ethnology and Folklore Studies with Ethnographic Museum – BAS (IEFSEM), Sofia, Bulgaria. Currently he is Assistant Professor at the Institute. The major fields of his research interest are: migration studies, border regions and border studies, issues of identity, cultural heritage and local development, family and kinship.

Bruno Meeus is a Postdoctoral Research Associate in the Sint-Lucas School of Architecture in Brussels, Belgium and Postdoctoral Research Fellow at the University of Leuven, Belgium. His main research interests build further on his PhD and revolve around the intersection between political economy, transnational migration and housing studies. His current postdoctoral project, financed by INNOVIRIS, is titled: 'Between Local and Transnational Social Mobility of Eastern-European Migrants in Brussels'.

Domna Michail is Assistant Professor of Social Anthropology at the Department of Pre-Primary Education, the University of Western Macedonia, Greece. She graduated from the Aristotle University of Thessaloniki, Greece, and gained her MA in Social Anthropology at the University of Manchester, UK, and her PhD from the London School of Economics, UK. Her academic interests include theories of nationalism and ethnicity, minorities, migration, the anthropology of education and the anthropology of migration.

Sergiu Porcescu is a PhD student at the Institute for Legal and Political Studies, the Academy of Sciences of Moldova (ASM), Moldova. His research focuses on the impact of European values and migration on the modernization of the Moldovan political system. He is also Head of the Moldovan Office for Science and Technology in Brussels.

Maja Povrzanović Frykman is Professor of Ethnology at the Department of Global Political Studies at Malmö University, Sweden, affiliated to the Malmö Institute for Studies of Migration, Diversity and Welfare. Her migration-related research focuses on concepts and practices in the domains of diaspora and transnationalism, highly skilled migrants and material practices.

Gabriela Tejada is a scientist at the Cooperation and Development Center (CODEV) at the Ecole Polytechnique Fédérale de Lausanne (EPFL), Switzerland, where she is Project Leader of research on scientific diasporas and skilled migration. Her research interests include the linkages between skilled migration and home country development, and

NOTES ON CONTRIBUTORS

diaspora transnationalism. She has research experience in countries such as Moldova, India, South Africa, Colombia and Mexico.

Vitalie Varzari is a senior specialist at the Department for European Integration and International Cooperation (DEIIC), Academy of Sciences of Moldova (ASM), Moldova. He is also an early-career scientist with academic interests in highly skilled migration and development, democratization of post-Soviet countries, national and European security.

Julie Vullnetari is Lecturer in Human Geography at the University of Southampton, UK. She holds a DPhil in Migration Studies from the University of Sussex where she also worked as a Postdoctoral Research Fellow for several years. Her research interests span a range of migration-related areas such as the dynamics of development, intersectionality, ageing and care.

Migration, transnationalism and development on the Southeastern flank of Europe

Russell King[a,b], Maja Povrzanović Frykman[c] and Julie Vullnetari[a]

[a]Sussex Centre for Migration Research, School of Global Studies, University of Sussex, Brighton, UK; [b]Malmö Institute for Studies of Migration, Diversity and Welfare, Malmö University, Malmö, Sweden; [c]Department of Global Political Studies, Malmö University, Malmö, Sweden

The South-east Europe and Black Sea region presents a fertile terrain for examining recent international migration trends. A wide range of types of migration can be observed in this region: large-scale emigration in many countries, recent mass immigration in the case of Greece, return migration, internal migration, internal and external forced migration, irregular migration, brain drain etc. These migratory phenomena occur within the context of EU migration policies and EU accession for some countries. Yet within this shifting migration landscape of migrant stocks and flows, the fundamental economic geography of different wealth levels and work opportunities is what drives most migration, now as in the past. This paper sets the scene for the special issue in three ways: first, by defining the three key concepts of migration, transnationalism and development; second, by setting the geographical scene, with the aid of relevant statistics on the migration, development and remittance trends in the various countries of the region; and third, by summarizing the highlights of the papers in this issue of the journal, which range in their coverage from Ukraine and Moldova in the north, to Greece and Albania in the south.

Introduction

The geographical area covered by this journal – especially the line of countries running from Ukraine and Moldova down to Albania and Greece – corresponds to the Southeastern flank of Europe and to a corridor of countries which have been witness to a variety of intense migration processes in recent decades. Some of these migrations – for instance those from Former Yugoslavia – have their origins in the European 'guest-worker' recruitment of the 1960s; others, including population movements in 'post-Yugoslavia', are more recent flows of the 1990s and 2000s. The purpose of this special issue is to present a coherent but diverse set of papers which explore several aspects of the migration dynamics of this border zone.

The papers derive from a workshop entitled 'Migration, transnationalism and development in the Balkans and South-East Europe' held in Amsterdam on

29 August 2012 within the framework of the Ninth Annual IMISCOE conference (IMISCOE is a European research network on 'International Migration, Integration and Social Cohesion in Europe').[1] Much of IMISCOE's work to date has concentrated on the situation of migrants in the main European destination countries and has focused on such issues as the labour market, citizenship, social integration, identity and migration policy. Our workshop was part of a recent initiative within IMISCOE to shift attention to some of the secondary countries, especially those positioned close to Europe, and to the interplay of emigration, return migration, transnationalism and development within these 'borderland' countries.

The call for papers yielded 33 abstracts – far more than we anticipated and far more than could be accommodated within our allotted conference time for one day. In the end, we squeezed 13 papers into the programme: all had pre-circulated drafts to facilitate discussion at the workshop and rapid publication thereafter. The refereeing process honed the papers down to the nine included in this special issue.

The purpose of this introductory paper is threefold: to define the key terms of migration, transnationalism and development; to set the scene in terms of the wider phenomena of migration, geopolitics and development in the European arena; and to overview the papers that follow, highlighting their most significant contributions.

Migration, transnationalism and development

These three concepts and their interactions constitute the *raison d'être* of the collection. Although we never 'imposed' these definitions and understandings on the contributors, all of them subscribed to a more or less common interpretation, with only minor deviations, which are usually context dependent. And all of the papers, each in their own way, address the triple nexus of migration–transnationalism–development.

For the purpose of the papers in this special issue, *migration* means *international migration*. In affirming this, we follow the general tendency to equate migration with international migration evidenced in many recent textbooks – for example *The Age of Migration* (Castles and Miller 2009). But we are also conscious that this is an unfortunate elision which ignores the fact that, on a global scale, as well as in most of the countries within 'our' region, internal migration is on a larger numerical scale than international migration (King and Skeldon 2010).[2] All the papers which follow concern themselves with international migration and leave aside internal movements, except for the briefest mentions. Yet we also acknowledge that blurring the distinction between the two can occur. Movements within the European Schengen area are seen as 'internal' and are unfettered by border controls or even visible borders, yet such movements *do* cross international borders. In the case of the Former Yugoslavia, what was once internal migration has become international through the creation of new states and national borders, some of them, like Croatia and Slovenia, not so easy to cross.

It is self-evident that (international) migration involves crossing an international border; less straightforward is deciding on the amount of time that has to pass before a 'visitor' or 'tourist' becomes a 'migrant'. Many authors defer to the United Nations' threshold of 12 months, but this overlooks short-term migrations which are seasonal or temporary. Particularly around the eastern fringes of Europe, there are forms of cross-border movement, variously called shuttle migration, pendular migration, to-and-fro migration etc., which are constrained by the short time limits set on visitor or tourist visas, the only means of legal entry. Are these to be considered 'true' migration, or do they exemplify some other regime of hybrid mobility? There are few widely accepted definitions or criteria in this area, and our reaction therefore is to promote a flexible conceptualization of migration (sometimes substituting the more apt terms 'movement' or 'mobility') and not to get too hung up on precise statistical criteria.[3] Having said that, we can clearly distinguish between temporary and permanent migration, with or without return, even if what is intended as temporary migration often subsequently becomes permanent settlement. We also recognize the widespread diffusion, especially in many of the countries considered in this collection of articles, of back-and-forth migration and mobility – which leads us to the next term.

Transnationalism has come to be the defining optic in anthropological and sociological studies of international migration over the past 20 years. Although the term had early incarnations in international relations and in studies of multinational firms or 'transnational corporations', its main thrust came from grounded studies of migrants' everyday lives that revealed, to quote a well-worn definition, 'multi-stranded relationships – familial, economic, social, religious and political – that span borders and link societies of origin and settlement' (Basch, Glick Schiller, and Szanton Blanc 1994, 7). The transnational paradigm was effective in countering a simplistic linear vision of international migration whereby migrants moved to another country where, over time, they integrated or assimilated, with some, those either who 'failed' to integrate or who achieved their 'target', returning to their home country at some point in their migration trajectory (cf. Cerase 1974).

Most literature on transnationalism has been crafted in the US context, via studies of Latin American or Caribbean migrants such as Levitt's *The Transnational Villagers* (2001), about Dominican migrants, and Smith's *Mexican New York* (2006). These are studies of long-distance transnationalism where physical distance is a barrier to be overcome for migrants and their non-migrant kin – although recent advances in communication technologies help to overcome the frictions of distance and cost, for those who have access to them. Studies of migrant transnationalism have also been conducted in Europe (see, e.g. Bryceson and Vuorela 2002; Faist 2000); this special issue helps to enrich this field. Particularly relevant in the latter context is the aspect of physical distance between the region under focus here and areas of destination in Europe, enabling travel over relatively short distances, reachable via cheap flights within an hour or two, or by low-cost coach trips of a day or so. Moreover, the possibility of cheap and frequent travel (except where irregular status or homeland conflict prevents this) gives rise to a greater range of intensity of transnational links, including those who do not move but are deeply imbricated in transnational relations. Brunnbauer (2012) endorses the utility of the transnational approach to the study of migration from and within the Balkans and South-east European region, with the proviso that the term be used carefully since 'nation' and 'state', let alone ethnicity, are not synonymous or coterminous in this part of Europe (see also Povrzanović Frykman 2008).

Boccagni (2012, 297) has set out a useful typology of transnational links and activities. Economic transnationalism embraces the sending and receiving of remittances, both financial and in-kind (gifts etc.); investments in land, housing and businesses in the country of origin; and the trading and consumption of goods from the home country (whilst abroad) and from abroad (for those in the homeland). Political transnationalism includes patriotism, long-distance nationalism, homeland-related political activism, distant voting, and the exercise of dual citizenship. Social and cultural transnationalism comprises the largest list: nostalgia and identification with the culture and folklore of the homeland; the 'myth of return' (always waiting or intending to return but never doing so); visits to kin and friends left behind; various forms of non-corporeal communication (phone, email, Skype, Facebook etc.); participation in or support for a variety of civic, recreational, religious or cultural initiatives and events. It is worth noting that the transnational linkages can also flow in the 'other' direction, i.e. from homeland to migrants abroad. Examples are 'reverse remittances', the sending of 'ethnic' goods such as foodstuffs, visits by non-migrants to migrants abroad, and the 'reversal' of transnational links when migrants return-migrate and want or feel the need to keep in close touch with relatives and friends who are still abroad.

It needs to be acknowledged that the transnational paradigm has not been without its critics. This is not the place to enter into this wide-ranging debate with its merry-go-round of exhaustive citations. Key elements of the critique include a tendency to over-extend the term to all international migrants (Portes 2003, 876 affirmed that 'regular involvement in transnational activities characterizes only a minority of immigrants'); an over-exaggeration of the newness of the phenomenon (migrants were also transnational in the past, we just did not use the term); and a tendency to deterritorialize transnationalism and therefore the need to bring back space, place and territory (Mitchell 1997).

This last point is certainly taken on board in several of the articles that follow; moreover, the papers also develop new elaborations on the transnational concept. Anna Amelina, in the next paper, extends the notions of transnational social space (Faist 2000; Pries 2001) and transnational social field (Levitt and Glick Schiller 2004) to arrive at her key concept of 'transnational scientific field' which she then applies to the mobile behaviour of Ukrainian scientists. In the paper that succeeds Amelina's, Gabriela Tejada, Vitalie Varzari and Sergiu Porcescu talk about 'scientific diasporas' and 'transnational communities of knowledge' when referring to the Moldovan scientific and professional migrants studying and working abroad. In another article in the set, Eralba Cela, Tineke Fokkema and Elena Ambrosetti quantify transnational behaviour by a series of survey variables converted into a single index of transnationalism which is then correlated with different types and measures of migrant integration. And finally, Ivaylo Markov points out the inappropriateness of the concept of transnationalism when applied to ethnic-Albanian migrants from the Republic of Macedonia, preferring instead notions of 'translocality' and 'transterritoriality'.

Boccagni's (2012) categorization of transnational linkages into economic, political and socio-cultural provides us with a bridge to our third key term: *development*. It is through transnational practices such as sending remittances to support family members, making business investments in the homeland, returning and developing an enterprise or contributing new ideas and behavioural norms ('social remittances', Levitt 1998) that migrants have the potential to stimulate the development of their home communities and countries. But what, exactly, do we mean by 'development'?

Traditionally, development was considered a purely economic concept and was therefore measured in strictly economic terms, using indicators such as per capita income and the growth rate in gross domestic product (GDP). The economic approach, however, paid no explicit attention to the distribution of income and resources within a country, nor to the broader social components of development such as health, education and other aspects of 'well-being'. Increasingly, however, development *has* come to be conceptualized as a process which is much broader than economics alone – although economic aspects do remain crucial. Some 20 years ago the United Nations Development Programme (UNDP), inspired by the work of 'social economists' Mahbub ul Haq and Amartya Sen, introduced the Human Development Index (HDI). The standard HDI[4] is an amalgam of three elements: *a long and healthy life* (measured by life expectancy at birth), *access to knowledge* (school enrolment and literacy rate), and a decent standard of living (GDP per capita at 'purchasing power parities', i.e. adjusted for different countries' costs of living). The HDI ranges from 0 to 1. A value of 0.9 + indicates very high development, above 0.8 is high, above 0.5 medium and below 0.5 low development (UNDP 2009, 15).

The reconceptualization of development away from a concern only with economic growth and towards recognizing the social, cultural and human rights dimensions of life corresponds to a shift in focus from measuring the wealth and commodities owed by people in a country to evaluating the broader well-being and freedoms of people – 'how human lives are going'. In the view of Dannecker (2009, 121), development is increasingly conceptualized as a dynamic, multidimensional and multiscalar process whose progression is not 'neutral', nor indeed irreversible, but mediated and transformed by the several factors involved. What this view of development means in practice is expanding individuals' opportunities to live long and healthy lives, to be well-housed, well-clothed and well-fed, to have access to adequate healthcare and education, to choose their own lifestyle (within socially responsible limits), to enjoy personal safety and to have the freedom to participate in public debate without fear of recrimination.

Where does migration fit into the evolving discourse on development? First, we distinguish between three levels of interaction and impact: the *micro level* (between migrants and their family members back home); the *meso level* (between the villages or hometowns of origin and the groups or associations of migrants abroad); and the *macro level* (country-wide effects activated by mass migration). These different contexts in turn shape ongoing migration processes, thus forming a dynamic, multi-level interactive system. For labour migrants coming from poor home-country backgrounds, migration can lead to two contrasting transnational family/household models, each with different effects on development. One is where the migrant leaves on his or her own in order to support remaining family members left behind. Remittances are the main transnational economic transaction, and through these, the migrants' spouse, parents, children and siblings in the place of origin can benefit not only from higher purchasing power, but can also afford better healthcare and education. The second model is where the nuclear family migrates as a unit (or achieves family reunification as a follow-on stage of the first model). When this happens the 'migration project' is geared towards making progress in the host society through integration and improved prospects for all concerned, especially the second generation. Remittances fall away, with transnational obligations limited to supporting elderly parents.

Whatever the scale of remittances, villages and towns of migrants' origin can benefit from the multiplier effects of such transfers; even more so if these are meso-scale 'collective remittances', sent as part of migrant hometown associations to improve community facilities such as schools, roads, clinics etc. Social remittances – skills, ideas, attitudes, behaviours etc. – are also potentially part of this 'development through migration' process.

The above picture of how migration can 'work for development' constitutes the positive scenario now in vogue in international policy circles such as the United Nations and World Bank (UNDP 2009; World Bank 2011). This is only one interpretation of what has come to be known as the 'migration–development nexus' (Van Hear and Nyberg Sørensen 2003). Another one, diametrically opposite, and taking its inspiration from Marxist political economy and Latin American dependency theory, sees migration as *under*development locked together in a vicious circle: underdevelopment 'produces' migration, but this takes away the cleverest ('brain drain') and the physically strongest ('brawn drain'), leading to the reproduction of underdevelopment in the emigration countries (Delgado Wise and Marquez Covarrubias 2009). De Haas (2010) has reviewed these competing optimistic and pessimistic scenarios and concludes that the jury is still out as to which bears the closest resemblance to reality. Both models – neoliberal optimist and neo-Marxism pessimist – involve some rather sweeping generalizations and assumptions as well as certain logical inconsistencies; moreover, empirical evidence is extremely mixed too. To the extent that access to migration and mobility has proved to be a route out of poverty for millions in different parts of the world, we endorse the more optimistic scenario and UNDP's arguments for 'overcoming the barriers to mobility' (UNDP 2009). But we should not overlook the harsh fact that we live in a very unequal world where inequalities, both between and within countries, are becoming more marked. Hence the structural factors which shape migration – the unequal distribution of wealth, capitalism's predatory tendencies, the retreat from state welfare provision, global geopolitics and the ability of some powerful countries and supranational entities to control migration – must always be appreciated. With this thought in mind, we turn to the region where the papers in this special issue are set.

Setting the geographical scene

Looking back over the six decades or more since the start of postwar labour migration to Western Europe, and paying particular attention to the countries featured in this journal issue, two major initiatives stand out as fundamental in shaping the migration patterns that subsequently unfolded. The first was the *establishment of the European Common Market* and the inscription into the Treaty of Rome (1957) of the principle of the free movement of labour (and goods and capital). Subsequently, of course, an ever-more 'integrated' Europe progressively enlarged from the original six countries to the current 27.[5] The original intention in 1957 had been to facilitate the movement of poverty-stricken southern Italians to work in the booming industrial economies of France and Germany; but it became apparent that the economics of labour demand was the overriding factor, and the prosperous and fast-growing economies of North-West Europe soon put in place bilateral labour recruitment agreements with a range of non-EEC Mediterranean countries stretching from Portugal across to Turkey as well as the Maghreb states. Two South-east European countries featured in papers in this special issue were drawn into this state-sponsored 'guest-worker' system: Greeks migrated in large numbers to West Germany during the years 1961–1973, whilst migrants from the Former Yugoslavia, who were free to migrate after the mid-1960s, went mainly to Germany and Switzerland (see Fielding 1993; King 1993 for details of this period).

The oil crisis of 1973–1974 closed down this mass labour migration system, although family reunion and marriage migration enabled the flows to continue over the ensuing decades. Meantime, during the 1980s, the southern EU countries, with Spain, Portugal and Greece 'joining the club', started to transform from sources of emigration to countries of immigration, this immigration reaching mass proportions after 1990.

The second turning-point in the evolution of pan-European migration patterns came with the *fall of the Berlin Wall* and the 'liberation' of a whole constellation of Eastern European and Former Soviet Union states from the straightjacket of banned emigration. The problem was that the doors of the EU and other Western European countries were not open to them, except for some refugee flows from the wars in Yugoslavia (mainly Bosnians and Kosovans). Yet there are problems with the 'Fortress Europe' metaphor, which cannot overcome the myth of zero migration (Tsianos and Karakayali 2010, 376). In reality, migration continued to take place and still does, and several papers in this issue show the agency of migrants in rendering the borders permeable. A common strategy was that labour migration became camouflaged as tourist or visitor mobility, or took other irregular forms, at least until some of the former Eastern European countries became incorporated into the EU in the 2000s.

Let us now focus more specifically on the mosaic of countries that form the southeastern border zone from the Black Sea down to the Mediterranean: Ukraine, Moldova, Romania, Bulgaria, the post-Yugoslav states, Albania and Greece. These are a group of mainly small-to-medium-sized countries which have experienced particularly intense migration flows in recent years – in most cases outflows but, in the case of Greece, inflows.[6] Table 1 sets out a range of data for the countries which are the focus of this special issue, although not all the countries listed are covered in equal depth in the following papers. The data refer to the late 2000s, more or less concurrent with the time periods of the research and field data included in the individual papers. In some cases, more recent data are available (for instance the results of the 2011 Albanian census, which reveal a population shrunk to 2.8 million,

Table 1. Selected Black Sea and South-east European countries: population, development, migration and remittances (2007–2010).

	Popn (million)	HDI	Per cap. GDP (PPP US$)	Stock of emigrants		Stock of immigrants		Remittances (US$)	
				000	% popn	000	% popn	per cap.	% GNI
Albania	3.2	0.818	7041	1438	45.4	89	2.8	412	10.4
Bosnia-H.	3.8	0.812	7764	1461	38.9	28	0.7	570	12.3
Bulgaria	7.6	0.835	11,222	1201	16.0	107	1.4	205	3.5
Croatia	4.4	0.871	16,027	754	17.1	700	15.9	335	2.4
Greece	11.3	0.942	28,517	1210	10.8	1133	10.1	179	0.6
Macedonia	2.0	0.817	9096	447	21.9	130	6.3	201	4.3
Moldova	3.6	0.720	2551	770	21.5	408	11.4	336	20.9
Romania	21.5	0.837	12,369	2769	13.1	133	0.6	229	3.0
Serbia	7.3	0.826	10,248	196	2.0	525	5.3	740	12.9
Slovenia	2.0	0.929	26,753	132	6.5	164	8.1	140	0.6
Ukraine	46.0	0.796	6914	6531	14.4	5258	11.6	115	4.8

Note: Data for Kosovo and Montenegro unavailable (except Montenegro HDI 0.834, per capita GDP 11,699).
Source: UNDP (2009); World Bank (2011).

making the scale of emigration even more dramatic), but the earlier data are used in order to preserve vertical consistency down the columns of the table.

Bearing in mind the earlier discussion on HDI and its components and thresholds, we note that the majority of countries in the table have 'high' development (above 0.8 and below 0.9), albeit towards the lower end of the band (except Croatia, 0.871). Two countries have 'very high' development (Greece and Slovenia), although again their scores are at the low end of the class (the migrant recipient countries of Switzerland, Austria, Germany and Italy are all higher). Two countries, Ukraine and Moldova, are at the top end of the 'medium' development category, 0.5 to 0.8.

If the overall figures for HDI for the countries in Table 1 appear somewhat higher than might be expected from the prior discussion, then two comments put the data in a more rational, relational perspective. First, the indices for less developed countries are much lower (e.g. Morocco 0.654, Ghana 0.526, Ethiopia 0.414, Afghanistan 0.352), whilst the top-ranking countries are a bit higher (e.g. Norway 0.971, Iceland 0.969, Netherlands 0.964). Second, the socialist history of most of the countries on the list has boosted literacy rates, health care and longevity so that, for example, countries like Albania, Bulgaria, Moldova, Romania and the post-Yugoslav states are all ranked higher in global rankings on life expectancy and literacy than they are on per capita GDP.[7]

Moving across Table 1 to the migration statistics, several countries – Albania, Bosnia and Herzegovina (BiH), Macedonia and Moldova – have rates of emigration equating to between 22 and 45% of their in-country populations. These ratios are amongst the highest, not only in Europe, but in the world. For post-Yugoslav countries, however, the migration data need to be interpreted with caution: high rates of emigration from BiH and Macedonia and high numbers of migrants from Croatia and Slovenia reflect a history of *internal* migration which the events of the 1990s and the break-up of Yugoslavia turned into 'international' migration. The relatively high number of immigrants in Moldova and Ukraine is largely made up of Russians who moved there before the collapse of the Soviet Union. The other figure to draw attention to is the large stock of immigrants in Greece – 1.1 million or one in ten of the population of Greece – which numerically corresponds closely to the stock of emigrants from Greece, 1.2 million, deriving from an earlier postwar history of emigration from Greece to Germany, North America and Australia.

A final way of measuring the scale and relative impact of migration is through remittance flows, the last element on Table 1. The data show that the economic weight of remittances is especially strong in Albania, BiH, Moldova and Serbia, accounting for between 10 and 21% of Gross National Income. Comparison of these figures with the global rankings in the World Bank's *Migration and Remittances Factbook* (World Bank 2011) shows that these are amongst the highest remittance dependency rates in the world, exceeded only by island micro-states.

The papers

In providing an overview of the papers which follow, we do not merely summarise them – this can easily be done by referring to their abstracts. Rather, what we try to do is highlight the significant and original statements that each paper makes. For want of a better alternative, we order the papers geographically: from the north of the region (Ukraine, Moldova, Romania) through Italy and Switzerland and 'receiving' countries of migrants from Eastern Europe and Kosovo, respectively, to the South-east Europe of the Balkans (Albania, post-Yugoslav states, Greece).

In the first paper, **Anna Amelina** makes two significant contributions to conceptualizing the unfolding dynamics of East-West migration in the post-socialist era, taking as her case material the mobility of Ukrainian scientists to Germany. The first contribution is the innovative concept of a *transnational field of science*, created by the cross-border mobility of scientific personnel, often orchestrated around specific bilateral or multilateral scientific networks, many of which have key personal relationships at their core. The second conceptual advance is to view this transnational scientific space as an *unequal playing field* with an asymmetrical and hierarchical distribution of material, organizational and symbolic resources. Ukrainian mobile scientists define themselves as an *exploited elite*; yet at the same time they are aware of the privileges their transnational connections and experiences give them, especially in their home universities in Ukraine. Gender introduces another dimension into the transnational academic hierarchy, as female mobile scientists are identified as having the most disadvantaged positions – a conclusion which resonates with earlier research on the intra-EU scientific mobility of women (Ackers 2004). In unpacking the complex intersectional relationships involved in this particular form of transnational mobility, Amelina suggests the term *paradoxical ethnicization* to explain the contradictory ways in which Ukrainians (and other Eastern European scientists) are 'welcomed' in German universities, but are then treated (at least in the Ukrainian scientists' eyes) as cheap labour (but this is also manoeuvred by processes of self-exploitation and self-ethnicization), whilst fully being viewed as privileged academics in their home institutions – as one interviewee said, 'My students [in Kiev] say I am their idol'.

The theme of scientific mobility is continued in the next paper, by **Gabriela Tejada, Vitalie Varzari and Sergiu Porcescu**, which is a study of skilled (i.e. graduate) Moldovans abroad and their potential contribution to home-country development. Tejada et al. deploy the notion of *scientific diaspora* to refer to Moldovan postgraduate students, researchers and university-educated professionals working or studying abroad. They emphasize that Moldova has experienced a dramatic loss of its qualified personnel since 1991 due to the country's problematic political transition and low levels of economic and social development. Like Amelina's paper, this one too engages with debates on 'brain drain', 'brain circulation' and 'brain return', but with a different methodological approach. Whereas the previous paper was an in-depth qualitative study of a relatively small number of research participants, the main empirical evidence for Tejada et al. comes from an online survey ($N = 197$) of the Moldovan scientific diaspora. Following the post-1990s rise in the popularity of the transnational paradigm as a relevant theoretical framework for examining how migration interfaces with development, Tejada et al. recognize scientific diaspora as *communities of knowledge* with the potential to act as agents of change in their home countries. Here, their focus is less on remittances (a key element of low-skilled Moldovan migrants' contribution to poverty alleviation and the national balance of payments), and more on knowledge circulation, business investment, and return migration or return visits. On the whole, skilled Moldovans consider themselves professionally or academically successful and well-integrated abroad; however, this does not prevent them from cultivating active transnational links with their home country, nor from having aspirations to help in its development. The areas that the scientific diaspora see as promising include joint scientific research, academic exchange and knowledge sharing, and business development. However, only 1 in 10 of the survey respondents plans to return to Moldova within the next five years. The main perceived barriers to return are the lack of encouragement from the Moldovan government, political instability, the hostility of local society towards successful emigrants and returnees, a general climate of mistrust, low incomes, and inadequate infrastructure.

Romania is the third country in this sequence of northern Black Sea countries with very high rates of recent emigration. **Bruno Meeus** develops a highly original analysis which refreshingly departs from conventional linear descriptions of emigration, labour market insertion, (non-)integration, remittances and their use for development. Based on a critical political-economy theoretical stance, his conceptual take is to view Romanian work migration as a form of welfare which supports the withdrawal of state support of vulnerable people in the neoliberal era. The Romanian migration is thus seen as underpinning a 'grassroots' *transnational labour market and welfare system* which has become a structural element of Romanian society, economy and government policy. The systematic nature of Romanian migration functions as a 'spatial vent' (Samers 1999) which creates a *safety valve* for the population's survival. But, and here's the rub, the safety valve is located in the southern EU countries of Italy, Spain, Portugal and Greece, all of whose economies are now in profound crisis, with severe austerity measures choking off, at least for the time being, employment opportunities. In these stricken Mediterranean economies, local employers' ability to hire Romanian workers in sectors such as construction, small industries, and domestic and care work, is hit by shrinking incomes, falling profits and, in particular, the collapse of the building industry. As the Mediterranean safety valve closes, Romanian migrants are put in a double squeeze by the fact that the financial crisis has hit the Romanian economy as well, which Meeus illustrates with a case-study of the Bistrita Valley (ex-) industrial region. Caught between a rock and a hard place, most Romanian migrants hunker down and stay put rather than return; or they look for new, more favourable opportunities in Northern Europe.

Romanians (997,000), Ukrainians (224,000) and Moldovans (148,000), alongside Albanians (492,000) and Poles (112,000), are some of the largest migrant communities in *Italy* (data from Caritas-Migrantes 2012). Surveys with these migrant groups provide the raw material for the next paper in this issue, by **Eralba Cela, Tineke Fokkema and Elena Ambrosetti**, which examines the relationship between transnational orientation (the dependent variable) and integration and duration of residence (hypothesized independent variables), for Eastern European migrants (the groups enumerated above) living in Italy. Reflecting the special issue's commitment to methodological pluralism, these authors carry out a principal components analysis of the above-mentioned dependent and independent variables, along with a battery of control variables (age at migration, gender, partner and parent status, religion, and country of origin). Data come from a special questionnaire survey, the Integrometro study, carried out during 2008–2009 with a sample of 3484 East Europeans in Italy. *Transnational orientation* was measured by several individual variables including remittance-sending, return intention and feelings of belonging to the home country. *Duration of residence* was a single-factor variable. *Integration*, the most complex of the three main operational variables, was captured by a wide range of measures which could be divided into *economic integration* (employment status, education, perceived economic condition) and *socio-cultural* *integration* (language proficiency, friendship patterns, acceptance of exogamous marriage, feelings of belonging to Italy, etc.). The main original contribution of this paper lies in its findings. In a nutshell, transnationalism is positively related to economic integration and negatively related to socio-cultural integration; and transnational behaviour decreases with length of residence in the host country. Amongst the stand-out control variables, men are more transnational than women.

For the next set of papers, we now move across the Adriatic Sea to the Western Balkans. **Bojana Babić** offers unique insights into the ongoing dynamics within the migration–development nexus in Bosnia and Herzegovina. Based on a close involvement with events on the ground, including interviews with returnees and community development workers in six municipalities, three in the Federation of BiH and three in the Republika Srpska, she reveals the incongruencies in perception of development possibilities and results between development policy staff on the one hand, and returnees and locals on the other. The paper is built around a case-study of the *Center for Local Development and Diaspora* (CLDD), a local development model sponsored by the City of Stockholm (reflecting the fact that Sweden hosts 80,000 people of Bosnian origin). Whilst the CLDD staff perceive initiatives to be underway, particularly in the involvement of some refugee migrants in Sweden in rebuilding houses and allied infrastructures, the view of returnees, and many diasporans, is that only their own remittances, savings and personal/family networks have been effective in supporting the population in BiH. There are complaints about local corruption and calls for structural reform and more efficient and transparent involvement of the BiH authorities.

One of the strengths of the paper by **Bashkim Iseni**, on the shifting transnational orientations of the Albanian-speaking population in Switzerland, is the quantity of ethnographic and interview evidence that it draws on. Long-term participation by the author, himself a member of the Swiss Albanophone community since 1991, is combined with three interview-based studies carried out in the mid-late 2000s and in 2011. Although the main focus of the paper is Albanians from Kosovo, reference is also made to migration from the ethnic-Albanian populations of Montenegro, Macedonia and southern Serbia.

Setting the scene, Iseni identifies three waves of Albanian migration to Switzerland. Low-skill migration from the ethnic-Albanian regions of the Former Yugoslavia, which corresponded to the most underdeveloped parts of this country, started in the mid-1960s and continued until 1973. Migration was temporary, and overwhelmingly of men. After a lull during the oil crisis and its aftermath, these emigration channels were reactivated during the 1980s; again mostly men remitting to their families left behind. The third wave was triggered by the conflict in Kosovo and consisted of asylum seekers and refugees, culminating in the main exodus in 1999. These departures were more family-based, and were accompanied by family members joining earlier-settled labour migrants. Woven into the latter stages of this chronology was the increasing diasporic political activism of the Kosovo Liberation Army, whose main followers came from the Kosovan diaspora in Switzerland.

The main fulcrum around which the paper's analysis is hinged is the switch in *transnationalism* from a strong *orientation to the territories of origin* before the 1990s to an increasing *focus on integration in Switzerland*. Long-delayed family reunion and a final 'settling down' in Switzerland have redefined the nature of transnationalism: remittances and a plan to return have been replaced by investment in families' future in Switzerland. Now, for the first generation, transnationalism means annual return visits; definitive return is made unlikely by the poor living conditions and economic prospects of post-conflict Kosovo, which are even more unappealing to the Swiss-born second generation.

With the next paper, by **Ivaylo Markov**, we zoom into the ethnic-Albanian area of western Macedonia (FYROM) to look in more detail at the local dynamics of migration, remittances, development and social change in this region of traditionally high emigration. Unlike Iseni, who concentrated his interviews in the destination country, Markov's fieldwork (54 interviews plus participant observation and photographic documentation) was in the area of origin, from which migrants go to, return from, and shuttle back-and-forth between, a variety of destination countries – Switzerland, Austria, Germany, and more recently, Italy.

Four concepts guide his analysis: the *culture of migration*, which not only denotes the intense migration outflow from this area but also is ingrained in people's everyday lives and imaginations; *social remittances*, which connote the transformations in patterns of consumption, social ranking, interpersonal relations and behaviour in the places of origin; *social network theory*, employed to grasp the relations between emigrants, returnees and non-migrants; and *transnationalism*, in order to describe the back-and-forth nature of migrants' movements within their transnational social spaces. However, Markov is critical of the use of 'transnationalism' within the ethnic-Albanian (and wider Balkan) context because of the assumption of equivalence of state, nation, nationality, ethnicity and citizenship. Finding 'translocal' too spatially confining a substitute concept, Markov follows Pichler (2009) in opting for the term 'transterritorial', which more adequately conveys the meaning of a non-national, non-local Albanian ethnic space combining different places of migrant origin and destination. The migration history of this Albanian ethnic space – male labour circulation to German-speaking countries during the 1960s and 1970s, followed by family reunion abroad and then renewed emigration in the two post-Yugoslav decades – justifies the use of the transterritorial concept since, in the rest of Macedonia, local rural-urban migration, rather than emigration, has been the norm.

In the rest of the article, the impacts of this intense emigration on the territory of origin are documented, with a sensitive feel for the landscape aesthetics wrought by large-scale investments in housing ('Alpine' and 'Mediterranean' styles contrast with the local vernacular architecture), consumer goods, businesses and community projects. With family reunion and family migration, however, some of the dynamics change, and new dilemmas and shifts in transnational orientations take place (the same changes as described by Iseni in the preceding paper). The summer return visit becomes the opportunity to display wealth and social prestige through expensive cars and lavish weddings, since only in the eyes of other local-origin migrants and the non-migrant population can the status achievements of migration be displayed and appreciated. The co-existence of two types of migration – one where entire families go abroad and the other when only the men work abroad coming home at regular intervals – gives rise to complex social networks and family and household structures. Declining patriarchy and changing gender relations are also evident.

Albanians, but this time from the Republic of Albania, are also the focus of the next article, by **Domna Michail**. Her innovation is to provide an empirically-grounded account of the impact of the Greek financial crisis on Albanian immigrants in this country. There has been much anecdotal comment in the Greek and international media concerning the effects of the Greek economic meltdown on the country's million-plus immigrants, especially the Albanians who make up around

60% of the immigrant population (see, e.g. 'Albanians in Greece: Heading home again', *The Economist*, 14 January 2012); but little by way of concrete and rigorous research. Michail uses a questionnaire approach ($N = 217$) supported by in-depth interviews ($N = 35$) to first- and second-generation Albanians in various parts of Greece to answer two main research questions. First, what has been the impact of the crisis on migrants' livelihoods, legal status and family development projects? Second, what is the second generation's positionality with regard to issues of 'return' to Albania, identity and belonging? Research was carried out during 2010–2011, hence during the third year of the crisis.

At a time when (to quote one of Michail's interviewees) 'there is not enough bread, even for the Greeks', Albanians' employment opportunities have certainly shrunk. This leads to a series of negative ramifications for the immigrants: falling incomes, declining material standards, inability to send remittances, and antagonism between Albanians and Greeks over the little work available. Unemployment threatens legal status, so a rise in insecurity occurs. Albanian families in Greece exist in a state of limbo, no longer able to sustain a decent standard of living there, but equally unlikely to be able to create a new and viable livelihood back in Albania, which remains poor and disorganized. Michail concludes by pointing to a new *transnational rupture* within Albanian migrant families. In an earlier phase, during the early and mid-1990s, families were split when the men migrated and their wives, children and parents remained in Albania. Then, family reunion and family formation took place in Greece. Now, the older generations (the middle-aged migrants and their parents, in those cases where the latter have followed the former in Greece) think of a possible return to Albania, but the second generation sees its future in Greece or elsewhere in Europe.

In the final paper, **Jennifer Clarke** shifts the analysis to the meso scale and looks at the role and efficacy of *migrant organizations* in Greece as *transnational actors* capable of promoting change and development in migrant countries of origin. A comparative perspective is provided by bringing in reference to migrant organizations in the UK and the Netherlands. Compared to these two latter countries, where both immigration and the founding of migrant organizations started much earlier, and where migrant organizations can be counted in their thousands, in Greece there are an estimated 128. Moreover, in Greece such organizations are mainly volunteer-run and exist on a shoestring, lacking government or NGO funding; whereas in the UK and the Netherlands many such organizations benefit from government funding and have paid, professional personnel in their employ. However, the most stunning of Clarke's findings is that none of the Greek migrant organizations seems to be engaged in any form of home-country development initiative; their main functions relate to assisting recent migrants with food, shelter and, where relevant, asylum advice; lobbying the government on migrant issues; putting on cultural events in Greece; and teaching the Greek language.

Notes

1. Funding for the travel expenses, accommodation and conference fees of selected workshop presenters was provided by a grant from IMISCOE to the Sussex Centre for Migration Research, and by a contribution from Malmö Institute for Migration (Diversity and Welfare).

2. UN figures for 2009–2010 commonly quoted are 214 million international migrants worldwide (i.e. people living in a country other than that of their birth) and 740 million internal migrants.

3. For a useful textbook which clearly distinguishes between different types of migration and thresholds and techniques for measuring migration in its various forms (including internal migration), see Boyle, Halfacree, and Robinson (1998).

4. There have been subsequent refinements, including HDI variants more oriented to measuring poverty or gender inequality – see UNDP (2009, 208) for a useful chart of these variations. However, the basic HDI remains the standard and most widely used measure.

5. Although concerns over likely 'excessive' migration resulted in multi-year 'transition periods' before free movement for work became fully operational in the case of the 'southern' enlargement in the 1980s (Greece in 1981, Spain and Portugal in 1986) and the major 'eastern' enlargement in 2004 (the so-called A8 countries), as well as the accession of Bulgaria and Romania (A2 countries) in 2007.

6. However, in the current period of deep financial crisis, Greek emigration, especially of highly educated graduates and professionals, has started again as a response to rising unemployment and falling living standards. The impact of the crisis on immigrants in Greece is examined by Domna Michail in her paper in this issue.

7. See UNDP (2009, 171–2) for the detailed evidence. For example, Albania's overall HDI ranking is 28 places higher than its per capita GDP figure.

References

Ackers, L. 2004. Managing relationships in peripatetic careers: Scientific mobility in the European Union. *Women's Studies International Forum* 27, no. 3: 189–201.

Basch, L., N. Glick Schiller, and C. Szanton Blanc. 1994. *Nations unbound: Transnational projects, postcolonial predicaments and deterritorialized nation-states*. Langhorne, PA: Gordon and Breach.

Boccagni, P. 2012. Even a transnational social field must have its boundaries: Methodological options, potentials and dilemmas for researching transnationalism. In *Handbook of research methods in migration*, ed. C. Vargas-Silva, 295–318. Cheltenham: Edward Elgar.

Boyle, P., K. Halfacree, and V. Robinson. 1998. *Exploring contemporary migration*. London: Longman.

Brunnbauer, U. 2012. Labour migration and transnationalism in the Balkans: A historical perspective. In *Migration and identity: Historical, cultural and linguistic dimensions of mobility in the Balkans*, ed. P. Hristov, 11–24. Sofia: Paradigma.

Bryceson, D., and U. Vuorela, eds. 2002. *The transnational family: New European frontiers and global networks*. Oxford: Berg.

Caritas-Migrantes. 2012. Immigration statistical file 2012. Rome: Idos [in Italian].

Castles, S., and M.J. Miller. 2009. *The age of migration*. 4th ed. Basingstoke: Palgrave Macmillan.

Cerase, F.P. 1974. Migration and social change: Expectations and reality. A study of return migration from the United States to Italy. *International Migration Review* 8, no. 2: 245–62.

Dannecker, P. 2009. Migrant visions of development: A gendered approach. *Population, Space and Place* 15, no. 20: 119–32.

de Haas, H. 2010. Migration and development: A theoretical perspective. *International Migration Review* 44, no. 1: 227–64.

Delgado Wise, R., and H. Marquez Covarrubias. 2009. Understanding the relationship between migration and development: Toward a new theoretical approach. *Social Analysis* 53, no. 3: 85–105.

Faist, T. 2000. *The volume and dynamics of transnational social spaces*. Oxford: Clarendon Press.

Fielding, A. 1993. Migration, institutions and politics: The evolution of European migration policies. In *Mass migration in Europe: The legacy and the future*, ed. R. King, 40–62. London: Belhaven-Wiley.

King, R. 1993. European international migration 1945–1990: A statistical and geographical overview. In *Mass migration in Europe: The legacy and the future*, ed. R. King, 19–39. London: Belhaven-Wiley.

King, R., and R. Skeldon. 2010. Mind the gap! Integrating approaches to internal and international migration. *Journal of Ethnic and Migration Studies* 36, no. 10: 1619–46.

Levitt, P. 1998. Social remittances: Migration driven local-level forms of cultural diffusion. *International Migration Review* 32, no. 4: 926–48.

Levitt, P. 2001. *The transnational villagers*. Los Angeles, CA: University of California Press.

Levitt, P., and N. Glick Schiller. 2004. Conceptualizing simultaneity: A transnational social field perspective on society. *International Migration Review* 38, no. 3: 1002–39.

Mitchell, K. 1997. Transnational discourse: Bringing geography back in. *Antipode* 29, no. 1: 101–14.

Pichler, R. 2009. Migration, architecture and the imagination of home(land): An Albanian-Macedonian case study. In *Transnational societies, transterritorial politics: Migrations in the (post-) Yugoslav region, 19th–20th century*, ed. U. Brunnbauer, 213–35. Munich: Oldenbourg Verlag.

Portes, A. 2003. Theoretical convergences and empirical evidence in the study of immigrant transnationalism. *International Migration Review* 37, no. 3: 874–92.

Povrzanović Frykman, M. 2008. South east European connections: Towards an ethnography of immigrants' transnational practices. In *MESS and RAMSES II, proceedings of the Mediterranean ethnological summer school, vol. 7*, ed. J. Repič, A. Bartulović, and K. Sajovec Altshul, 147–67. Ljubljana: University of Ljubljana.

Pries, L., ed. 2001. *New transnational social spaces: International migration and transnational communities in the early 21st century.* London: Routledge.

Samers, M. 1999. 'Globalization', the geopolitical economy of migration and the 'spatial vent'. *Review of International Political Economy* 6, no. 2: 166–99.

Smith, R.C. 2006. *Mexican New York.* Berkeley, CA: University of California Press.

Tsianos, V., and S. Karakayali. 2010. Transnational migration and the emergence of the European border regime: An ethnographic analysis. *European Journal of Social Theory* 13, no. 3: 373–87.

UNDP. 2009. *Human development report, 2009. Overcoming barriers: Human mobility and development.* Basingstoke: Palgrave Macmillan.

Van Hear, N., and N. Nyberg Sørensen, eds. 2003. *The migration–development nexus.* Geneva: International Organization for Migration.

World Bank. 2011. *Migration and remittances factbook.* Washington DC: World Bank.

Hierarchies and categorical power in cross-border science: analysing scientists' transnational mobility between Ukraine and Germany

Anna Amelina

Faculty of Social Sciences, Goethe-University Frankfurt am Main, Frankfurt am Main, Germany

Using the results of qualitative research in Germany and Ukraine, the article provides evidence to how the short-term and circular geographic mobility of Ukrainian natural scientists between Ukraine and Germany contributes to the formation of a cross-border scientific field. Combining Bourdieu's field theory with the transnational field approach and the intersectional perspective, the article indicates how unequal access to scientific reputation is structured across borders. In sum, the complex interplay of ethnicity-, class- and gender-related categorizations pushes mobile scientists to define themselves as an exploited elite. At the same time, female mobile scientists are identified as having the most disadvantaged positions in the transnational academic hierarchy.

Introduction: from permanent migration to short-term mobility

The collapse of the socialist regimes in Eastern and Central Europe and the fall of the Iron Curtain at the end of the 1980s led to large-scale emigration from the former socialist countries to Western Europe. During the 1990s and later, after the 2004 and 2007 enlargements of the European Union, emigration flows from Central and Eastern to Western Europe steadily decreased and permanent emigration was gradually replaced by short-term and circular mobility (Wallace 2002).

This article focuses on the changing nature of migration from Eastern to Western European countries and addresses two issues. First, it examines how the cross-border mobility of scientists from one Eastern European country contributes to the formation of a 'transnational field of science'. My second purpose is to identify the conditions which influence the unequal distribution of symbolic, organizational and material resources within this transnational field. These issues are closely connected and are discussed using the example of natural scientists' geographical mobility between Ukraine and Germany. The discussion is based primarily on the results of 16 semi-structured interviews the author carried out between 2010 and 2012 with natural scientists (mathematicians, physicists and biologists) who regularly travel between Eastern and Western Europe. The interviews were conducted in various localities in Germany and Ukraine using methods inspired by multi-sited ethnography (Amelina 2010).

The focus on the Eastern European social and historical context is promising for three reasons. First, immediately after the breakdown of the socialist regimes at the beginning of the 1990s, international geographical mobility was one of the main strategies for individuals and households to improve their social mobility (Heyns 2005). Second, the transformation of the political and economic regimes of Eastern and Central European countries led to comprehensive modifications of their migration and welfare regimes (Cerami and Vanhuysse 2009). The welfare gaps which emerged served as an additional stratifying force within the social orders of the sending countries. Moreover, in the second half of the 1990s, researchers realized that migration from Eastern and Central European countries had a significant influence on the transformation of the migration and welfare regimes of some of the receiving countries in Western Europe (Banting 2000). Third, the enlargement of the European Union has not only produced new mobility and welfare regimes on the supra-national level, but has also created new peripheries of Europe which include, amongst others, countries such as Russia, Ukraine, Belarus and Moldova. Consequently, migrants from these new European peripheries who continuously move between the sending and receiving countries experience different forms of oppression and exploitation than migrants from those Eastern and Central European countries which are now EU member states (Jandl 2007).

This article addresses the question of how the changing nature of scientific migration between the Eastern European periphery and Germany encourages the formation of unequal social positions within the social field of science. In particular, it goes beyond the study of scientists' geographical mobility as a process that influences an economic transformation of the immigration country or of the emigration country. It also does not discuss the conditions of social mobility of the migrant scientists in the receiving country. Instead, it provides evidence of how social inequality – understood as a hierarchy in terms of access to symbolic, organizational and material resources – emerges within the transnational field of science. In doing so, I seek to overcome the nation-state-centred focus (Amelina and Faist 2012) and to explore inequality formation in the context of cross-border mobility.

The article begins with a brief overview of the current state of research on the geographical mobility of highly skilled migrants and a discussion of the brain drain and brain circulation approaches. The concept of the *transnational field of science* is then introduced and its underlying premises explained. The final section presents the results of the author's qualitative study, which shows the significance of multi-dimensional hierarchies that are emerging in the field of cross-border science. In sum, the article provides evidence to how cross-border mobility generates new social realms and sheds new light on inequality patterns, which emerge beyond national container-spaces.

International migration of scientists: neither brain drain nor brain circulation

One of the scientists interviewed during my fieldwork was Oleg, a 28-year-old mathematician who was employed as a junior professor at the University of Wiesenbad.[1] The following paragraph briefly introduces his professional biography which allows us to address the concerns of this article.

Oleg began his career at Kiev State University, where he studied Mathematics. He graduated at the age of 20. The supervisor of his diploma thesis, who held professorships at the Universities of Kiev and Wiesenbad, suggested to Oleg that he obtain his PhD at a German university. Oleg completed his doctoral studies at the age of 22, winning the prize for the best dissertation at the Department of Mathematics in Wiesenbad. Later, Oleg's PhD supervisor helped him to get a research position at the same university. Like his PhD supervisor, Oleg has been teaching at Kiev University on a regular basis, even though he is a full-time research fellow at Wiesenbad. This is possible because the academic terms at German and Ukrainian universities do not overlap, so that Oleg can spend several months teaching in Kiev.

In the interview, Oleg said that he experienced high work pressure at the university in Germany. According to him, to be accepted, an Eastern European scientist is expected to work 'twice as hard' as a German colleague. However, he also stated that his research position at the German university not only gives him access to current research trends, financial (research) resources and Europe-wide collaboration opportunities; it also offers certain benefits at the university in Ukraine, where he is given additional opportunities to participate in decision-making and restructuring processes concerning the curriculum.

The above brief account of one interviewee's scientific career is a good example of the changing, increasingly multi-directional nature of (Eastern European) scientists' migration, which is better understood as short-term and circular mobility rather than as permanent emigration.[2] It also reflects the ambivalent social position of transnational scientists who experience some degree of exploitation at the university of the receiving country, but at the same time have opportunities to build a scientific reputation, participate in decision-making and obtain research funds at the university of the sending country, not least because of their simultaneous commitment to two universities: in the immigration and emigration countries.

This portrayal of Oleg suggests two questions as eminently relevant. Which theories can be applied to examine this kind of transnational scientific career from a social inequality perspective? Or, more generally: which approaches address the relationship between the formation of unequal social positions and the cross-border mobility of scientists? The twin concepts of brain drain and brain circulation dominate the current state of thinking on scientists' international mobility in an enlarged Europe. These analytical tools will be briefly reviewed below.

The existing studies on scientists' migration from Eastern Europe in the early 1990s appear to generally confirm the *brain drain approach* (Vizi 1993). They address emigration from countries such as Bulgaria, former Czechoslovakia, Poland, Hungary and Romania, as well as from Russia and other post-Soviet republics. Analysis of the available statistical data suggests that, immediately after the fall of the Iron Curtain in 1990 and 1991, up to 20% of emigrant populations from these countries were scientists from professional fields such as medicine, biology, chemistry, engineering, information technology, mathematics and physics. The studies regard the emigration of scientists as a loss of 'intellectual resources', which has a negative influence on the economic growth of the sending countries (Ivakhnyuk 2006). However, studies on structural factors also identify difficult economic conditions such as a lack of research funding, low salaries and 'better research opportunities' abroad as the main factors that cause scientists to emigrate (Ivakhnyuk 2006). Studies of scientists' motivations for emigrating conducted immediately after the fall of the Iron Curtain showed that the limitations of a scientific career and the declining prestige of the scientific profession were amongst the major reasons for scientists to emigrate (Vizi 1993, 104). It is worth noting that these studies implicitly refer to the world-systems theory, which originally framed the brain drain approach (Portes and Walton 1981).

The brain drain approach concerns the interrelation between scientists' international migration and the formation of *economic* inequalities as a result of the international division of labour (Portes and Walton 1981). Focusing primarily on the economic development or underdevelopment of states, it rarely takes the transformation of social positions of individuals or groups into consideration. This is why it does not focus on how cross-border mobility influences scientists' access to the symbolic, organizational and material resources *within* their professional field. The institutional transformation of science as a particular social field is rarely addressed in this regard.

However, current studies on the migration of highly skilled populations from Eastern European countries (Wallace 2002) call the premises of the brain drain theory into question. The pessimistic world-systems notion of the exploitation of the periphery by the centre is replaced by an analysis of multi-directional migration as a resource for the economic development of both the receiving and sending countries. Researchers use the term *brain circulation* (Baláz, Williams, and Kollár 2004) to reflect the fact that the elimination of geographical mobility constraints in Europe has led to unique migration conditions which promote temporary mobility rather than permanent migration (Wallace and Stola 2001). In addition, these studies predict a convergence of economic development of the new and the old EU member countries in the long run (Straubhaar and Wolburg 1999; Wallace and Vincent 2007), which is expected to promote temporary mobility rather than permanent emigration as well. Finally, current return migration policies of sending countries, which aim to create appropriate employment possibilities for highly skilled migrants, also encourage the mainly temporary mobility of skilled migrants in general and of scientists in particular (Laczko 2001).

The concept of *brain circulation* (Barre et al. 2003; Kuznetsov 2006; Saxenian 2002) indicates the relevance of transnational network ties in encouraging the structural interconnection and economic exchange between the economies of migration-sending and migration-receiving countries. In this context, transnational linkages of highly skilled professionals are understood to be both a competitive advantage in establishing high-tech businesses and a resource to increase the economic growth of both countries. In general, studies on brain circulation between Eastern and Western European countries focus mainly on the economic dimension of inequality, and the fact that economic divergence between sending and receiving states is reduced due to transnational linkages amongst highly skilled professionals and amongst companies which operate across borders. In doing so, they rarely address social mechanisms which determine the stratification of access of highly skilled professionals to the symbolic and organizational resources in the context of cross-border mobility.

Despite their conflicting views on the impact of international migration on economic disparities between the immigration and emigration countries, the brain drain and brain circulation approaches have similar weaknesses. First, they tend to reduce social inequality to economic inequalities between nation states. Second, they extrapolate the research results for the meso-level of organizations or networks to the macro-level, in this case again the nation states. Third, although the two approaches address the global and transnational settings of inequality formation, they focus primarily on nation states as the main framework of analysis.

These approaches to the mobility of scientists fail to consider three factors. In the first place, they do not acknowledge the multi-dimensional understanding of social inequalities proposed, amongst others, by intersectional studies (e.g. Anthias 2001; Walby, Armstrong, and Strid 2012), which avoid reducing social inequality to economic inequality. In the second place, they ignore the current approaches to the transnationalization of social inequalities (e.g. Amelina and Faist 2012; Beck 2007), and focus exclusively on the unit of the nation state. In the third place, they fail to consider the impacts of scientists' mobility on the (re)structuring of the non-national scientific field. To address these research gaps, the next section discusses the formation of scientists' unequal social positions within the *scientific field* using the transnational and field approaches.

Cross-border mobility and the hierarchy of scientists' positions: towards the transnational field approach

The transnational perspective allows researchers to study social inequalities in two ways. The first approach addresses the structural conditions which determine the positions of individuals or collectives within the transnational class hierarchy (Sklair 2001). The second approach focuses on the inequality of individuals' positions within the transnational social fields (Levitt and Glick Schiller 2004).

This study builds on the second approach because it allows us to consider the internal logic of science as a particular social field, using the idea of field-specific hierarchies to examine inequality between scientists' positions. In contrast, the transnational class approach focuses on the vertical inequality of social positions in the realm of global society as a whole. Moreover, the field perspective can be more easily combined with the notion of multi-dimensionality of social inequalities, as will be discussed later.

Multi-locality of professional commitments as a constitutive element of the transnational field of science

According to the field approach, science is organized around practices of truth and knowledge production. It is internally divided into sub-fields of disciplines and into various disciplinary approaches and schools which govern the everyday practices and experiences of scientists. Inequality within this field thus emerges with respect to field-specific symbolic and organizational resources, such as symbolic power and access to positions in scientific organizations (Bourdieu 2001). This section discusses the *transnational* dimension of the field of science and then examines the unequal distribution of these resources in detail.

The interview with Oleg suggests that multi-local professional involvement is decisive for the constitution of the transnational field of science. According to Levitt and Glick Schiller (2004), who explicitly draw on Bourdieu's (1985) field theory, the ability of individuals, organizations and institutions to participate in multiply located, dense, long-term social networks that spread over nation states, cities and localities is crucial for the formation of cross-border fields. This implies that there are not only mobile scientists who are defined as relevant field players, but also immobile scientists 'who do not move themselves but maintain social relations across borders through various forms of communication' (Levitt and Glick Schiller 2004, 10).

According to this view, the *transnational scientific field* is organized around multi-local professional linkages that are based on a network of social relationships which emerge from multiple memberships of scientists in universities or institutes in immigration, emigration or even third countries. Mobile and immobile actors who are unable to get access to interpersonal and organizational transnational networks are excluded and predestined to remain players only in national scientific landscapes. Transnational geographical mobility, which is characterized by its unfinished and multi-directional nature, appears to be a constitutive element of transnationalization.

The summary of Oleg's scientific career indicates three structural dimensions of transnationalization within the cross-border field of science. The first dimension concerns ways of accessing the transnational field. The *interpersonal networks* allowed Oleg not only to begin his PhD studies in Germany, but also to maintain his professional contacts with Ukraine. These networks are, however, gendered and ethnicized, as will be discussed in the next section.

The second dimension worth noting is *transnational membership* in scientific organizations such as universities. Scientists who enjoy transnational membership hold temporary or permanent teaching and/or research positions in the immigration country and the emigration country. Under certain circumstances, holders of transnational membership also have privileged access to the symbolic power and the institutional and material resources in various organizations of a scientific field.

Third, the *institutional level* of the scientific field makes *international visibility* of research one of the leading criteria for a distinguished scientific reputation. Transnational scientific reputation is reflected in the pressure exerted on scientists to produce a great number of peer-reviewed publications in national and international journals. The only way for researchers to build a transnational reputation is to have their research results recognized by relevant communities of academic disciplines both in and outside their home country. Recognition can come in various forms, such as honorary degrees and visiting professorships.

My ongoing research suggests that these three aspects are essential parts of the process of transnationalization of science. However, the transnational prospect taken does not suggest a transnational scientific landscape as based on mutual solidarity and equal opportunities in the scientific careers of transnational players. The following section draws on Bourdieu's field approach to address the issue of inequality of scientists' positions in more detail.

Understanding inequalities within the transnational field of science: combining Bourdieu and the intersectional approach

How does the field approach address social inequality in the scientific sphere? Pierre Bourdieu's theory of social fields provides evidence of how social relations are fixed by power. He distinguishes between the economic, cultural, political, scientific and bureaucratic fields and assigns to each of them a specific logic (the *nomos*), insisting that the particular field logic organizes the routines to manage practices and experiences within the field (Bourdieu 1985).[3] Although Bourdieu's field theory is used here heuristically, this article follows the understanding of the social field as created by the relational positions of actors who are involved in the fight over power of definition and symbolic resources. In this context, social inequality is defined as the inequality of social positions within a particular field that results from the specific rules of the field and the actors' access to the field-specific resources (Bourdieu 1985). However, the transnational perspective suggests that access to demanded resources and scientific reputation is evaluated against the background of the transnational landscape of scientific organizations. Because this study analyses inequality as inequality between prominent scientists, holders of symbolic power and newcomers by whom these positions are formed, my principal concern here is the question of whether and under what conditions transnational linkages contribute to scientists' access to the symbolic and other powers within this specific field.

Although Bourdieu's field approach provides insights into how social inequality emerges within a particular field, it also acknowledges the relevance of multiple forms of capital, such as economic, cultural and social capital, which co-determine actors' social mobility, although they are somewhat less relevant than the field-specific capital most prevalent in the particular field structure. However, apart from the capital (i.e. the class dimension), the field approach rarely considers the dimensions of ethnicity (including 'race') and gender. By ignoring these dimensions, we risk overlooking dominant stratifying forces within the transnational field in question. The biographical account of Oleg suggests that the transnational positioning of scientists is characterized by a specific ambivalence. On the one hand, some of the interviewees mentioned 'exploitation' at the universities of the receiving country, which appeared to be connected with processes of (self-)ethnicization. This suggests that *ethnic categorizations* might become highly relevant stratifying forces in cross-border science.

On the other hand, the analysis of interview transcripts indicates that *gendered categorizations* are relevant as well. For example, some interviewees believe that the fact that there are only a small number of female transnational scientists is explained by 'women's natural ability to have and rear children, which potentially makes female scientists immobile' (28-year-old male researcher, mathematician, place of interview: Germany). Consequently, scholars benefit from addressing gendered categorizations as relevant for the genesis of unequal social positions in cross-border settings. The combination of field theory and the intersectional lens for an inequality analysis is, therefore, a promising conceptual tool to reconstruct the unequal social positions within a cross-border setting.

Approaching inequality of social positions within the transnational scientific field: towards the power of categorization

The empirical field and the guiding research questions

The data for the analysis of transnational hierarchies were collected according to the multi-sited research strategy (Marcus 1995), which includes the localities in both immigration and emigration states in the research design. First, using the Social Network Site 'Ukrainian Scientists Worldwide',[4] I conducted an ethnographic observation of online conversations and posts. After content analysis of the conversations, I contacted the German universities which platform members identified as the target universities: Aachen Technical University, Technical University Berlin, Bielefeld University, Göttingen University and Würzburg University. After conducting 12 semi-structured interviews with natural scientists (mathematicians, physicists and biologists) based at these universities, four additional interviews were conducted in Ukraine (National University of Kiev). These contacts were provided by the interview partners in Germany. The age of interview partners varied between 25 and 45. Gender balance in the sample was almost achieved (nine men and seven women). The subsequent data interpretation included a two-step procedure. First, the analysis was based on the open coding of interviews, which follows the premises of grounded theory (Strauss 1987). Second, selected interview paragraphs were analysed according to hermeneutic sequence analysis (Amelina 2010). This integrated approach allowed illuminating cultural systems of classification, which actors use to interpret social praxis.

As indicated above, the research results were interpreted from an intersectional perspective on social inequality (Anthias 2001; Walby, Armstrong, and Strid 2012). First, this approach considers various inequality dimensions such as class, gender and ethnicity/race as central principles for determining unequal life chances and life conditions. These different sets of unequal social relations cannot be reduced to each other; which means, for example, that gender or ethnic divisions cannot be reduced to class inequalities.

Second, this theory draws on post-structuralist ideas (West and Zimmerman 2002) to highlight the *power of social categorization* spread over different social fields, institutional regimes or organizations. This approach analyses the genesis of multi-dimensional hierarchies by identifying the *making* of social boundaries between ethnicities, gender positions or classes.

Third, in addition to focusing on the multi-dimensionally formed hierarchies within society as a whole, intersectional analysis can also be used to address internal hierarchies within social fields. The following analysis introduces paradigmatic examples of how ethnicity-, gender- and class-specific categorizations – *categorical mechanisms* in the terminology of Charles Tilly (2000) – co-produce unequal positions within the cross-border field of science, and how they are connected to the unequal distribution of field-specific resources.

Consequently, the guiding question of this analysis is: what practices of categorization generate unequal positions within the transnational scientific field? The focus is on the advantaged and disadvantaged positions amongst scientists who commute between Ukraine and Germany.

'Highly welcome talents', 'cheap labour' and 'patriots': natural scientists between ethnicization and self-ethnicization

Ethnicization, as a boundary between 'us' and 'them' (Wimmer 2008), is relevant in the scientific organizations and networks of both immigration and emigration countries, if in a different way. At universities in Germany, natural scientists from Ukraine are confronted with ambivalent ethnic labelling. First, they are ethnically labelled in a positive way as 'highly welcome talents', the main reason being that the educational institutions from which scientists originate in the emigration country enjoy a good scientific reputation in Germany (as well as in other European countries and the USA). Most of the individuals interviewed for this study mentioned particular schools of mathematics and physics. Affiliation with these institutions opens doors to employment at universities in Germany and other countries. However, Eastern European scientists also feel that they are regarded as cheap labour:

I think that you know perfectly well what happened after the breakdown of the Soviet Union. All mathematicians went to the West. (…) Take a look at the publication lists of German scientists and at how they have changed since the 1990s. You will notice that German mathematicians really benefit from us: the frequency of their publications increased enormously. (…) Also look at the names: you will find Slavic-sounding names in all co-authored publications. (30-year-old researcher, mathematician, place of interview: Germany)

The interviewees also state that their employers, i.e. German universities, expected them to perform additional duties not defined in their employment agreements. For example, all the interviewees were involved in the preparation of research proposals for their employers, an activity not specified in their contracts. However, they emphasized that this extra work was important because it gave them the opportunity to demonstrate 'commitment' and 'willingness to get ahead'. Young scientists in particular justified this extra work as an opportunity to show that they are strong enough to pursue a scientific career in the West. Interestingly, all of the interviewees used ethnic categorizations to justify the extra work (or, to use the Marxist term, exploitation):

We Ukrainians, no, (…) even more generally, (…) we Eastern Europeans are expected to work twice as hard (…) no, three, four times as hard as the natives. Who are we? NO-BO-DY (…) They [the employers] make us feel that way every day. The only way to earn some respect is to work more: to publish, to speak at conferences and to obtain external funds. (…) But you also know, we are tough (…) compared to what WE experienced in the '90s, we will manage somehow. (28-year-old researcher, mathematician, place of interview: Germany)

This passage indicates not only how mobile scientists at German universities are ethnicized, but also how scientists ethnicize themselves: 'Being strong enough' is a (socially constructed) ethnic trait which is perceived as a condition for successful performance at universities in Germany and other countries. In addition, 'being strong enough' is related to the difficult shared past. Interestingly, 'being a Ukrainian' appears to be less relevant in this regard than the shared experience of being Eastern Europeans after the dramatic breakdown of socialism.

Mobile scientists are also affected by ethnic labelling at the scientific organizations of the sending country, since they commute between Ukraine and Germany. Universities in Ukraine benefit from the scientific know-how and international contacts of transnational scientists, as the following passage shows:

When I found a position at this laboratory in Kiev, I was made highly welcome because I knew the particular brain cell modification method of [names the method]. Actually, I originally co-developed this method with my boss in Schönefeld [name is fictitious]. I also continued to publish with him on this topic. (…) However, my new boss [at a laboratory in Kiev] suddenly decided to be the co-author. What does that mean? She certainly benefited from the new international reputation I helped her build. (…) But this is why she also pushes my career ahead. (34-year-old researcher, cell biologist, place of interview: Kiev)

In addition, in the emigration context transnational scientists are positively labelled as 'some of us' or 'our best' for being able to get access to new audiences and communities:

How am I welcomed in Kiev? That's great! [laughs] My students there often say I am their idol. (28-year-old researcher, mathematician, place of interview: Kiev)

Another interviewee expressed a similar view:

What happens during my stays in Kiev [at the laboratory]? Actually, I feel like a ruler: everybody listens to me and (…) I enjoy a great reputation. (34-year-old researcher, cell biologist, please of interview: Kiev)

At Ukrainian universities, transnational scientists ethnicize themselves as part of the national scientific community. In particular, the contentious nation-building processes after the breakdown of the Soviet Union have promoted patriotic terms and definitions in the scientific-political discourse in Ukraine as well (Gnatyuk 2005). This is also a reason why the Ukrainian ministry of education and science regards scientific publications in Ukrainian as more relevant than publications in English when appointing professorships and other scientific positions. 'Being a patriot' is therefore an important element of the scientific-political discourse in Ukraine because it has considerable influence on whether or not researchers can pursue a scientific career. According to the interviewees, during their stays at the Ukrainian universities, they often use patriotic terms publicly to acknowledge their affiliation to the home institutes.

The preliminary conclusion is that, as evidenced above, the complex process of ethnicization is highly relevant for mobile scientists' simultaneous access to and maintenance of membership in the universities of the immigration and emigration countries. One could even use the term *paradoxical ethnicization* because on the one hand the ethnicization of mobile scientists from Ukraine as 'cheap labour' encourages their (self-)exploitation in the receiving context. On the other, the patriotic discourse of the emigration context re-defines the extra work as an honour. In other words, mobile scientists' extra work is embedded in the mechanism of *opportunity hoarding* (Tilly 2000). Whilst the mobile scientists' extra work at German universities ensures access to organizational resources, publication opportunities in international peer-reviewed journals, international awards and the accumulation of a scientific reputation, at Ukrainian universities they act as a 'strategic group' which is able to provide access to the latest international scientific subjects, methods and international networks. (Male) mobile scientists screen and use various opportunities at various organizational sites to reach the top of the transnational hierarchy, thus gaining access to symbolic power (Bourdieu 1985).

The question of how these ethnic categorizations are embedded in class-specific categorizations is addressed in the next section.

Class-related categorizations: the self-description of 'being the exploited elite'

One of the first results of this study suggests that class-related categorizations are embedded in ethnic categories and, thus, in the process of (self-)ethnicization. At first glance, one may think of transnational scientists as the 'transnational middle class', a group of people whose academic degrees are readily accepted in different nation-state contexts. However, the interviews suggest that these positions are more likely to intersect with ethnic categorizations. Whilst Ukrainian scientists at the universities of the receiving country are perceived as lower-middle-class because of their ethnic background ('cheap labour'), their colleagues at the universities of the emigration country honour their international employment status in a country of higher economic development, thereby actually assigning a higher class position to them ('the best of *us*'). From the latter perspective, geographically mobile scientists appear to be upwardly socially mobile because they have a higher income than immobile scientists in the sending country and 'enjoy cosmopolitan lifestyles', which include international collaboration, participation in international conferences and international travel. This perception also results from objectified differences in living expenses and wage levels between the two countries.[5]

In sum, the self-positioning of my interviewees is that of an 'exploited elite'. Mobile scientists are well aware of the extra work they are expected to put in outside Ukraine, but they also regard employment abroad as an opportunity to pursue an international career. Paradoxically, this self-perception of being privileged and disadvantaged at the same time is not addressed or discussed by them as a contradiction in terms.

Why are female natural scientists at a disadvantage? Between 'post-socialist' and 'Western' interpretations of gender equality

The research conducted for this study suggests that female mobile scientists in particular face considerable challenges in pursuing international scientific careers and that these challenges are significantly different from those facing male scientists.

Engendering, as a social boundary between 'male' and 'female' practices in the scientific field, is both discipline specific and context specific (depending on the types of networks and organizations in which the scientists are involved). Scientific organizations in Western and Eastern European countries have been making efforts to achieve gender equality, but this trend is framed by different institutional discourses and strategies of legitimization. At German universities, the gender equality discourse (which includes a discourse on the strategy of 'gender mainstreaming') began in the early 1970s and was institutionalized by the end of the 1990s. Socialist feminism, which was part of the official Soviet ideology, became relevant in scientific organizations of the USSR much earlier, in the 1930s. The main idea of 'socialist feminism' involved gender equality in terms of income and access to professional positions and decision-making processes (Dudwick, Srinivasan, and Braithwaite 2002). Soviet universities and research institutes in particular, including natural science institutes, followed this policy of gender equality until the end of the 1980s. The natural sciences were not completely dominated by female scientists in the USSR, but nor were they exclusively the domain of male researchers (Linkova 2007). For reasons of space, this article cannot discuss particular gender discourses and gender orders in greater detail. Instead, the intention is to emphasize the increasingly shared institutional semantics of gender equality in the universities of both countries.

An interesting finding here is that, despite the formally institutionalized gender equality arrangements, there are, in particular, mobile female scientists who give up their international careers on the grounds that they are excluded from relevant resources. Here is a typical example. One of the interviewees had successfully completed her PhD in Biology at a German university and had been employed on an innovative research project, but then decided to terminate her contract to return to Ukraine. She stated that Kiev was the more favourable environment to make care arrangements after the birth of her child. Although she continued to work at a research institute in Kiev, she did not have the same access to funding and technologies. As a result, she was unable to submit publications with innovative research results to internationally renowned journals. Indeed, this interviewee explicitly reflected on her downward mobility, stating that the loss of professional opportunities was strongly connected to particular stages in the life-course such as pregnancy and childbirth. The interviewee also remembered very well what happened when she told her German employer about her decision to leave the job:

> This happened during the mandatory Christmas party at our office [at a German university]. When my boss, (...) you know, she is a successful female professor (...) opened the party, she said to everybody, 'Look at her! She got pregnant and now she's leaving us! What better way to ruin a scientific career!' (...) Later, however, she apologized, though not in public, not in front of the others. (28-year-old researcher, cell biologist, place of interview: Kiev)

This account is important because balancing motherhood and a scientific career is not a contradiction in terms, according to socialist feminist ideology, which is still quite a powerful tradition in post-socialist Ukraine. The gender equality discourse in Germany and other non-socialist countries, by contrast, places great emphasis on equal professional opportunities, but still rarely treats the balancing of parenthood and a successful professional career as something to be taken for granted (Pfau-Effinger and Magdalenić 2009).

The process of social categorization, which relates to biological differences (pregnancy, childbirth), creates a categorical distinction between 'male' and 'female' that is still relevant in the context of scientific organizations. The interesting finding here is that transnational scientists organize their careers at the crossroads of multiple national and institutional gender orders of the scientific field. However, the post-socialist gendered career pattern (the balancing of parenthood and professional activities) is in conflict with the non-socialist feminist discourse and results in the exclusion of female mobile researchers from career opportunities.

Concluding remarks

The results of the study suggest that neither the brain drain nor the brain circulation approach explain the genesis of transnational inequalities because their main interest is the economically quantifiable advancement of particular nation states which are connected by migration flows. Therefore, this article calls migration scholars to organize the research beyond exclusive frameworks of particular nation states. It also casts doubt on the traditional view that social inequality always results from economic inequality between nation states or that it is a class order within particular national societies. By contrast, my study provides evidence on how the multi-dimensional process of hierarchization is organized within the multi-local setting. In the context of cross-border science, social inequality is thus understood as inequality in scientific reputation in the sense of a field-specific resource which implies access to publication opportunities, research funding and positions in organizations. The hierarchy within cross-border science, as shown in the example of mobile natural scientists, is conceptualized as a continuum of social positions which is reflected in scientists' degree of ability to accumulate *multiple memberships in and affiliations to* scientific organizations in different national landscapes. Moreover, by adopting the intersectional perspective, the article has illuminated the complex interplay between various types of social categorizations: it has been argued that access to the field-specific resources and positions is grounded in and influenced by *social practices of categorization*, which include ethnicity-related, class-related and gender-related systems of classification. However, these specific categorizations are not just powerful in fixed national settings, but also bring about an ambivalent power and rather contradictory positions in a multi-locally organized transnational realm. The narrative of 'exploited elite' is the paradigmatic example for such contradictions.

In sum, this process of hierarchization, its multi-dimensionality and its contradictions could not have been examined without the transnational perspective, which has identified cross-border mobility as crucial for the transformation of social orders. As the study of cross-border mobility of natural scientists between Germany and Ukraine has shown, this perspective provides worthwhile avenues for future research on cross-border inequality patterns.

Notes

1. The German university is given a fictitious name here to protect the identity of the interviewee. The names of the interviewees in this paper are also pseudonyms. All interviews were conducted in Russian; translation of quotes is by the author.
2. Whilst migration is conventionally defined as one-year stay abroad, mobility is specified as the residence abroad which lasts less than one year.
3. The relation between particular fields is hierarchical. The fields are subordinated to the larger field of power relations.
4. Which is the most prominent online platform for scientific mobility in the Ukrainian language (http://www.usw.com.ua).
5. The average monthly income in Ukraine is around €250.

References

Amelina, A. 2010. Searching for an appropriate research strategy on transnational migration: The logic of multi-sited research and the advantage of the cultural interferences approach. *Forum: Qualitative Social Research* 11, no. 1. http://nbn-resolving.de/urn:nbn:de:0114-fqs1001177 (accessed January 1, 2011).

Amelina, A., and T. Faist. 2012. De-naturalizing the national in research methodologies: Key concepts of transnational studies in migration. *Ethnic and Racial Studies* 35, no. 10: 1707–24.

Anthias, F. 2001. The material and the symbolic in theorizing social stratification: Issues of gender, ethnicity and class. *British Journal of Sociology* 52, no. 3: 367–90.

Baláz, V., A.M. Williams, and D. Kollár. 2004. Temporary versus permanent youth brain drain: Economic implications. *International Migration* 42, no. 4: 3–34.

Banting, K.G. 2000. Looking in three directions: Migration and the European welfare state in comparative perspective. In *Immigration and welfare: Challenging the borders of the welfare state*, ed. M. Bommes and A. Geddes, 67–89. London: Routledge.

Barre, R., V. Hernandez, J.B. Meyer, and D. Vinck. 2003. *Scientific diasporas: How can developing countries benefit from their expatriate scientists and engineers?* Paris: Institute for Development Research.

Beck, U. 2007. Beyond class and nation: Reframing social inequalities in a globalizing world. *British Journal of Sociology* 58, no. 4: 679–705.

Bourdieu, P. 1985. The social space and the genesis of groups. *Theory and Society* 14, no. 6: 723–44.

Bourdieu, P. 2001. The peculiar story of scientific reason. *Sociological Forum* 6, no. 1: 3–26.

Cerami, A., and P. Vanhuysse, eds. 2009. *Post-communist welfare pathways: Theorizing social policy transformations in Central and Eastern Europe.* Basingstoke: Palgrave Macmillan.

Dudwick, N., R. Srinivasan, and J. Braithwaite. 2002. *Ukraine: Gender review. Environmentally and socially sustainable development.* Washington DC: World Bank.

Gnatyuk, O. 2005. *The leave of Empire: The discourse of the Ukrainian identity.* Kiev: Kritika [in Ukrainian].

Heyns, B. 2005. Emerging inequalities in Central and Eastern Europe. *Annual Review of Sociology* 31: 163–97.

Ivakhnyuk, I. 2006. Brain drain from Russia: In search for a solution. In *Brain drain or brain gain – a global dilemma: The transatlantic security challenges and dilemmas for the European migration policy project*, ed. K. Gma and K. Iglicka, 83–98. Warsaw: Center for International Relations.

Jandl, M. 2007. Irregular migration, human smuggling and the Eastern enlargement of the European Union. *International Migration Review* 41, no. 2: 291–315.

Kuznetsov, Y. 2006. *Diaspora networks and the international migration of skills: How countries can draw on their talent abroad.* Washington DC: World Bank.

Laczko, F. 2001. *New challenges for migration policy in Central and Eastern Europe.* The Hague: TMC Asser Press.

Levitt, P., and N. Glick Schiller. 2004. Conceptualizing simultaneity: A transnational social field perspective on society. *International Migration Review* 38, no. 3: 1002–39.

Linkova, M. 2007. Moving target: Gender equality in science in enlarged Europe. *Context* 1, no. 5: 1–13.

Marcus, G. 1995. Ethnography in/of the world system: The emergence of multi-sited ethnography. *Annual Review of Anthropology* 24: 95–117.

Pfau-Effinger, B., and S. Magdalenić. 2009. Formal and informal work in the work-welfare arrangement of Germany. In *Formal and informal work: The hidden work regime in Europe*, ed. B. Pfau-Effinger, L. Flaquer, and P. Jensen, 89–116. London: Routledge.

Portes, A., and J. Walton. 1981. *Labour, class, and the international system.* New York, NY: Academic Press.

Saxenian, A. 2002. *Local and global networks of immigrant professionals in Silicon Valley.* San Francisco, CA: Public Policy Institute of California.

Sklair, L. 2001. *The transnational capitalist class.* Oxford: Blackwell.

Straubhaar, T., and M. Wolburg. 1999. Brain drain and brain gain in Europe: An evaluation of East-European migration to Germany. *Journal for Economics and Statistics* 5, no. 6: 574–604.

Strauss, A. 1987. *Qualitative analysis for social scientists.* Cambridge: Cambridge University Press.

Tilly, C. 2000. Relational studies of inequality. *Contemporary Sociology* 29, no. 6: 782–5.

Vizi, S. 1993. Reversing the brain drain from Eastern European countries: The 'push' and 'pull' factors. *Technology in Society* 15, no. 1: 101–9.

Walby, S., J. Armstrong, and S. Strid. 2012. Intersectionality: Multiple inequalities in social theory. *Sociology* 10, no. 1: 1–17.

Wallace, C. 2002. Opening and closing borders: Migration and mobility in East-Central Europe. *Journal of Ethnic and Migration Studies* 28, no. 4: 603–25.

Wallace, C., and D. Stola. 2001. *Patterns of migration in Central Europe.* Basingstoke: Palgrave Macmillan.

Wallace, C., and K. Vincent. 2007. Recent migration from the new European borderlands. *Review of Sociology of the Hungarian Sociological Association* 13, no. 2: 19–37.

West, C., and D. Zimmerman. 2002. Doing gender. In *Doing gender, doing difference: Inequality, power, and institutional change*, ed. S. Fenstermaker and C. West, 3–24. London: Routledge.

Wimmer, A. 2008. Elementary strategies of ethnic boundary making. *Ethnic and Racial Studies* 31, no. 6: 1025–55.

Scientific diasporas, transnationalism and home-country development: evidence from a study of skilled Moldovans abroad

Gabriela Tejada[a], Vitalie Varzari[b] and Sergiu Porcescu[c]

[a]*Cooperation and Development Center, Ecole Polytechnique Fédérale de Lausanne, Lausanne, Switzerland;* [b]*Department of European Integration and International Cooperation, Academy of Sciences of Moldova, Chisinau, Moldova;* [c]*Institute for Legal and Political Studies, Academy of Sciences of Moldova, Chisinau, Moldova*

This paper discusses the Moldovan 'scientific diaspora' made up of students, researchers and those engaged in professional activities abroad, and their propensity to either return or engage in home-country development initiatives. Moldova has suffered a significant loss of its qualified personnel since 1991, due to a difficult political transition and current low level of development. An online survey, supplemented by follow-up interviews, enabled the authors to outline the parameters of the Moldovan scientific diaspora and its current and potential future transnational activities. Although skilled Moldovans do feel positive about their study and work experiences abroad, they are also keen to help in the development of their home country. However, several determinants are necessary to make this happen: information about institutional initiatives, political stability, improved socio-economic prospects and an adequate infrastructure, a shared vision of the diaspora role, as well as specific instruments for engagement. Policy options are discussed in the conclusion.

Introduction

Large-scale emigration by scientists and skilled professionals from developing and transition countries in search of better opportunities and career prospects in high-income industrialized countries, commonly known as 'brain drain', is a major concern for the respective home countries. Yet, the emigrated human capital can also act as a bridge between the home and host countries, promoting the transfer of ideas, skills and knowledge. Examples have shown that foreign-based scientists and skilled professionals often undertake transnational actions that benefit the communities in home countries in the form of training, education and research collaborations that reinforce local capacities, as well as through investment and entrepreneurial activities. One such example is that of Romanian scientists abroad who were mobilized through the creation of the Ad-Astra Network in the early 2000s in favour of the reform of the education and research sector in Romania (Nedelcu 2008). Other

---

© 2013 The Author(s). Published by Taylor & Francis. This is an Open Access article. Non-commercial re-use, distribution, and reproduction in any medium, provided the original work is properly attributed, cited, and is not altered, transformed, or built upon in any way, is permitted. The moral rights of the named author(s) have been asserted.

instances include those of Indian and Chinese skilled professionals and technicians living in the United States who in the 1990s contributed to a strengthening of their countries' scientific and technological capacities through knowledge and technology transfers as well as investment linkages (Saxenian 2005; 2006). Finally, Colombian scientists based in Swiss academic and research institutions have boosted bilateral scientific collaboration for more than two decades strengthening a critical mass in key areas for the development of Colombia (Tejada 2012).

When considering skilled migration within the migration and development nexus, both academic research and policy discourse tend to refer to two main inter-related topics: firstly, the brain gain vs. brain drain debate and the challenges of retaining and attracting scientists and skilled professionals; secondly the diaspora option, encouraging interconnections between home and host countries allowing the transfer of various resources such as knowledge, technology, investments and financial remittances.

For Eastern European countries, the impact of skilled migration on development and the role of diasporas are new issues on the public agenda. In the Republic of Moldova, the mass emigration of skilled human capital is a tough challenge that has hindered the advancement of science, research and innovation in the 20 years since independence. Severe economic crises and a long political transition saw science neglected as a national priority until recently. The ensuing limited availability of infrastructure, employment opportunities and income prospects led to the massive emigration of scientists and skilled professionals. Over the past few years, the government has implemented specific initiatives under the auspices of the Academy of Sciences of Moldova (ASM) to counteract this loss, thereby opening up cooperation possibilities with Moldovan scientists abroad. Recognizing that scientists abroad can remain interconnected and contribute, Moldova offers an example in the region of policy strategies being set-up to address brain drain through the mobilization of scientific diasporas, and specifically by encouraging their involvement in activities related to research, technological development, innovation and education. Nevertheless, we still lack empirical evidence as to what the Moldovan scientific diaspora's transnationalism has been in practice and the opportunities and constraints that influence transnational ties and cooperation mechanisms in the home and host countries. By focusing on skilled migration from Moldova, this article seeks to fill some of the gaps in existing research. Based on the findings of a recent study, it provides an analysis of primary data on skilled Moldovans abroad collected through both an online survey and qualitative interviews.

The Republic of Moldova boasts a significant tradition of excellence in science, research and education; yet it lags behind in the various international rankings on prosperity. Therefore, it is crucial to address the brain drain challenge in both research and policy discussions about the relationship between migration, transnationalism and development. The Moldovan case study can serve as an example to examine the problems and prospects that arise within Eastern European countries going through a transitional phase, with regard to how they deal with the challenge of linking scientists abroad to national strategies for socio-economic progress. Since economic enabling factors such as precarious environments for scientific research, limited infrastructure, low salaries and restricted scientific and career prospects have led to the emigration of human capital, this study suggests that structural development conditions in Moldova need to improve if the country is to tap into the diasporas' potential.

Our paper has several objectives. Firstly, it seeks to promote a focus on the scientific diaspora option in research and discussions on the migration and development nexus. Secondly, it looks at the theoretical implications of this option. Thirdly, it offers an evidence-based analysis aimed at identifying the determinants of the transnationalism of skilled Moldovans and their cooperation activities with the national scientific community. Finally, it provides specific policy recommendations for Moldova.

The Moldovan context

To put the Moldovan case study into context, we offer a brief overview of the socio-economic and political situation of the country. Like other Eastern European countries, the Republic of Moldova underwent considerable pressure during its transition from a totalitarian and centralized economic system to a democracy and market economy after independence in 1991. During the 1990s the country faced a period of transformation with a significant deterioration of economic and social indicators, very limited access to basic public services and the impoverishment of large sections of the population. Moldova's political instability and a lack of complete control over its entire territory after the self-declared de facto independence of the state of Transnistria represented additional challenges. The complexity and magnitude of these challenges have prevented the country from equalling its pre-1991 GDP levels up to now, and today it is considered the poorest country in Europe with a GDP per capita of US$2900 and 65% of its population living below the poverty line (UNDP 2011a). Moldova ranked 111 worldwide amongst the 187 countries included in the 2011 UNDP Human Development Index (UNDP 2011a), showing the country still has a very long way to go towards an effective poverty eradication. Notwithstanding modest growth in recent years, the National Human Development Report shows a decrease in the employment rate from 55% in 2000 to 40% in 2009, confirming the unsustained nature of poverty reduction (UNDP 2011b). A further problem in the country is the lack of a strong and cohesive national identity. The multi-ethnic population, many minority groups and historically rooted clashes, as well as opposing sides representing competing political positions, make it difficult to establish a Moldovan identity amongst the population, and this constantly influences a political discourse divided between pro-Russian and pro-Western forces.

Today Moldova has one of the world's highest emigration rates. Estimates show 600,000 to 1 million Moldovans living outside the country. The UNDP figures show 23% of the total active population working abroad in 2009 (UNDP 2011b). There have been different stages of Moldovan emigration. The first stage, between 1991 and 1998, saw small-scale migration flows mainly for ethnic and political reasons and family reunification, particularly to Israel, the USA and Germany. After 1998, migration flows increased as a consequence of the regional economic crisis. The lack of opportunities and the poor quality of life forced many Moldovans to leave in search of better prospects in several destinations mostly in the Commonwealth of Independent States, principally Russia, and in Western Europe. According to the International Organization for Migration (IOM), the total number of emigrants living abroad grew from slightly less than 100,000 in 1999 to more than 400,000 by the end of 2005 (Lücke, Mahmoud, and Pinger 2007). This stage started with migration flows involving unskilled workers mostly, but in recent years the trend has changed with increasing flows of scientists, skilled professionals and students. Gaugas (2004) emphasizes the lack of connection between the educational system and the labour market. As a result, the increasing number of higher education graduates competing for scarce positions is an important push factor forcing skilled Moldovans to search for options abroad. A recent OECD (2012) study shows that 56% of people aged between 15 and 24, and 37% of those with a third-level education would leave permanently if they had the opportunity. Financial remittances represent a remarkable 23% of Moldovan GDP, placing the country amongst those with the highest remittance inflows in relation to GDP worldwide (World Bank 2011). The importance of these remittances is enormous as 26% of Moldovan households depend on them for their daily and basic consumption needs; yet they hardly influence or ameliorate structural constraints (Lücke, Mahmoud, and Pinger 2007; Orozco 2008).

Science and technology was a neglected sector in the country for almost 15 years after independence. Public investment in science and technology fell drastically between 1990, when it was 0.73% of GDP, and 2000, when it was only 0.18% of GDP (ASM 2010). Science, research and innovation activities suffered major degradation due to a lack of proper funding, adequate wages and up-to-date infrastructure. At a management level, the methods of organizing science remained conservative and the legislative framework had a regressive rather than a stimulating character. However, the scientific excellence of Moldovan researchers and the reputation of the country's science schools remained high; but this alone could not prevent many scientists from emigrating in search of better opportunities abroad, and indeed it even acted as a push factor. Others left the national research system to join other fields of activity in the country, where they were overqualified in most cases. As a result, the scientific potential of Moldova fell by 83% in 15 years, dropping from a total of 30,000 scientific researchers in the early 1990s to less than 5000 in 2004 (ASM 2010). By 1 January 2011, the country had only 5216 employees registered in the research and development R&D area.[1] The year 2004 marked a turning point with Parliament's ratification of the Code on Science and Innovation and the adoption of the Partnership Agreement between the Government and ASM, aimed at ensuring sustained support for science and R&D-related activities and offering better conditions to scientists. As a result, state investment in science and technology increased systematically, reaching 0.74% of GDP in 2008. Additionally, the ASM launched a focused strategy in 2008 to encourage linkages with skilled Moldovans abroad with a view to overcoming the brain drain challenge. Two complementary initiatives have been implemented recently, opening up cooperation possibilities between Moldovan scientists abroad and the national scientific community. The first is the IOM-ASM temporary return programme for Moldovan scientists and young researchers, implemented within the framework of the EU-Moldova Mobility Partnership.[2] The second is the ASM–EPFL research project providing knowledge-based evidence on Moldovan skilled emigration, transnational links and development impact.[3] In recent years, the country has also tried to involve skilled Moldovans abroad in the promotion of its integration into the European Union (EU). However, although Moldova participates in the European Neighbourhood Policy (ENP) and is already integrated into the European Research Area through its recent association with the EU FP7 Programme, accession to the EU will certainly not happen overnight.

Conceptual considerations

The increasing scale and scope of international migration offers new concepts and perspectives for both research and political discussion as they seek to explain its intersections with development. These include a new vision of the emigration of human capital, examining challenges and opportunities resulting from the transnationalism of skilled migrants and reverse knowledge transfers to home countries.

If we take a quick look at the evolution of the academic debate on migration and development over the last few decades, and skilled migration in particular, we can see how the pessimistic and sceptical brain drain option of the 1970s and 1980s underwent a significant change from the 1990s. This switch involved more thorough or pluralist alternatives influenced by the new economy of labour migration and the opening up of national resources within a knowledge-based economy; accordingly related perspectives started to focus on migrant transnationalism, networks and cooperation links with home countries. This new standpoint arose when, in an attempt to move from general formulations to the generation of policies that could deal with this phenomenon, the limitations explaining the loss of human capital became obvious, leading to alternative proposals promoting the use of skilled migrants' resources through knowledge transfer and circulation strategies. This is how scientists and skilled professionals abroad started to be perceived as available capital, susceptible to being mobilized to benefit home countries (Gaillard and Gaillard 1999; Johnson and Regets 1998; Meyer 2001).

Following this paradigm change, optimistic functionalist visions acquired prominence from 2000 onwards, making transnationalism a popular theoretical framework in the most recent studies on migration and its interfaces with development. This vision emphasizes financial remittances as an important source of growth for home countries (Adams 2003; Agunias 2006; de Haas 2005) and it praises the transnational ties migrants have with their communities of origin (Portes 2001; Vertovec 2004). Transnationalism sees individuals as carriers of their own identity without being uprooted from their home country, and they belong to several places simultaneously whilst building up and maintaining links over borders (Levitt and Glick Schiller 2004; Vertovec 2001). Several empirical studies underline the possibility of migrants acting as agents of development (de Haas 2006; Katseli, Lucas, and Xenogiani 2006; Lowell and Gerova 2004) and attempt to identify conditions and factors necessary to generate positive impacts. Continuing along similar lines, other studies have shown how international migration and the mobility of human capital can lead to a strengthening of the scientific and technological capacities of home countries. Examples from India and China (Saxenian 2005; 2006) illustrate the contributions that engineers and technicians make to their home countries through knowledge, investment and technology transfers. In other cases, countries affected by brain drain have benefitted from temporary returns and circular migration schemes (Agunias and Newland 2007; Wickramasekara 2011).

Another recent evolution is the recognition of *scientific diasporas* as new development actors (Barré et al. 2003; Tejada and Bolay 2010). Scientific diasporas bring together groups of scientists, engineers and skilled professionals acting mainly to produce new knowledge and collectively create cooperation opportunities with home countries. Their networking actions are based on the logic of connectivity and the multiplier effect of a personal interest to participate in a community project (Meyer 2001). The knowledge circulation dynamics of scientific diasporas see them considered as *knowledge communities* (Foray 2004) with the potential to act as agents of change back home (Tejada 2012). In some cases, scientific diasporas form networks using information and communication technologies to boost their connectivity with home countries. Whilst many scientific diaspora networks promote knowledge circulation through collective transnationalism, their efficiency to create an impact and their sustainability over time have been questioned; and there are many failed examples (Meyer 2011). Network benefits for migrants are more apparent at an individual level, providing social contacts (Bruggeman 2008) and sustained access to social capital (Bourdieu 1986).

Specific factors are highlighted in the literature as influencing diaspora transnationalism. These include the reasons for emigrating, migrants' socio-demographic profile, as well as their length of stay and main activity in the host countries. The conditions of migrants in host countries, and specifically their level of integration, are also shown to exert important influence. Many studies have examined the link between integration and transnationalism, considering transnational ties and incorporation in the host society as entwined and concurrent social processes (Itzigsohn and Giorguli-Saucedo 2002). Yet, the different alternative views in the analysis of the options suggested by this correspondence of processes make the discussion inconclusive as to whether one facilitates or hinders the other. Migrants' return planning is another key factor inducing diaspora transnationalism, and its interplay with integration is often referred to in the literature (de Haas and Fokkema 2011). By considering their appraisal of what their future plan may look like, migrants tend to invest their time and resources in activities related to such a priority project. If they plan to return to the home country, it is likely that they will attach significant importance to maintaining their transnational ties, and place less importance on integration. Similarly, it is assumed that migrants' integration in the host countries weakens their transnational ties and decreases return intentions. Nonetheless, here the discussion also remains inconclusive, and a recent study by de Haas and Fokkema (2011) into the impact of integration and transnational ties on return migration plans disputes the theoretical arguments that conceptualize return migration and transnationalism as a cause or an effect of integration failure.[4]

The value of group mobilization and structures in the form of networks or associations has been shown to be a condition for encouraging a diaspora's collective transnationalism. Saxenian (2006) refers to organized collective actions in the form of diaspora networks of technicians or engineers linked by their international exposure and shared cultural ties, as determinants of the duration of collaborations with home countries over time. From a diaspora standpoint, we should see both a common cultural, ethnic or national identity and a collective relation of solidarity with the home country, as the glue binding migrants together in communitarian actions. Such actions in the form of collective transnational practices are indeed a result of diasporas' shared identity (Bordes Benayoun and Schnapper 2006; Butler 2001).

Whilst the significance of knowledge and ideas embedded in human capital as a development catalyst is widely recognized, the relationship between diasporas' transferred skills and knowledge, on the one hand, and socio-economic progress on the other, is not straightforward; and in reality we can see that local society does not benefit from these practices in many cases. Furthermore, the potential positive impact of skilled migration is not similar for all countries. The discussion remains complex and far from conclusive, mainly as a result of two issues. First of all, the divergent approaches are often based on different analytical levels entailed in the multidimensionality of the development concept, which may refer specifically to the distinct micro, meso or macro levels of the impacts. Secondly, the enabling environment in the home country matters and the diverse contexts across countries help to explain why migration can play a positive development role in some cases but not in others. As de Haas (2008) argues, the extent to which migrants' contributions can influence positive socio-economic change in home countries depends on broad structural conditions. He suggests paying greater attention to the relevance of structural problems that limit diasporas' interventions in home countries and to the role that state and other actors, including international organizations, can play in creating favourable environments. Indeed, the specific country setting under which migration occurs determines its development impact, and examples have shown that benefitting from diaspora knowledge transfer and circulation is only possible when home countries offer an adequate scientific and technological infrastructure.

What role do these determinants play in the case of skilled Moldovans abroad? What are the main challenges and opportunities that Moldova has to capitalize for an effective scientific diaspora transnationalism? To respond to these questions, we will now consider the above conceptual considerations and use a transnational standpoint as an analytical framework to provide a complementary vision of the host and home countries. By examining the transnational links of skilled Moldovans abroad, and specifically their cooperation actions with the scientific community based in Moldova, we hope to shed light on the influence that the aforementioned determinants can have on their transnational actions.

Methodology

The rest of this article draws on an analysis of the experiences of skilled Moldovans abroad aimed at understanding the determinants of their transnational cooperation actions with Moldova.[5] We are particularly interested in their conditions and experiences in host countries, the ties with the home country, as well as their perceptions of both the environment in the host countries and the situation in Moldova, which affect their transnational interventions and cooperation prospects, and their migration plans.

The data presented here were collected between 2011 and 2012 using a primary online survey applied to a target group defined as 'members of the Moldovan scientific diaspora'. This refers to Moldovan scientists, researchers and skilled professionals living abroad, as well as postgraduate students (MA and PhD) from all disciplines, professional areas and sectors. Respondents were asked about their motivations for emigrating, experiences in host countries, links with Moldova, future plans, and perceptions of their role in home-country development. The survey was answered by 197 members of the Moldovan scientific diaspora. To complement this, 27 qualitative face-to-face interviews were conducted with Moldovans selected from the same group. Given the impossibility of precisely knowing the entire population of skilled Moldovans abroad, the purposive sampling method was applied.[6] To recruit the sample, we used both formal channels (email invitations sent to people on ASM lists, ASM newsletter subscribers, diaspora associations and organisations, and consulates and embassies); and informal channels such as social networks and the snowball principle. As the response rate was initially lower than expected, a second round of email messages was despatched after four months. The following sections present some of the observations of the survey and are complemented with excerpts from the testimonies of the Moldovans interviewed.

Empirical evidence of skilled Moldovans abroad

The basic parameters of the survey respondents are as follows. Most of the 197 Moldovans surveyed are aged between 26 and 35; mostly female (58%); half are married and less than half have children. Half of them hold a Master's degree, and half have either a PhD or a Bachelor's degree, in the main disciplines of economics, social and political sciences, and management and business. Two-thirds left Moldova between 2000 and 2010 and around one-third before the year 2000.

Migration determinants and conditions in host countries

Skilled Moldovans mainly choose their destinations on the basis of opportunities offered and less because of geographical and cultural proximity or a shared language. The main destination countries for the respondents surveyed are in Western Europe (Germany, France, Belgium, Spain, the Netherlands, UK and Switzerland), the Commonwealth of Independent States and neighbouring countries (Russia, Ukraine and Romania), and North America (the USA and Canada). We observed that push factors in Moldova are stronger than pull factors in destination countries, because the home-country context is the main catalyst behind skilled Moldovans deciding to emigrate. Political and economic instability and the consequential lack of professional prospects and the precarious life quality are major push factors. Skilled Moldovans emigrate in search of better living standards, improved career prospects, further education and scientific advancement. Moldovans also see migration as a means of moving to a new professional context offering better rewards for labour and fairer competition which they think are lacking in Moldova. The relevance of international exposure for their scientific careers is an important migration determinant. One scientist highlighted his desire to learn new research methodologies and to access modern infrastructure which was impossible during Soviet years:

> Until 1991 researchers from Moldova had no access to international publications, scientific events or research projects, and when the opportunity opened up for me to apply for a research grant, I went to Germany.

The search for further training abroad is another important motivation. Indeed, more and more skilled Moldovans emigrate as students. Moldovans feel their migration project will provide international exposure and valuable experience that will be appreciated in Moldova, and they expect to use the acquired knowledge for its benefit.

The most important factor behind the decision to leave is personal motivation, as indicated by 80% of respondents; the influence of family, colleagues and friends on their decisions is less important. Therefore, skilled migration from Moldova may be understood as the result of individual strategies established to improve personal conditions at both a professional and private level. The families back in Moldova view their departure with a sense of pride for having accomplished their professional or educational project abroad. The emigration process is seen as an achievement, and parents prefer to see their children depart and succeed abroad rather than remain dissatisfied at home under precarious conditions.

Skilled Moldovans have a positive perception of the environment offered by host countries, particularly regarding employment and career opportunities, income level, level of scientific research and the living environment. However, the ease of doing business and obtaining a residence and/or working permit is a constraint they still face. Most Moldovans believe they are well integrated socially in the host countries because of their good knowledge of local languages and their participation in local organizations and associations. More than half hold temporary residence status; less than half are permanent residents or citizens of the host country. With regard to their professional integration, we can see that the majority of those in paid employment consider themselves to be well established professionally and show a high level of satisfaction with their jobs in the host country. If Moldovans are working within their field of specialization and feel their positions correspond to their qualifications, they consider that their technical and scientific competences have improved during their stay abroad and that their skill levels have increased.

With regard to students, we can see that they choose their destinations according to the prestige of institutions or academic programmes or they are guided by scholarships. Their selection is also influenced by expected employment opportunities after graduation and their perception of policies in destination countries enabling such migration projects. Policies in some destination countries, mostly in North America and Western Europe, focused on attracting skilled human capital, are increasingly enabling international students to become part of the labour force. We can see that completing their studies in host countries is a general trend even for those Moldovans who emigrated for professional reasons. In order to adapt their qualifications to the requirements of the labour market in the host country, they pursue further training there as a necessary step towards accessing better employment opportunities. The discussion indicates that 'probationary immigration' (Kuptsch 2006) by Moldovan students is usually a precursor to labour migration, encouraging the transformation of students into qualified workers. Whilst Moldovans generally complete a Master's degree in their country of destination as a primary means of entering the local labour market, some opt to do a PhD.

Moldovans participate in professional associations and networks established abroad, which can be differentiated into two types. The first type are associations or professional networks of an exclusive nature focused on specific areas or disciplines, open to members from any country. Through their participation, skilled Moldovans establish transnational linkages with scientists across the world and have access to collaboration opportunities, which Moldova could also benefit from. The second type are associations that bring the Moldovan community abroad together and promote an exchange of experiences and the implementation of collective projects in favour of the home country. Compared to the first type, these are less exclusive (beyond, that is, the criterion of being Moldovan) and have significant implications thanks to their capacity to forge links amongst the diaspora, gather scattered individual efforts and promote collective action. However, their actions remain sporadic and are mostly focused on promoting cultural and social activities. Beyond these two types, apart from some emerging exceptions, there is no formal collaboration mechanism exclusively for Moldovan scientists and skilled professionals abroad in the form of a specialized scientific diaspora association or network which could boost the magnitude and impact of diaspora knowledge transfers (Meyer 2001). We can see that the lack of a collective identity within the Moldovan diaspora, which reflects the existing national identity problem and hinders collective transnationalism, is nonetheless evolving to more structured communitarian-focused initiatives; this is also related to the fact that mass emigration is still a recent phenomenon in Moldova. These observations are consistent with the concept of an 'emerging diaspora' (Buga 2011), which shows that the associative activities of

Moldovans abroad are made up of small informal networks created by Moldovans living in the same countries to promote shared cultural values and channel common efforts to benefit Moldova. These collective actions are seen as a 'sample of the evolution of the process of structuring the Moldovan diaspora towards a desire to affirm themselves as a group' (Buga 2011, 331).

Transnational links and development impact

Moldovans tend to cultivate their transnational links with the home country, and they communicate regularly with relatives, friends and colleagues back home. The majority return to Moldova once or several times a year, mainly to visit relatives and friends and to a lesser extent for scientific and academic exchanges. We observe that permanent settlement abroad and integration in the host societies does not necessarily result in a decline in the intensity of Moldovans' ties with their family and community back in Moldova. However, being able to determine whether the transnationalism of skilled Moldovans is concurrent with their integration in the host country (Itzigsohn and Giorguli-Saucedo 2002) or whether it works as a distinct path (Portes, Haller, and Guarnizo 2002) remains an empirical question still to be concretely answered.

In order to shed light on the feelings of skilled Moldovans about contributing to the progress of their home country and to identify the influence of their main activity in the destination country, we divided the respondents into three different groups based on their activity profile – students, scientists and researchers, and professionals.[7] Interest in Moldova's development is high for all three groups of respondents. They believe they could generally contribute to Moldova through their activities abroad and more precisely in terms of improving the image of Moldova, increasing the pool of better trained students, promoting investment, and improving the quality of science and research. We can see that, whilst students believe they can contribute through the education and skills gained abroad, professionals think they can promote an increase in foreign investment in Moldova. Scientists and researchers feel an attachment to Moldova through science and believe they can contribute through reverse knowledge transfers within their field of study.

There are some important qualitative differences between the transnational cooperation of Moldovan scientists and researchers, on the one hand, and those of students and professionals, on the other. These differences have mostly to do with the value of scientific exchange and collaboration, and the knowledge circulation created. Provided that Moldovan scientists have attained stable positions and a critical mass through their international exposure and networks, their transnational cooperation actions bridging science and innovation between scientists in the home country and their colleagues in host countries may open opportunities for new collaboration projects, which might generate important gains for Moldova. Concretely, systematic scientific collaboration may progressively enable advances in research, the reinforcement of local capacities and trigger further positive knowledge spillover effects back to Moldova. Since scientists believe Moldovan society can absorb direct benefits from their activities, they may be more willing to address issues of critical importance to the development of Moldova in their scientific and research endeavours. One researcher living in France said:

I believe Moldovan scientists have a great deal to contribute in the form of collaboration projects between scientists in Moldova and counterparts in Europe.

Other Moldovans pointed out the value of transnational cooperation:

People should see what we make in the West. What cannot be done in Moldova may be done in European institutions; [but] to achieve a common thing we need to work together.

Moldovan scientists think that knowledge transfer and the implementation of cooperation activities is difficult because of the lack of funding and scarce recognition of skilled Moldovans abroad, insufficient infrastructure in Moldova for host projects and a lack of time to undertake transnational cooperation. The difference in terms of working conditions and responsibilities is another barrier to cooperation with scientists based in Moldova. One researcher said:

Scientists who have settled in richer countries are available for various projects because their situation is different from those following a scientific career in Moldova. Here more time is devoted to research than in Moldova where teaching absorbs a great part of their time.

Whilst the incidence of cooperation projects implemented is higher for scientists and researchers than for students and professionals, the readiness to collaborate and contribute to Moldova's advancement was apparent across the three groups. Most Moldovans (86% or 151 persons) believe they can play an important role in the socio-economic advancement of Moldova and they are interested in getting

Table 1.   Transnational cooperation actions of skilled Moldovans abroad.

Knowledge sharing
Joint participation in seminars and/or international conferences
Sharing scientific knowledge and information with colleagues working in the same area
Better understanding of Moldovan problems through PhD topics chosen
Publication of scientific work in Moldova
Providing technical advice on key development issues
Information on scholarship opportunities abroad
Joint research
Involvement of Moldovan partners in international research projects
Joint publications in collaboration with Moldovan scientists
Helping Moldovan scientists to submit proposals for international research grants
Academic exchange
Temporary visits to research centres and universities
Sharing support materials for university courses
Giving lectures in Moldova
Co-mentoring Moldovan PhD students
Participation in the creation of academic programmes and syllabus design
Investment and business
Investment promotion projects
Other
Interventions in public administration reform

Source: ASM—EPFL survey of the Moldovan scientific diaspora (2011–2012).

involved in specific initiatives such as temporary visits, joint research projects, public policy advice, technology transfer and investment promotion. A Moldovan respondent working in France mentioned:

> I am open to participating in any projects that are linked to Moldova's development that might help improve its situation.

Table 1 shows examples of transnational cooperation actions carried out by skilled Moldovans abroad.

Future plans and perceptions of enabling conditions

Migration projects are related to perceptions of the opportunities offered. The future plans of Moldovans depend on the options they feel both host countries and Moldova will offer them to accomplish their projects. Our study therefore also sheds light on the plans of migrant Moldovans to return in the future. We found that students are the most likely to return to Moldova (47%), followed by scientists and researchers (35%) and finally by professionals (28%). Whilst their return intentions are related to their perceptions of opportunities available such as professional and private prospects, their interest to contribute to Moldova's socio-economic development is the most important reason to plan a return, with the desire to be with family and friends the second most important.

We also asked skilled Moldovans about their plans for the next five years. We find that 60% plan to stay in their current host country, whilst 16% plan to move to a third country and 10% plan to return to Moldova. There were interesting differences in terms of profile. Scientists and researchers have the highest share (14%) amongst respondents planning to return to Moldova, followed by students (12%) and professionals (6%). Whilst 72% of scientists and researchers and 60% of professionals plan to stay in their current host country, only 40% of students intend to do so. We can also see that students are more uncertain about their short-term future plans than scientists and professionals in paid employment. This is probably because they are younger and without family responsibilities, but also because their stay in host countries is shorter and their situation less stable than the other two groups; yet they appear to be more open to opportunities. The discussion indicates that Moldovan students abroad do not limit their migratory plans to specific time frames or places, but rather they follow a strategy where their options are kept deliberately open. Migrants' deliberate hesitation is significant when they are uncertain about the chances that the future will offer them. Accordingly, we might conclude that the mobility behaviour of international students changes according to the opportunities available and perceptions of the environments in the host and home countries, as well as in third countries. The intentions of students to return and those actually doing so may increase if they believe Moldova can offer them a safe and trustful environment with a specific career and future prospects.

Moldovans who do not intend to return remain sceptical of Moldova being able to offer them such prospects. They think the situation of poor scientific and career options, a low quality of life, and political and socio-economic instability will not change soon and so they feel a brighter future awaits them elsewhere. Whilst students have more trust in job opportunities that may be offered, scientists rate scientific advancement options in Moldova more highly. In overall terms, skilled Moldovans are willing to contribute to Moldova's progress, but are discouraged by the attitude of the Moldovan government, which they feel is not interested in engaging them in development efforts, and also by the hostility of Moldovan society towards scientists abroad. Despite negative perceptions of the home-country environment, transnational cooperation of Moldovan scientists is expected to rise in the years to come. There are several reasons for this. Firstly, the institutional programmes and specific brain gain policies of the Moldovan government have encouraged transnational collaboration and other forms of interaction between emigrated scientists and the national scientific community in recent years, and further incentives are expected. Secondly, recognition and visibility of the capacities of Moldovan scientists abroad are increasing. Thirdly, new opportunities for international collaborations are boosted by Moldova's recent association with the EU FP7 Programme.

As part of the enabling environment, adequate policies are perceived as crucial both for encouraging bottom-up transnational collaboration initiatives from the diaspora, and in the form of top-down incentive programmes. We can observe that Moldovans know very little about the existence of institutional programmes that the government has recently implemented to engage skilled Moldovans abroad.[8] The main reasons for not participating include a lack of interest in supporting the government and a distrust of these initiatives. A US-based researcher said:

> I am very interested in participating, but the majority of these programmes are not advertised properly.

The discussion indicates that whilst top-down policies implemented by the government include valuable programmes, the scientific diaspora appears to lack ownership of these initiatives and this is necessary to boost bottom-up practices.

Conclusions

Today, Moldova is undergoing a series of important reforms aimed at advancing economic growth and poverty reduction. These include a specific strategy to boost science, research and innovation, encourage international cooperation and acknowledge the role of the scientific diaspora in helping the country strengthen its competitiveness. The situation leads us to believe that the country's committed support for specific policies boosting linkages with the diaspora is based on two complementary points. Firstly, recognition of the potential gains the home country can obtain from collaboration with Moldovan scientists abroad, which goes beyond the general advantages of research collaboration; for example, through temporary visits or circular migration that might lead to a permanent return, or through engagement in policy design or the promotion of entrepreneurial activities and investments. Secondly, the belief that the Moldovan national system of science, research and innovation is sufficiently adequate and capable of benefitting from international scientific collaboration.

The objective of this study was not to magnify the role of scientists and skilled professionals abroad in the development of their home country. Rather, our interest was to provide an evidence-based analysis of opportunities and challenges for skilled migrants' transnationalism, which might contribute to advancing academic discussion on the development impact of migration and make some specific recommendations for Moldova. The evidence shows that although skilled Moldovans abroad do have the motivation and potential to benefit the home country through collaboration with the scientific and professional community in Moldova, this can only be accomplished if adequate conditions are put in place and maintained over time. The evidence gathered indicates that skilled Moldovans will continue to emigrate, but it also shows that return skilled migration could occur. However, if economic and political conditions in Moldova remain unclear, it could happen that migrants intending to return might decide to settle abroad and maintain their transnational ties. Likewise, return results in the transfer of skills and knowledge only when returning human capital can be utilized in the home country. Therefore, the country's structural situation must improve significantly and adequate policies need to be put in place.

A number of specific policy recommendations drawn from this study could help. First of all, since the collective actions of the skilled Moldovans abroad are still weak, notwithstanding early signs of an evolution towards better cohesion, there is a need to recognize them as an important asset and to promote their associative activities, supported by well-advertised diaspora policies. Secondly, a suitable environment to validate the knowledge and resources transferred within the local socio-economic context needs to be secured, and this should include political stability and governability. Thirdly, both the sustained return and a continuous enhancement of diasporas' transnational cooperation need to be secured through improvements to the local structural situation. Such improvements include a systematic institutional commitment to science and education; the creation of conditions to guarantee good employment opportunities and access to resources and infrastructure; ensuring coherence between higher education programmes and labour market needs; enabling the transfer of skills gained abroad upon return (ensuring jobs–qualifications matching); and making sure the transferred scientific research and knowledge can become useful to local society. For this, cooperation with key national and international actors is necessary in order to create appropriate environments to trigger brain gain for Moldova.

Notes

1. National Statistics Office, 3 May 2012, http://www.statistica.md/newsview.php?l=ro&id-c=168&id=3744 (accessed November 7, 2012).
2. During recent years, IOM-Moldova has been an important player in moving forward the debate on migration and development in the country, including highlighting the role of diasporas, as well as in pushing this issue on the national agenda, for which concrete policies have now been designed and adopted.
3. The project was carried out through a collaboration agreement between the ASM and the Ecole Polytechnique Fédérale de Lausanne (EPFL) between 2010 and 2012 and it was financed by the SCOPES Programme of the Swiss National Science Foundation and the Swiss Agency for Development and Cooperation.
4. See also the paper by Cela, Fokkema, and Ambrosetti (2013) in this issue.
5. This study is based on the ASM–EPFL research project, which sought to advance knowledge on Moldovan scientists and skilled professionals abroad and thereby provide specific policy recommendations about how to benefit from collaboration opportunities with the Moldovan scientific community.
6. The sampling strategy and the lower than hoped-for response rate to that expected indicate that a response bias could influence the findings, such as an over-representation of respondents interested in development or those who are professionally well established abroad. In this sense, the possible positive effects of migration might be exaggerated. Therefore, we should try not to place too much trust in the extent to which the findings

of the survey can be generalized. However, this first attempt to identify skilled Moldovans abroad will help in extracting general trends and opening new paths for future research. Furthermore, the methodology and research tools will be useful for additional studies of a similar nature.

7. We collected responses from 36 students, 41 scientists and researchers employed in a research or academic institution, and 88 professionals in paid employment or self-employed.

8. Examples are the IOM-ASM temporary return programme, the creation of the council of scientists of Moldovans abroad, the PARE 1+1 programme promoting an entrepreneurial use of remittances, and the Moldovan Diaspora Congress.

References

Academy of Sciences of Moldova (ASM). 2010. *Annual reports on the activities of the Academy of Sciences of Moldova: Years 1990–2009*. Chisinau: ASM Printing House [in Romanian].

Adams, R. 2003. International migration, remittances and the brain drain: A study of 24 labor-exporting countries. Policy Research Working Paper 3069. Washington DC: World Bank.

Agunias, D.R. 2006. *Remittances and development: Trends, impacts and policy options. A review of the literature*. Washington DC: Migration Policy Institute.

Agunias, D.R., and K. Newland. 2007. *Circular migration and development: Trends, policy, routes and ways forward*. Policy Brief. Washington DC: Migration Policy Institute.

Barré, R., V. Hernández, J.-B. Meyer, and D. Vinck. 2003. *Scientific diasporas: How can developing countries benefit from their expatriate scientists and engineers?*. Paris: Institute de la Recherche pour le Développement [in French].

Bordes Benayoun, C., and D. Schnapper. 2006. *Diasporas and nations*. Paris: Odile Jacob [in French].

Bourdieu, P. 1986. The forms of capital. In *Handbook of theory and research for the sociology of education*, ed. J.G. Richardson, 241–58. New York, NY: Greenwood Press.

Bruggeman, J. 2008. *Social networks: An introduction*. New York, NY: Routledge.

Buga, N. 2011. Diasporas as resources of integration in the global economy. PhD diss., Pierre Mendès France University [in French].

Butler, K. 2001. Defining diaspora, refining a discourse. *Diaspora* 10, no. 2: 189–219.

Cela, E., T. Fokkema, and E. Ambrosetti. 2013. Variation in transnationalism among Eastern European migrants in Italy: The role of duration of residence and integration. *Southeast European and Black Sea Studies* 13, no. 2: this issue.

de Haas, H. 2005. International migration, remittances and development: Myths and facts. *Third World Quarterly* 26, no. 8: 1269–84.

DEVELOPMENT IN SOUTH-EAST EUROPE AND THE BLACK SEA REGION

de Haas, H. 2006. *Engaging Diasporas: How governments and development agencies can support diaspora involvement in the development of origin countries*. A study for Oxfam Novib. Oxford: University of Oxford, International Migration Institute.

de Haas, H. 2008. Migration and development: A theoretical perspective. Working Paper 9. Oxford: University of Oxford, International Migration Institute.

de Haas, H. 2011. The migration and development pendulum: A critical view on research and policy. Paper presented at the international conference 'Migration and development nexus revisited: State of the art and ways ahead', June 8–10, University of Trento, Italy.

de Haas, H., and T. Fokkema. 2011. The effects of integration and transnational ties on international return migration intentions. *Demographic Research* 25, no. 24: 755–82.

Foray, D. 2004. *Economics of knowledge*. Cambridge, MA: MIT Press.

Gaillard, A.M., and J. Gaillard. 1999. *The challenges of international scientific migration: From the quest for knowledge to the circulation of competencies*. Paris: L'Harmattan [in French].

Gaugas, P. 2004. Labour migration in Moldova: Contexts and controls. *Higher Education in Europe* 29, no. 3: 343–52.

Itzigsohn, J., and S. Giorguli-Saucedo. 2002. Immigrant incorporation and sociocultural transnationalism. *International Migration Review* 36, no. 3: 766–98.

Johnson, J., and M. Regets. 1998. *International mobility of scientists and engineers to the United States: Brain drain or brain circulation*. Issue Brief 316. Arlington, VA: National Science Foundation.

Katseli, L., R. Lucas, and T. Xenogiani. 2006. Effects of migration on sending countries: What do we know? Working Paper 250. Paris: OECD Development Centre.

Kuptsch, C. 2006. Students and talent flow – the case of Europe: From castle to harbour? In *Competing for global talent*, ed. C. Kuptsch and P.E. Fong, 33–61. Geneva: International Institute for Labour Studies.

Levitt, P., and N. Glick Schiller. 2004. Conceptualizing simultaneity: A transnational social field perspective on society. *International Migration Review* 38, no. 3: 1002–39.

Lowell, L., and S.G. Gerova. 2004. *Diasporas and economic development: State of knowledge*. Washington DC: Georgetown University, Institute for the Study of International Migration.

Lücke, M., T. Mahmoud, and P. Pinger. 2007. *Patterns and trends on migration and remittances in Moldova*. Chisinau: IOM.

Meyer, J.B. 2001. Network approach versus brain drain: Lessons from the diaspora. *International Migration* 39, no. 5: 91–110.

Meyer, J.B. 2011. A sociology of diaspora knowledge networks. In *The migration–development nexus*, ed. T. Faist, M. Fauser, and P. Kivisto, 159–84. Basingstoke: Palgrave Macmillan.

Nedelcu, M. 2008. Internet diaspora: How Romanian scholars abroad connect home. Working Paper 17. Florence: European University Institute, Research Network 1989.

OECD. 2012. *Strengthening ties with the diasporas: An overview of migrants' skills*. Paris: OECD [in French].

Orozco, M. 2008. *Looking forward and including migration in development: Remittance leveraging opportunities for Moldova*. Chisinau: IOM.

Portes, A. 2001. The debates and significance of immigrant transnationalism. *Global Networks* 1, no. 3: 181–94.

Portes, A., W. Haller, and L. Guarnizo. 2002. Transnational entrepreneurs: An alternative form of immigrant economic adaptation. *American Sociological Review* 67, no. 2: 278–98.

Saxenian, A. 2005. From brain drain to brain circulation: Transnational communities and regional upgrading in India and China. *Studies in Comparative International Development* 40, no. 2: 35–61.

Saxenian, A. 2006. *The new Argonauts: Regional advantage in a global economy*. Cambridge, MA: Harvard University Press.

Tejada, G. 2012. Mobility, knowledge and cooperation: Scientific diasporas as agents of development. *Migration and Development* 10, no. 18: 59–92.

Tejada, G., and J.C. Bolay. 2010. *Scientific diasporas as development partners: Skilled migrants from Colombia, India and South Africa in Switzerland. Empirical evidence and policy responses.* Bern: Peter Lang.

UNDP. 2011a. *Human development report 2011. Sustainability and equity: A better future for all.* New York, NY: UNDP.

UNDP. 2011b. *National human development report 2010/2011. Republic of Moldova: From social exclusion towards inclusive human development.* Chisinau: UNDP.

Vertovec, S. 2001. Transnationalism and identity. *Journal of Ethnic and Migration Studies* 27, no. 4: 573–82.

Vertovec, S. 2004. Migrant transnationalism and modes of transformation. *International Migration Review* 38, no. 3: 970–1001.

Wickramasekara, P. 2011. *Circular migration: A triple win or a dead end?* Geneva: ILO.

World Bank. 2011. *Migration and remittances factbook 2011.* Washington DC: World Bank.

Welfare through migrant work: what if the Romanian 'safety valve' closes?

Bruno Meeus

Sint-Lucas School of Architecture, Brussels and University of Leuven, Belgium

The Romanian work migration system came as an answer to the increased individual welfare risks caused by a particular form of Romanian neoliberalism. The system acts as a transnational labour market built up from the grassroots. Through its maturing, this migration system has acted as a 'safety valve' in Romania: neoliberal principles could be built into the Romanian welfare system. As such, migrant work abroad became a structural aspect of the Romanian welfare system. The austerity measures that are currently imposed on Mediterranean economies hosting Romanian migrants, and on Romania itself, therefore, create a double pressure on welfare in the latter, since they undermine the 'safety valve' capacity of the migration system.

Introduction

Recently, Smith and others (2012) stated that the current financial and economic instability in different places across Europe is not only symptomatic of the depth of the crisis of capitalism but also evidence of the interconnectedness of states, regions and cities across Europe. In this paper, I wish to endorse their statement. I will argue that the current economic crisis in Mediterranean Europe – Spain, Portugal, Italy, Greece – also hits those places in Romania that have increasingly become dependent upon a system of reproduction that grew bottom up through the migratory practices of Romanian migrant workers, these migratory practices having originated as a reaction to a previous round of austerity measures.

A critical political-economic perspective on work migration frames my argument. This perspective developed during the 1970s and 1980s when some scholars started to look at human mobility through the lens of historical materialism, arguing that the mobility of workers plays a central role in capitalism on two occasions (see, *inter alia*, Harvey 1982; Portes 1978; Sassen 1989). First, since capitalist production depends on individual workers who need an income, people have to be disconnected or 'freed' from the collective structures of reproduction in which they are embedded. The resulting 'mobilized' individual workers depend for their welfare on the accessibility of different markets: labour markets for a wage, housing markets for a home and so on. Secondly, people's mobility then becomes dominated by the spatial and temporal logics of the successes and failures of markets: the spatio-temporal logics of capital accumulation, the logics of cyclical growth and crisis in certain sectors of the economy and the rhythms of the working day (De Gaudemar 1976). This dependence on markets, however, increases individual risks, for instance the risk of having to pay for a house without finding a job. But, as Polanyi (1944) pointed out, society reacts against the devastating consequences of individualization in which the spatial and temporal logics of markets dominate welfare provisioning. The process of dis-embedding is followed by diverse societal grassroots reactions, some of which try to re-embed the economy in society through social struggle, whilst at the same time aiming at the re-collectivization of individual risks.

The goal of this article is to link these societal dialectics with Hirschman's classic migration model. In this model, Hirschman (1970) discerned three reactions to change in a certain place: staying and making the best out of it (loyalty), mobilization against change (voice) and leaving the place (exit). But whilst these three options were considered by Hirschman as mutually exclusive, I endorse Hoffmann's (2008) argument that Hirschman's migration paradigm needs to be recontextualized in order to avoid 'methodological nationalism'. Indeed, the overlapping and simultaneity of 'exit', 'voice' and 'loyalty' are precisely the most important features of 'transnational' migration (Vertovec 2009). Within a critical political–economic framework, there are at least three ways in which this overlapping can occur.

First of all, transnational political mobilization can be seen as 'voice resulting from exit'. Guarnizo and Smith (1998) and Samers (2002), amongst others, have argued that transnational migrant networks (can) enable new forms of democratic participation and transnational political mobilization.

Secondly, 'exit' can itself be seen as a form of mobilization ('voice'). In reality, migration is no individual undertaking. Instead, the migrant networks literature suggests that existing social networks are mobilized in order to succeed in receiving information about employers, wages and housing abroad. As such, migration is a form of collective agency that builds on existing structures that enable mobility and out of which new patterns, pathways, migration industries and other migration-enabling structures develop (Goss and Lindquist 1995; Meeus 2011; Morawska 2001).

Thirdly, 'loyalty' and 'exit' are intertwined as well. Contrary to Hirschman, who maintained that exit equals the cutting of bonds between places of origin and destination, the transnational turn in migration research has pointed exactly to the fact that migrants retain these ties. Indeed, they develop hybrid identities that reflect diverse degrees of loyalty (Swyngedouw and Swyngedouw 2009). This persistent dual loyalty forms the basis of my argument, since the exploitation of Romanian migrants' loyalty by West European economies as well as by the Romanian state, is the underlying cause of the current double welfare crisis in Romania.

Indeed, the argument advanced by Burawoy (1976), Piore (1979), Castles and Kosack (1985), Freeman (1986) and Samers (1999), amongst others, about the systemic function of labour migration can be re-iterated here. These migration scholars argued that the re-embedding of citizen workers in receiving nation states in post war Western capitalism created 'closed' welfare systems for their citizens (Freeman 1986). However, since capitalist production in the West still needed workers prepared to fill in the vacant jobs in mining and construction work, such workers were imported, thereby creating a de facto dual labour market (see also Kloosterman, van der Leun, and Rath 1999). The reproduction of these workers was outsourced to the sending nation states. For Burawoy (1976), this typical 'migration system' was not characterized by a form of permanent migration, i.e. cutting the bonds. Instead, temporary or circulatory migration was organized in order to produce the spatial segregation of two types of welfare: maintenance welfare or the day-to-day reproduction of migrant workers, in the receiving states; and renewal welfare or labour's long-term reproduction, in the sending states. For the receiving states, this 'guest-worker system' had the advantage of not having to bear the responsibility for the 'renewal' of workers, since families and children were supposed to stay behind. As such, production in the receiving state capitalized on the persistent loyalty of 'guest-workers' who were encouraged or forced to leave again at the moment when insurgency developed (Samers 1999). Seen from the perspective of the sending state, a similar outsourcing of social reproduction occurs. If workers make use of transnational networks of social support, the sending state also does not have to bear full responsibility for the reproduction of its citizens (Piore 1979). Sending states also capitalize on migrants' loyalty: migrants work abroad in order to secure social reproduction 'at home'. Moreover, their migrant work acts as a 'safety valve' for the sending state: migrants' welfare is ensured, they do not mobilize against the welfare policies of the sending state, and the sending state does not have to invest in collectivizing the social risks of all its citizens.

Based on this framework, I focus on three main points in this article.

First, I argue that the Romanian work migration system evolved as a response to the increased individual welfare risks caused by a particular form of Romanian neoliberalism. The system acted as a transnational labour market and was built up from the grassroots. Secondly, through its maturing, this migration system acted as a 'safety valve' in Romania. Geographical proximity of informal work opportunities for over two million Romanians meant that neoliberal principles could be built into the Romanian welfare system, making migrant work a key structural aspect. Therefore, and my third point, the austerity measures that are currently imposed both in the Mediterranean economies and Romania cause a double pressure on welfare in Romania, since they undermine the 'safety valve' capacity of the Romanian migration system.

Dis-embedding in Romania: reform and the decline of 'voice'

Particularly important for understanding Romania's starting position on the road to post-socialist neoliberal reform was the specific heritage of the years of austerity preceding the 1989 revolution. Ceausescu's repayment of Romania's debts could only succeed through major cuts in domestic consumption and in public welfare at large. As a consequence, at the start of the reform period, popular support for state socialism was at its lowest level. At the same time, Western European industries and banks, backed by important lobby groups such as the European Roundtable of Industrialists (Balanya et al. 2003), were eager to 'redevelop' Eastern Europe in search of cheaper and non-unionized labour and an expanding market for consumption products, insurances, credit-takers and the like. The redevelopment involved two instances, as Ivanova (2007, 360) argues: first, the fundamental destruction of the socialist state through a retreat from its redistributive and investor function; and second, the creation of a strong neoliberal state that could effectively discharge its duties as legislator and guardian of the free market, creating and safeguarding favourable conditions for business operations. However, as Ivanova (2007) points out, the destruction of the state in Bulgaria and Romania has been so profound that what emerged was not fully capable of defending the interests of the foreign capitalist class.

There is no space in this article to give a complete historical overview of all the domains of social reproduction that were privatized. Instead, I focus on three issues: the shift of some key aspects of welfare from state responsibility to individual bodies; how this process accelerated when the influence of the IMF and the EU increased in 1997; and how Hirschman's 'voice', under the form of unions' protest, gradually declined. The remainder of this section draws considerably on Ban's (2011) recent work – the first systematic study of Romanian neoliberalism.

The power of the unions and the deterioration of welfare at the beginning of the 1990s

Reform in Romania started in the 1990–1991 period when the first post-socialist cabinet under President and former 'apparatchik' Iliescu made a first attempt at implementing neoliberal principles by declaring price and wage liberalization, privatization and the withdrawal of industrial subsidies as their most important objectives (Ban 2011, 364). As part of these measures, it was decided that state-owned companies should be split up in two kinds: 'regii autonome' which stayed in the hands of the state in order to keep control over strategic sectors of the economy and to secure employment, and 'commercial corporations' that were to be privatized.

However, the implementation of neoliberal principles proved to be much more difficult than in other Central and Eastern European countries. This was due to two key factors. First, the country lacked neoliberal technocrats placed in strategic positions. Second, working-class mobilization against price and wage liberalization was strong. Not only were the energies of the 1989 mass mobilizations still alive, but the austerity measures of the 1980s did not leave much manoeuvring space for further cuts in welfare such that industrial production continued to be dominated by large and very large state-owned enterprises where unions remained powerful. Labour mobilization ultimately led to the end of the first post-socialist government when the Jiu-valley miners went on strike and forced the government out of power at the end of 1991.

After this short period, a new cabinet under President Iliescu came into power and compiled an alternative to the neoliberal model between 1992 and 1997. It was based on an industrial policy that mainly tried to secure employment, renew the existing industrial stock and placate labour union resistance to privatization (Ban 2011, 380). However, the continuous expenditure on full employment channelled state funds away from much-needed investments in welfare provisioning. This had an important influence on the legitimacy of the reform policy amongst Romanians. Having not seen any serious investment in welfare since the beginning of the 1980s, they were now faced with a dilapidated welfare state which was a far cry from their expectation of enjoying a considerable improvement in their living standards after the revolution.

Indeed, both political periods had a significant impact on welfare since important parts of the already deteriorated socialist redistribution function were either privatized or left in deteriorating condition due to limited budget resources.

Three key areas reflect this well. The first is related to the countryside and the privatization of agricultural land that proved to be a lengthy and conflictual process. The land of collective farms, which represented 74% of Romania's arable land, was restituted to those who owned it before collectivization (1948–1962), whilst the state retained control of the land in the state farms. However, few land recipients could assemble the other production factors necessary for commercial farming. Consequently, a large share of the land was handed over to newly formed producers' cooperatives called 'associations' or was leased to emerging 'super-tenants' (Verdery 2003).[1]

The second focus concerns urban areas and the privatization of housing there. Most of the 1960s' and 1970s' dwellings built in urban areas were blocks of flats, usually 30 flats per block (Dan and Dan 2003). Although flats were equipped with installations and facilities, they were of a low quality, which often led to major problems concerning central heating, gas and running water. From the 1980s onwards, the housing crisis became increasingly acute. During the last decade of socialism, building activities slowed down causing increasing overcrowding. The 1990 elected government decided to sell the state housing stock to the tenants for symbolic prices. By transferring a difficult-to-manage, low-quality housing stock into private hands, the state essentially escaped from a significant responsibility.

The third point spans rural and urban areas and relates to healthcare provision and its deterioration over the years. Free access to medical services for everybody, equity in distribution of medical provision and easy access to physicians at all rural and urban places improved the health status of the population during the first decades of socialism. All of this changed during the austerity years of the 1980s. 'Unproductive' sectors such as healthcare were underfinanced and life expectancy decreased at the beginning of the nineties. There were no major changes in the Romanian health system during the period of 1990–1996 as a consequence of a lack of budgets, although the population's expectations were high.

The super-shock, the rise of the technocrats and the decline of the unions

The 1997 elections resulted in a change of power and a new period of privatization dawned. The 'ex-communists' lost the elections and the 'Democratic Convention' now in power gave neoliberalism a real chance. The economic reform authorized by the Convention was the most radical 'shock therapy' package tried anywhere in the East European region (Pop-Eleches 2009). Government spending on public services was halved, a massive withdrawal from the ownership of industrial assets was initiated and support for agriculture was suddenly stopped. The 1997 stand-by agreement with the IMF put the focus squarely on accelerating privatization, with one of the IMF criteria being the closure of loss-making enterprises. 'Voice', under the form of union protest, however, stopped the closure of several large enterprises whilst deficit figures kept rising. As Ban (2011) states, Romania experienced the worst of all worlds since the fragile Convention government lost IMF and World Bank financial support whilst pushing on with austere and pro-cyclical fiscal and monetary policies.

In the meantime, two important political power shifts occurred: first, a consolidation of a Romanian network of befriended technocrats and politicians; and second, decreasing public support for the influence of the unions' actions. As Ban (2011) again demonstrates, at the end of the 1990s, the vague structures of a particular form of Romanian 'Third Way' neoliberalism started to take shape. On the one hand, aided by German social-democrats, the former communists started to incorporate the latest Third Way ideas in the 2000 election manifesto of their 'Social Democratic Party' (PDS). On the other hand, due to increased international mobility of students of economics and the rise of externally funded Romanian 'think tanks', a small army of neoliberal technocrats began to develop.

A gradual shift in the public discourse about the transformation occurred as well. The 'company manager' became increasingly the central figure of the transforming economy. He was seen as the actor of change who was hindered in his freedom of enterprise by the power of unions and by the different workforce protection measures that were built into the privatization procedures by the former government. Notwithstanding their remaining power in some large enterprises, trade unions increasingly became the scapegoat. Over the course of the first post-socialist decade, unions and workers were largely depicted as symbolic reminders of a dark past, as trouble-makers that literally blocked the possibility of creating a new Romania (see also Kideckel 2008). This association was further strengthened by the fact that unions were mainly active in the former state-owned enterprises but were almost non-existent in new companies.

The 2000 elections brought the ex-communists of Iliescu, this time with prime minister Nastase, once again behind the steering wheel but now in a different power constellation. The new party programme was interlarded with Third Way ideas: a combination of macro-economic orthodoxy, privatization, deregulation and free trade coupled with tax cuts for business and an industrial policy centred on attracting FDI; a plea for increasing investments in welfare but with a focus on individual responsibility, activation and conditionality of benefits.

Under this Nastase government, privatization progressed at a fast pace as especially the large state-owned enterprises were sold leading to large-scale restructuring and lay-offs. The formerly strategic heavy industry – the petrochemical, oil as well as the electricity and gas companies – was sold to foreign owners, whilst the telecommunication and financial markets were deregulated.

The influence of the neoliberal period on social welfare

The massive growth of unemployment that followed and the policy to shrink benefits and to grant them for only half a year was accompanied by an increasing privatization and corporatization of social welfare. Several indicators testify to this.

Firstly, the price of houses and particularly flats in large urban areas increased dramatically after the legalization of mortgage loans in 2002; at the same time, the average rent for apartments and flats rose sharply (Panait 2009). Mortgage lending requires a stable income and thus a fixed job, as well as a deposit of at least a quarter of the price. The 2009 banking crisis made the borrowing of mortgages so difficult that the Romanian government introduced successive 'Prima Casa' programs – starter mortgages guaranteed by the state – to stimulate the building sector. At the same time, the number of foreign investors capitalizing on the Romanian housing market increased.

Secondly, in 2001, the general reform of the social insurance system was mainly built around a renewal of the pay-as-you-go pension system and resulted in the anchoring of private pension funds in the pension system (Goedemé 2006).

Thirdly, since the 1990s, different legislative changes in the social health insurance system were undertaken. The period until 2000 was characterized by a rapid process of polarization (Rebeleanu 2008), which saw a large segment of the population only marginally covered for health services. This was most pronounced in rural areas where overall coverage as well as access to medical services decreased. Furthermore, collateral payments (official co-payment of public services and unofficial informal payments to medical staff) and the rising price of medicines as a consequence of their price liberalization were heavy to bear at a time of decreasing consumption power. Medicines were especially vital in cases of chronic diseases that were often related to unhealthy work circumstances in mines and the paper and chemical industries. Access to healthcare depended further on the conditional social aid. Especially the Roma population was over-represented in the category of those not covered by social aid and consequently lacking health insurance (European Roma Rights Centre 2006, 29).

A case study: Piatra-Neamt and the privatization of the Savinesti platform

The above sketch of the main lines along which the Romanian public welfare system restructured has revealed that 'neoliberalism' was only gradually introduced in Romania. In order to illustrate how this slow introduction turned out 'in the field', the case of the Savinesti industrial platform, located in the Neamt region of northeast Romania, is revealing. The Romanian northeast is characterized by extensive socialist industrialization and urbanization and was, therefore, highly sensitive to the different phases of post-socialist restructuring. The overall decrease in salaried employment in the region is indicated in Figure 1 where the different stages of privatization can be discerned. A first wave of closures and privatization at the beginning of the 1990s was followed by a period of employment stability corresponding to the ex-communists' policy choice for full employment. From 1997 until 2001, the 'super-shock' took place, followed by 'Third Way' neoliberalism in which a further decrease, mainly in manufacturing, occurred.

The Savinesti industrial platform, one of the many socialist industrial developments in the northeast, was part of the large-scale socialist industrial development of the Bistrita valley. Throughout the socialist period, Bicaz remained a mono-industrial town specializing in cement production. The Savinesti industrial platform, located between Roznov and the former 'timber town' of Piatra-Neamt, was created during the 1950s and gathered different chemical industries located next to each other. 'Azochim', producer of fertiliser, commenced its activity in 1956. Next to it, the 'Combinatul de fire si fibre sintetice Savinesti' (CFS), where synthetic fibres and yarn were produced, was erected. The platform was built downstream of the city of Piatra-Neamt and the nearby Roznov I and II hydropower plants formed its power source. Hence, the space between Roznov and Piatra-Neamt turned into a continuous industrial production space (see Figure 2).

The town Piatra-Neamt was redeveloped as the residential space of this new industrial centre. It was completely rebuilt in view of its new function: in 1974 some 95% of the town consisted of new apartment blocks and only a few historical monuments and buildings remained. In Roznov, housing was provided for the technical staff in order to make fast interventions possible in case something went wrong. Hence, Piatra-Neamt, Roznov and the new town of Bicaz, as well as the communities in between, grew excessively in this period, based on immigration of

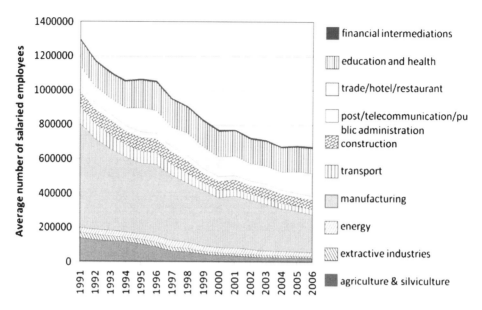

Figure 1. Number of salaried workers in the Romanian northeast.
Source: Institutul National de Statistica (2007).

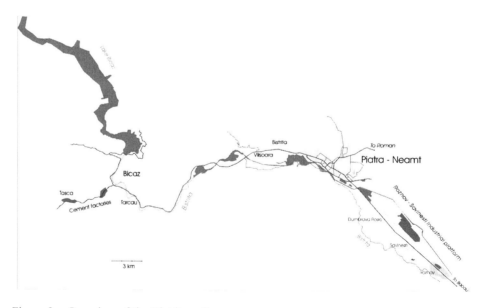

Figure 2. Overview of the Bistrita valley.
Source: Author's drawing based on the fieldwork data of 2007.

young families from other parts of the country. In 1968, the average age of employees was 27, which illustrates the young population that started a new line in the history of the region at the time. A special school, directed towards the production of technical personnel specialized in synthetic fibres, was erected next to that of vocational and higher education specializing in woodworking. The Savinesti factory formed part of the new identity of Piatra-Neamt, forged further as cultural activities were organized through the factory. This included in particular a handball team called 'Savinesti' that were several times national champions. Hence, the presence of the Savinesti platform influenced local citizens from cradle to grave.

The Savinesti case is illustrative of how, after the creation of state-owned 'commercial corporations' at the beginning of the 1990s, the privatization of these industrial mastodons developed slowly. However, this situation changed dramatically at the end of the 1990s following the neoliberal path taken by the Romanian government of that time.

In 1991, following the first privatization law, Azochim and the former 'CFS' were transformed into different 'commercial corporations' from which Fibrex, Melana and Rifil were the largest (with more than 500 workers each). Rifil, created in 1973 with a mix of state and private Italian capital, remained operative during the 1990s and succeeded in consolidating its production of fibres, keeping a constant employment level of around 500 workers. The three other large employers, however, almost disappeared as soon as the political regime change took place.

The IMF requirement to privatize or close debt-accumulating state enterprises and the eagerness of the 1997–2000 government to comply with Western 'shock therapy' had enormous consequences for the three industrial giants, which all had outstanding public debts. Azochim, employing around 1700 workers in 1998, was sold to Interagro Bucuresti and its restructuring resulted in a residual of 143 workers. The commercial company Melana, consisting of four different units and employing around 1200 workers in 1998, saw three of its units closed in 1999. The largest company on the platform, Fibrex, employing more than 4700 workers in 1999, was sold to the Italian 'Radici' company in 2000. However, the privatization of Fibrex turned out to have unwanted consequences.

At the moment of privatization, Fibrex had a monopoly position on the synthetic fibre market in Romania due to the withdrawal from the market of a similar Romanian producer. Hence, the company in Savinesti remained the only manufacturer for some products (such as yarn) that were distributed to over 800 local textile industries as well as to overseas markets. Unions and the new Italian management agreed to reduce the number of employees in order to revive the finances of the firm. Those who would voluntarily leave the company would receive a compensation amount, depending on seniority, which would add to the redundancy payments provided by the regional government. As a result, in 2000, some 3336 jobs were retained. However, in about a year, the Radici group decided to stop most of the production units in Savinesti and started selling yarn produced in Italy directly to the broad network of Romanian textile producers that were dependent on the Fibrex nylon. As a result, the workforce was further reduced with 1936 workers remaining in 2001 and 1044 in 2002.

In a final step in 2005, what remained of the firm was split into two smaller companies: 'Yarnea', employing around 500 workers (but only 310 in 2009) and still producing some fibre; and 'Fibrex Nylon', with only 66 employees in 2009 and having an entirely different set of activities. Owning large parts of the former industrial platform's real estate, this small company became specialized in managing and providing drinking water, industrial water, sewage, electricity and a biological station to other (future) firms at the platform. Currently, encouraged by the Neamt local government that wants to attract new employment opportunities, 'Fibrex Nylon' has become a partner in regional development. In this role, it is mainly active as a real estate agent actively promoting the investment opportunities of the Savinesti platform in Western Europe and in Italy in particular. The focus is especially on the 'skilled labour force at very competitive costs'.

In 2005, what remained of the Azochim factory was bought by 'Ga-Pro-Co Chemicals' and is currently again an employer. In 2009, the company employed 679 workers but due to rising natural gas prices, around 500 of them were laid-off more recently.

Hence, the privatization history of the Savinesti platform is a rather sad one. In 10 years, the total number of jobs decreased from around 8100 in 1998 to around 1000 in 2009. Instead of providing employment, the Italian investor first cut jobs, the unemployment benefits being provided by the regional government, subsequently closed the main production units in order to eliminate a competitor in the Romanian market and finally became a real estate speculator.

From voice to exit: migration from grassroots reaction to safety valve

The dramatic restructuring of employment in Romania that I illustrated in the previous section with the case of the northeast followed a period of relative job certainty but limited investments in welfare. The bargaining capacity of unions declined due to the accelerated privatization of state enterprises and an increasingly hegemonic discourse which considered unions as trouble-makers. The structural disappearance of secure jobs and secure welfare resulted in the growth of different 'survival type' grassroots reactions. One of these was a return migration to the countryside which reflected the rural background of the northeast residents and the national restitution policy on agricultural land (Sandu 2002). In urban regions, on the other hand, an explosive growth of precarious flexwork, mainly in services, appeared as a reaction to the disappearance of secured salaried work. Figure 3 illustrates for the city of

Figure 3. Self-employment in a de-industrializing urban space.
Source: Author's fieldwork photo from Piatra-Neamt, 2007.

Piatra-Neamt the nature of some recurrent forms of flexwork activities: starting up a taxi service, a real estate office, video cassette renting, a Xerox shop, an internet café, a tourism office, etc. These are all small businesses that are often combined and sometimes result from investing small sums as starting capital, perhaps gathered through temporary work abroad.

The remainder of this article focuses on the importance of migration abroad as one of the key strategies to survive the negative consequences of such a dramatic restructuring. It draws mainly on data collected by means of an exploratory quantitative survey carried out in 2007–2008 amongst 916 work migrants who (temporarily) returned to their northeast hometowns. The structured questionnaires were administered by 200 students from the Iasi University in Romania, each of whom interviewed five returned migrants he or she knew in his or her own hometown in the northeast. This methodological choice resulted in sampling a diversity of departure sites in the northeast with a limited representation of rural areas (see Meeus 2011, 2012). The questionnaire was built around the personal life-course of the responding migrant worker. Besides their motivations for going abroad and returning to Romania, migrant workers were asked how they organized work, maintenance and renewal in sites abroad before and after they left Romania. The data were analysed using three techniques: exploratory, correspondence and cross-tabulation analysis (Meeus 2011). Exploratory data analysis revealed information about year of emigration, destination, age, the use of information before leaving, length of stay, access to housing and work abroad at first and subsequent trips, and respondents' socio-economic situation before and after departure. Correspondence analysis brought together groups of migrants with similar life-course motivations, whilst cross-tabulation analysis examined in more detail the characteristics of these groups. In the next two parts of this section, I discuss the development of work migration from Romania towards the Mediterranean economies, followed by an analysis of the role of this migration as a safety valve.

Migration as grassroots reaction

Figure 4 presents first departures from northeast Romania drawing on my own survey data and that of Sandu et al. (2006). The results of my survey indicate an increasing number of first departures for work abroad soon after the 'super shock' in 1997. Before 2002, destinations were still quite diverse. Building on the existing practice of cross-border petty-trading (Thuen 1999) but without much prior information about work, workers left in the direction of Turkey, Hungary and other neighbouring countries. Most of them looked for housing on an individual basis and operated on the rental markets or were housed by employers next to building sites or industrial plants. The ease with which the labour markets of these countries could be reached translated into sojourns of maximum three months. As a result, only few migrant workers settled for longer periods and thus no stable communities could develop in these destination places.

Parallel to these movements and building on the practices of travelling construction teams during socialism (Cingolani 2009), middle-aged men left for periods of around two years to Israel where a specific guest-worker system for construction workers with strict controls on residency status prevented permanent settlement but offered higher salaries. Many of the workers were directly recruited in Romania by

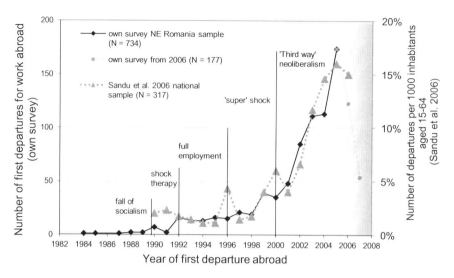

Figure 4. The evolution of first departures from northeast Romania.
Source: Author's survey and Sandu et al. (2006).
Note: From 2005, the graph is greyed since the decrease in the number of first departures from 2006 has probably more to do with the fact that many of the migrant workers who left in that period had not returned by the time the survey was conducted in 2007. A regression analysis between my survey results and the results of the national survey carried out by Sandu et al. (2006) who encountered the same problem shows a high correlation coefficient until 2005 of $R^2 = 0.94$.

Jewish construction companies and were housed on their building sites (Rosenhek 2003). Once again few workers settled permanently.

As the survey data indicate (Figure 5), more permanent forms of migration developed in the same period in the direction of France, Germany and the Mediterranean economies, especially towards Italy, Spain and to a lesser extent Greece. Here, as a consequence of administrative constraints related to mobility between Romania and these Schengen countries, work migration turned into sojourns of more than two years. For instance, less than 20% ($N=99$) of surveyed migrant workers who went to Italy before 2002 stayed abroad for only three months. These administrative constraints, combined with subsequent regularization programmes in host countries, stimulated the consolidation of Romanian migrant communities throughout Western Europe.

The evolution of these migration patterns during the second post-socialist decade reflected this opportunity structure. Thus, the increasing insecurity and the impossibility of family reunion in Israel made construction work there less attractive. Meanwhile, the relatively easy access to the informal labour markets in Italy and Spain, the increasing number of permanently settled Romanians there and the affinity with the Mediterranean culture made the track in the direction of these countries ever more attractive (see also Sandu et al. 2006). From 2002, the lifting of the Schengen visa requirement for Romanian citizens made it easier to reside on a tourist visa for three months in the Schengen zone and cranked up the practice of short-term work migration. According to my survey, almost 60% ($N=401$) of migrant workers who went to Italy for the first time after 2002 stayed abroad for only three months.

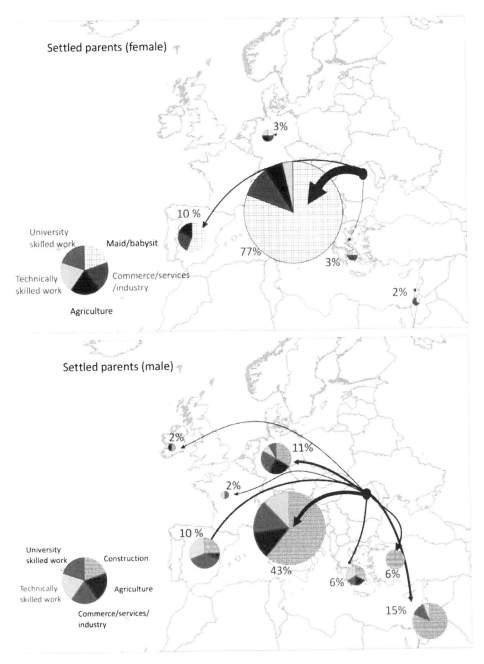

Figure 5. (a) and (b). Destination countries and sector of employment at first trip abroad from northeast Romania of the group of settled parents (5a, $N=151$; 5b, $N=109$).
Source: Author's survey.

The significant gendered demand for domestic work and elderly care secured (informal) employment opportunities for women (Figure 5a), almost half of whom were provided accommodation by the employing families themselves. The booming construction sectors and, to some extent, labour-intensive agriculture in Italy and

Spain, created a similar demand for male workers (Figure 5b) who were also housed by the employing companies or could find accommodation with friends and family. As migrants' number of trips abroad increased, the role of support networks composed by friends and family decreased as migrant workers built up their own experience and searched individually on the rental market. They further looked on their own for a better paid job or knew that their job was secured by the company or family in which they were employed. This form of security had an influence upon their mobility within the European Union. Therefore, only a relatively small group headed north to Ireland, the UK, France or Germany. Given that it was more difficult to access labour markets of North-Western Europe and the USA, the survey indicated that recruitment companies and temporary staffing agencies were much more important in enabling migrants to reach these destinations.

The safety valve: migration as a system of welfare provisioning through the life-course

Whilst the previous section focused on migration as a reaction to the way in which neoliberal reforms of the slacking post-socialist economy further individualized the welfare burden, this section centres its attention on the importance of temporary work abroad as a transnational form of reproduction that functions as a 'safety valve'. Results from the survey which was part of my doctoral research revealed that diverse life-course motivations lay at the basis of work migration (Meeus 2011). In the survey, 22 motivation parameters were included, on which scores from 0 to 10 could be given. The parameters were broadly constructed around mainte-nance and renewal issues (see Meeus 2011). In a first step, correspondence analysis revealed that respondents mainly differed on the basis of the scores that were given to the parameters: 'I needed money to support my children', 'I wanted to give my children a better future', 'I wanted the finances to live together with my spouse', 'Before starting up a family I wanted to save some money' and 'I wanted to save some money to buy/build a house'. Based on the scores given to these parameters, in a second step respondents were categorized into four groups and a new corre-spondence analysis between these four groups and the 22 motivation parameters made it possible to discern four different profiles of migrant workers.

Figure 6 plots the four groups and the motivation parameters on the two main dimensions of the correspondence analysis. The centre of this plane represents the average situation. The more a group of workers or a motivation variable diverges from the average situation, the further they are located from the centre. First, there were those in their early twenties who could be further divided into two groups: migrants for whom household creation was not yet an issue (*discoverers*, $N=289$), and those who were trying to pool resources to start up a new household unit (*family starters*, $N=249$). The former saw their work abroad mostly as a chance to get in contact with the West, to finance their vacations and eventually to save some money for their studies. The latter needed monetary income to leave their parents' household, to buy or build a house or an apartment, to get married and live together with their spouse. Children were not yet an important issue for them. The third group (*young parents*, $N=116$) was composed of migrants approaching their thir-ties, for whom the need for significant amounts of cash income was more urgent. These young parents, often sharing a house with their own parents, saw themselves faced with a situation in which they had children to raise and a future mortgage to

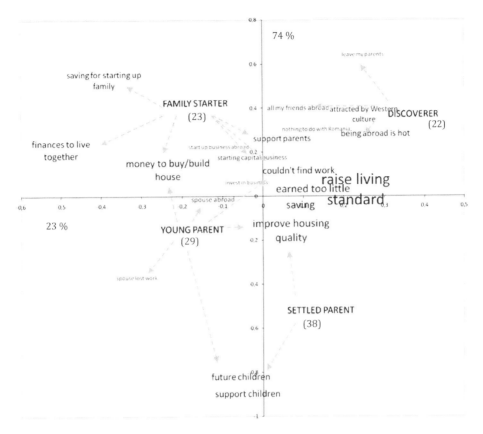

Figure 6. Work migration motivations over the life course.
Source: Author's survey (Meeus 2011).

pay, whilst wanting to maintain their own living standard and even enhance the future prospects of their children. A fourth profile consisted of people who had reached their forties (*settled parents*, $N=260$) and had to make a trade-off between their own social mobility and securing the future of their children. Especially older women went abroad and saved money to ensure their children's (higher) education.

The first three groups of migrants captured by the survey are all part of a generation or cohort that either never experienced or were too young to feel the true impact of 'actually existing socialism' (Verdery 1996). This is a cohort that has been growing up in a context of an ever-increasing migration, whereby many people around them go abroad for a certain period of time, in order to perform certain crucial steps in their life career. In contrast, the generation of their parents, including the group of 'settled parents' working abroad, which started having a family at a time when employment was secure and housing provided by the state, is faced with decreasing opportunities for social upward mobility. As such, during the implementation of neoliberal reforms in Romania, labour markets in the West formed a crucial resource to continue performing these life-career steps in Romania in a successful way. For the neoliberal Romanian governments too, migration acted as a 'safety valve', built up by entrepreneurial citizens from the grassroots, that could compensate for the accumulation of problems of social reproduction in certain areas of the country, such as illustrated by the case of Romania's northeast.

Conclusion: what if the safety valve closes?

At the dawn of the millennium, Favell and Hansen (2002) warned that, as a consequence of the increasing economic integration in Europe, markets were taking over from states the regulation of labour mobility in Europe. Despite attempts to define migration as a political phenomenon, they argued that migration and mobility between Eastern and Western Europe were beginning to resemble more a scenario in which self-regulating supply and demand factors are the ultimate determinants of why people move and where they end up. The consequence of this scenario, where market selectivity and flexibility become more important than the previous state-centred trajectory from migrant to citizen, is, the authors argued, the downgrading of citizenship and welfare rights for all those living within the territories of the sending and receiving states and the development of a precarious workforce, unprotected from the crisis-tendencies of the market.

The impact of the current financial crisis on European labour markets suggests that Favell and Hansen (2002) were right in their prognosis. As demonstrated by this article, Romanian migrant workers in Southern Europe work mainly in construction, services, domestic work and agriculture. Not only do these sectors often represent precarious and unhealthy work, but they are also highly sensitive to fluctuations in economic growth. In Spain, house prices tripled in the period 1985–2007, a speculation bubble that was mainly financed by cheap loans provided by German banks. In the wake of the financial crisis, the bubble exploded and the building sector collapsed resulting in massive unemployment. In the area of Castello for instance, between the first quarter of 2008 and the second quarter of 2010, employment in services fell by 11%, in agriculture and manufacturing by 25–26% and in construction by 50% (Bernat and Viruela 2011). In Italy, the construction market was also heavily affected by the financial crisis. Construction suffered a slowdown in 2007, a fall in 2008 and a further significant drop in 2009 (Mora 2010).

At the same time, however, the financial crisis has hit the Romanian economy hard as well. The crisis first reached the Romanian economy in the last quarter of 2008 as a consequence of a drop in exports due to the recession in Western Europe. Later on, access to external financing and FDI declined. Trade and industrial output dropped sharply, generating unemployment and downward pressure on wages. A combination of aggravating factors further created a public finance deficit (see Constantin, Goschin, and Danciu 2011). The deficit further worsened in 2009 as tax revenues diminished due to the crisis. The deficit forced Romania to borrow large amounts of money and in April 2009 the government concluded a stand-by agreement with the IMF for 20 billion Euros provided by IMF, the European Commission and the World Bank. This 'Troika' demanded a reduction in the budget deficit to a 3% target by 2012 by putting in place austerity measures, the consequences of which were 25% cuts in public sector wages, frozen pensions and VAT increases from 19 to 24% in July 2010.

As Constantin et al. (2011) point out, the economic crisis and its 'solutions' aggravate all the problems that existed in the labour market before the crisis: more unemployment, an increase in flexwork, a higher fiscal burden and reduced remittances. Once again, urban industries' offer of stable work diminishes. Counties with a high share of rural population suffer less directly from the crisis than more urbanized ones due to their reliance on subsistence agriculture. But in these counties, the current overall economic situation is overlaid on a previously low development level. Moreover, the situation for a considerable number of working-age inactive people in economically underdeveloped regions is worse than before the crisis in the sense that their already small chance of getting formal employment has further decreased (Goschin, Constantin, and Danciu 2010, 209–12).

As argued in this article, the 'safety valve', formed by the migration system that developed from the mid-1990s onwards, is currently eroding. This is happening at a moment when the Romanian government is once again forced by the 'Troika' to implement neoliberal austerity measures. The main question that arises now is what happens if this 'safety valve' closes?

Firstly, as some authors indicate, there is only a small-scale return to Romania from labour markets abroad. Bernat and Viruela (2011), for instance, document that the majority of the Romanians in the Castello region decide to stay. Especially when partners are abroad, return is less likely. Compared to Polish return from the UK and Ireland, Romanians' return from Spain is low since wage differentials between Romania and the host countries are still high (Barbulescu 2009). Mora (2010) adds that, in the shrinking Italian labour markets, Romanians are discriminated positively compared to African migrant workers. Yet, the number of Romanian migrant workers going abroad has stagnated and the authors indicate at least some return, especially of short-term workers, and a decreasing amount of remittances.

It seems that transmigration to Northern Europe is a second consequence of the crisis. For instance, the number of Romanian migrants in Brussels has increased sharply since the crisis started (8741 in 2008 and 19,377 in 2011 according to FOD Economie 2013). Here, it can be expected that the pressure on the existing informal labour markets and cheap housing markets will increase enormously.

Finally, to what extent does the current 'double pressure' on welfare stimulate 'voice' in Romania? In January 2012, for the first time since 1989, a countrywide demonstration against the austerity measures that followed the IMF stand-by agreement lasted for over a month. The demonstration led to the fall of the Emil Boc government and an enduring political crisis. The question remains to what extent this could be the first step towards new progressive mobilization of energies in a country in which those suffering most from the accumulation of reproduction problems did not take part in the demonstrations (Domnisoru 2012).

Acknowledgements

I would like to thank Julie Vullnetari, Russell King, Maarten Loopmans, Chris Kesteloot and Ionel Muntele for their useful comments on earlier versions of the paper. I would also like to thank the staff and students from the Geography department of the University Alexandru Ioan Cuza of Iasi who helped me with the Romanian survey. The usual disclaimer applies.

Note

1. The term 'super-tenants' was introduced by Verdery (2003) to indicate the different social situation of these tenants compared to restitution recipients, because of their easier access to financial capital, fertilizers, etc. and their engagement in the production of cash-crops.

References

Balanya, B., A. Doherty, O. Hoedeman, A. Ma'anit, and E. Wesselius. 2003. *Europe Inc.: Regional and global restructuring and the rise of corporate power.* 2nd ed. London: Pluto Press.

Ban, C. 2011. Neoliberalism in translation: Economic ideas and reforms in Spain and Romania. PhD diss., University of Maryland.

Barbulescu, R. 2009. The economic crisis and its effects for intra-European movement: Mobility patterns and state responses. The case of Romanians in Spain. Paper presented at the Annual COMPAS Conference, September 21–22, University of Oxford, in UK.

Bernat, J.S., and R. Viruela. 2011. The economic crisis and immigration: Romanian citizens in the ceramic tile district of Castello (Spain). *Journal of Urban and Regional Analysis* 3, no. 1: 45–65.

Burawoy, M. 1976. The functions and reproduction of migrant labor: Comparative material from Southern Africa and the United States. *The American Journal of Sociology* 81, no. 5: 1050–87.

Castles, S., and G. Kosack. 1985. *Immigrant workers and class structure in Western Europe.* 2nd ed. Oxford and New York, NY: Oxford University Press.

Cingolani, P. 2009. *Romanians of Italy: Migrations, daily life and transnational ties.* Bologna: Edizioni del Mulino [in Romanian].

Constantin, D.L., Z. Goschin, and A.R. Danciu. 2011. The Romanian economy from transition to crisis: Retrospects and prospects. *World Journal of Social Sciences* 1, no. 3: 155–71.

Dan, A.N., and M. Dan. 2003. Housing policy in Romania in transition: Between state withdrawal and market collapse. Paper presented at the round table on 'Globalisation, Integration and Social development in Central and Eastern Europe', September 6–8, University Lucian Blaga of Sibiu, in Romania.

De Gaudemar, J.P. 1976. *Labour mobility and capital accumulation.* Paris: François Maspero [in French].

Domnisoru, C. 2012. Counterproductive paradigms of poverty and the need for a socialist party in Parliament. *CriticAtac*, August 29, http://www.criticatac.ro/18196/counterproductive-paradigms-poverty-need-socialist-party-parliament/ (accessed January 11, 2013).

European Roma Rights Centre. 2006. *Ambulance not on the way: The disgrace of health care for Roma in Europe.* Budapest: European Roma Rights Centre, http://www.errc.org/cms/upload/media/01/E6/m000001E6.pdf (accessed January 11, 2013).

Favell, A., and R. Hansen. 2002. Markets against politics: Migration, EU enlargement and the idea of Europe. *Journal of Ethnic and Migration Studies* 28, no. 4: 581–601.

FOD Economie. 2013. Statistics Belgium, population by nationality. http://economie.fgov.be/nl/statistieken/cijfers/ (accessed January 11, 2013) [in Flemish].

Freeman, G.P. 1986. From foreign workers to settlers? Transnational migration and the emergence of new minorities. *Annals of the American Academy of Political and Social Science* 485: 51–63.

Goedemé, T. 2006. Pension systems in Western and Eastern Europe: A comparison of the old age pension provisions in Belgium and Romania. Paper presented at the 'Summer School in Governance and Social Protection Policy', June 26–July 1, Maastricht University, in The Netherlands.

Goschin, Z., D.L. Constantin, and A.R. Danciu. 2010. A regional perspective on the impact of the current economic crisis in Romania. *Romanian Economic and Business Review* 5, no. 3: 204–25.

Goss, J., and B. Lindquist. 1995. Conceptualizing international labor migration: A structuration perspective. *International Migration Review* 23, no. 2: 317–51.

Guarnizo, L.E., and M.P. Smith. 1998. The locations of transnationalism. In *Transnationalism from below*, ed. M.P. Smith and L.E. Guarnizo, 3–31. New Brunswick, NJ: Transaction.

Harvey, D. 1982. *The limits to capital*. London: Verso.

Hirschman, A. 1970. *Exit, voice and loyalty: Responses to decline in firms, organisations and states*. Cambridge, MA: Harvard University Press.

Hoffmann, B. 2008. Bringing Hirschman back in: Conceptualising transnational migration as a reconfiguration of 'Exit', 'Voice', and 'Loyalty'. Working Paper 91. Hamburg: German Institute of Global and Area Studies (GIGA).

Institutul National de Statistica. 2007. Average number of employees by main activity of national economy, www.insse.ro (accessed March 10, 2011) [in Romanian].

Ivanova, M.N. 2007. Why there was no 'Marshall plan' for Eastern Europe and why this still matters. *Journal of Contemporary European Studies* 15, no. 3: 345–76.

Kideckel, D.A. 2008. *Getting by in postsocialist Romania: Labor, the body, and working-class culture*. Bloomington, IN: Indiana University Press.

Kloosterman, R., J. van der Leun, and J. Rath. 1999. Mixed embeddedness: (In)formal economic activities and immigrant business in the Netherlands. *International Journal of Urban and Regional Research* 23, no. 2: 253–67.

Meeus, B. 2011. Migrant workers and postsocialism. A social reproduction perspective to work migration from NE-Romania. PhD, diss., University of Leuven.

Meeus, B. 2012. How to 'catch' floating populations? Research and the fixing of migration in space and time. *Ethnic and Racial Studies* 35, no. 10: 1775–93.

Mora, M. 2010. Immigrant workers in the Italian construction sector. Solidar, European Network Advancing Social Justice in Europe and Worldwide, http://www.solidar.org/IMG/pdf/ires_en.pdf (accessed January 11, 2013).

Morawska, E. 2001. Structuring migration: The case of Polish income-seekers to the West. *Theory and Society* 30: 47–80.

Panait, A. 2009. Old dwellings, the first to experience rent decreases [in Romanian]. *Adevarul* [Romanian daily], May 5. Bucharest.

Piore, M.J. 1979. *Birds of passage: Migrant labor and industrial societies*. Cambridge: Cambridge University Press.

Polanyi, K. 1944. *The great transformation*. Repr., Boston, MA: Beacon Press, 2001.

Pop-Eleches, G. 2009. *From economic crisis to reform: IMF programs in Latin-America and Eastern Europe*. Princeton, NJ: Princeton University Press.

Portes, A. 1978. Migration and underdevelopment. *Politics and Society* 8, no. 1: 1–48.

Rebeleanu, A. 2008. Health policy in the postsocialist Romania: Intentions vs achievements. *Studia Universitatis Babes-Bolyai-Sociology* 53, no. 2: 5–22.

Rosenhek, Z. 2003. Migration regimes and prospects for the creation of migrant associations: The case of Romanian workers in Israel. In *Visible but only few: Romanian migratory circuits*, ed. D. Diminescu, 137–47. Paris: Editions de la Maison des Sciences de l'Homme [in French].

Samers, M. 1999. 'Globalization', the geopolitical economy of migration and the 'spatial vent'. *Review of International Political Economy* 6, no. 2: 166–99.

Samers, M. 2002. Immigration and the global city hypothesis: Towards an alternative research agenda. *International Journal of Urban and Regional Research* 26, no. 2: 389–402.

Sandu, D. 2002. Emerging transnational migration from Romanian villages. Paper developed as Oxford College Hospitality Scheme invitee http://aa.ecn.cz/img_upload/f76c21488a048c95bc0a5f12deece153/Dumitru_Sandu____Emerging_Transnational_Migration_from_Romanian_Villages.doc (accessed January 13, 2013).

Sandu, D., A. Bleahu, V. Grigoras, A. Mihai, C. Radu, M. Serban, A. Toth, et al. 2006. *Living abroad on a temporary basis: The economic migration of Romanians, 1990–2006*. Bucharest: Open Society Foundation.

Sassen, S. 1989. *The mobility of labor and capital: A study in international investment and labor flow*. Cambridge: Cambridge University Press.

Smith, A., N. Coe, M. Baylina, and L. Labrianidis. 2012. Editorial. *European Urban and Regional Studies* 19, no. 1: 3–5.

Swyngedouw, E., and E. Swyngedouw. 2009. The Congolese diaspora in Brussels and hybrid identity formation: Multi-scalarity and diasporic citizenship. *Urban Research and Practice* 2, no. 1: 68–90.

Thuen, T. 1999. The significance of borders in the East-European transition. *International Journal of Urban and Regional Research* 23, no. 4: 738–50.

Verdery, K. 1996. *What was socialism and what comes next*. Princeton, NJ: Princeton University Press.

Verdery, K. 2003. *The vanishing hectare: Property and value in postsocialist Transylvania*. New York, NY: Cornell University Press.

Vertovec, S. 2009. *Transnationalism*. London: Routledge.

Variation in transnationalism among Eastern European migrants in Italy: the role of duration of residence and integration

Eralba Cela[a], Tineke Fokkema[b] and Elena Ambrosetti[c]

[a]Department of Economics and Social Sciences, Polytechnic University of Marche, Ancona, Italy; [b]Department of Social Demography, Netherlands Interdisciplinary Demographic Institute (NIDI), The Hague, Netherlands; [c]Department of Methods and Models for Economics, Territory and Finance, Sapienza University, Rome, Italy

Transnationalism of first-generation migrants, usually considered as a core element of their migratory projects, is nowadays taken somewhat for granted. Our aim in this paper is to examine empirically the relations of transnationalism with duration of residence and integration of Eastern European migrants in Italy, a country which evolved into a mass immigration one since the 1980s. Data come from the Integrometro survey 2008–2009, encompassing more than 4500 Eastern European migrants. We chose this group of migrants because East Europeans now constitute half of the foreign population in Italy and these nationalities have been overlooked by migration research on transnational topics. Our results show a positive relationship between migrants' economic integration and transnationalism, suggesting that economic resources facilitate the maintenance and development of cross-border ties. Being more integrated socio-culturally, however, is accompanied with weaker transnational practices. Moreover, the level of transnational behaviour decreases the more years Eastern European migrants spend in Italy, which cannot be fully attributed to a higher level of socio-cultural integration.

Introduction

In the aftermath of the oil crisis of 1973, Northern European countries, the main destinations of immigration in Europe during the early postwar decades, adopted restrictive immigration policies. Labour migration was no longer encouraged, although migration flows to Northern Europe did not stop because of family reunification and family formation. The direction of labour migration, however, diverted to Southern European countries, characterized thus far by emigration and transit migration, but not by legislation on immigration, thereby facilitating migrants' efforts to enter into Southern Europe and transform it into a region of final destination.

It is not surprising that Southern European countries attracted large numbers of immigrants. Their economies are characterized by a segmented labour market, widespread small-scale family enterprises that often are labour (not capital) intensive, an increasing education of native population who refuse to engage in low-paid employment in agricultural, construction and low-skilled service sector jobs, a widespread informal economy especially in the tertiary sector such as tourism and domestic and care services, as well as by important seasonal sectors like agriculture, fishing and tourism. These labour niches require a low-cost labour force to survive and to compete within the global economy. All these aspects contributed to affect migrants' trajectories, shaping a new map of European immigration (King 2002).

The new waves of migrants are no longer solely attracted by pull factors such as production. Instead, a variety of motivations are at play depending both on push factors and migrants' own characteristics as well as on the specific socio-economic environment of the destination countries, resulting in diversification of migration types. King (2000) has defined a 'Southern European Model of Migration'; he describes the immigration phenomenon in the northern Mediterranean Basin as characterized by features such as the globalization of origins (broad range of nationalities), increased proportion of women as independent migrants from specific countries, the spreading of migration into both urban and rural areas, the presence of some skilled migrants from wealthy families, and high levels of irregular migration.

Among Southern European countries, Italy represents a singular case for the intensity of migration flows and the presence of a wide variety of nationalities. The first migrants were mainly males from Muslim countries like Tunisia, Morocco and Senegal, political refugees from Vietnam and Chile, students from Iran and Greece, and mostly females from Catholic origins like the Philippines and Cape Verde. Since the 1990s, after the fall of the Berlin Wall and the end of the communist regimes in Eastern Europe, Italy experienced a renewed boom in migration, characterized by different waves. The first migrants arrived at the beginning of the 1990s from Albania, followed by migrants from Former Yugoslavia and Poland. Intensive flows from other Eastern European countries to Italy started in the early 2000s, in particular from Romania, Ukraine and Moldova.

Migration has thus become a structural element of Italian society. In the last ten years, the migrant population in Italy has more than tripled, passing from 1.3 million individuals reported in the 2001 census, to 4.6 million at the end of 2010, more than 7% of the total population, according to the National Institute of Statistics. Since 2007 the increase in immigrant stocks is largely attributed to flows of Eastern European citizens. Currently, Eastern Europeans (Romanians and Albanians) and Northern Africans (Moroccans) are the largest national-origin communities in Italy, followed by Far Eastern Asians (Chinese and Filipinos).

Although migration from Eastern Europe has been characterized by several waves, as described above, the migration motives are largely similar – i.e. the quest for job opportunities and escape from political and economic crisis. Nevertheless, each community is characterized by some specific features that are reflected in its sex and age composition. Romanian migration was at the beginning male-dominated, employed in the construction and secondary sectors; later on it was followed by female migrants employed in the (health and child) care sector. The current sex ratio of Romanians in Italy is 86 males per 100 females. Albanians are the second community of foreign residents in Italy. The migration flows from Albania to Italy were for a long time dominated by male temporary labour migration. Thanks to family reunification, however, Albanian residents in Italy have nowadays a sex ratio of 118 males per 100 females. Migrants from Moldova, Poland and Ukraine are essentially females, working in the care sector. Consequently, the ratio of males to females in these populations is low, respectively 52, 42 and 26.

The emergence of these mostly female communities from Eastern Europe has attracted scholarly attention into the multiple relations they maintain with their countries of origin. So far, the focus has particularly been on mothering practices at distance and conjugal relationships (Ambrosini 2005; Banfi and Boccagni 2011; Castagnone et al. 2007; Catanzaro and Colombo 2009; Vlase 2006). In addition, some studies have been conducted on both their integration patterns in Italy and their ties with relatives left behind (Ban 2009; Cela and Moretti 2011; King and Mai 2008). These studies, however, are almost exclusively qualitative in nature and restricted to one of the main communities, like Romanians, Albanians, Ukrainians or Poles. Accordingly, there is a lack of quantitative research on the prevalence and determinants of transnational relations across all migrants from Eastern Europe in Italy. Hence, this study examines the transnational behaviour among first-generation Eastern European migrants in Italy, with a special focus on the relationship between transnationalism on the one hand, and duration of residence and integration on the other hand. Data come from a unique dataset, the Integrometro survey, carried out at the Italian national scale between 2008 and 2009.

Interlinkages between duration of residence, integration and transnationalism

For a long time, migrants were assumed to assimilate inevitably over time. The classical assimilation theory argued rather convincingly that the longer migrants stay in the host society, the more they will be integrated and the less they will remain connected to their home country (Alba 1985; Alba and Nee 1997; Gordon 1964). A major shift of thinking occurred since the introduction of the concept of transnationalism into the migration debate in the 1990s, transnationalism being defined as the process 'by which immigrants build social fields that link together their country of origin and their country of settlement' (Glick Schiller, Basch, and Szanton Blanc 2006). The emerging transnational perspective pushed researchers to move beyond the study of migrants' process of integration in the host society and to focus also on migrants' multiple ties with their country of origin (Guarnizo, Portes, and Haller 2003; Portes and Rumbaut 2001; Portes and Zhou 1999). More particularly, it has challenged migration scholars to think more deeply and creatively about the linkages between duration of residence and integration on the one hand and transnationalism on the other hand. As a result, segmented assimilation theory emphasizes the importance of individual and contextual factors in determining the degree of integration and, contrary to the classic assimilation assumption, does not consider any more the ties with the home country as a barrier to integration processes (Basch, Glick Schiller, and Szanton Blanc 1994; Faist 2000; Glick Schiller, Basch, and Szanton Blanc 1992; Itzigsohn et al. 1999; Kivisto 2001; Levitt 2001; Portes, Guarnizo, and Landolt 1999).

To represent the broad range of transnational practices and to make the complexity of the relationship between transnationalism and integration more manageable, a number of researchers have identified typologies of transnationalism. For sure, the issue of time (duration of residence in the host society) is a key feature in understanding the evolution of transnational behaviour. Faist (2000), for instance, distinguishes three different typologies of transnational spaces. Firstly, there are *transnational kinship groups*, characterized by short-lived transnationalism and assimilation as time goes by, due to family reunification and/or death of first-generation migrants. The underlying assumption of this typology is a *positive* relationship between duration of residence and integration and a *negative* relationship of duration of residence and integration with transnationalism. Secondly come *transnational circuits*, typical in cross-border trading networks, characterized by mutual obligations among actors involved. In this second typology, we find the assumption of *positive* relationships between duration of residence, integration and transnationalism. Finally, *transnational communities*, such as diasporas or village communities, are characterized by enduring ties over time between migrants abroad and those staying behind; *no* relationship is assumed between duration of residence and integration on the one hand and transnationalism on the other hand.

Itzigsohn and Giorguli Saucedo (2002), in their attempt to analyze incorporation and socio-cultural transnationalism, also identify three forms of transnationalism. The *linear* form suggests that, as time passes, incorporation increases and transnationalism slowly decreases. This assumes a *positive* relation between duration of residence and integration into the host society, and a *negative* one between residence/integration and transnationalism. Second, *resource dependent transnationalism* implies that time and financial resources are necessary to engage in cross-border practices and hence, assuming thereby a *positive* relationship between duration of residence, integration and transnationalism. Thirdly, *reactive transnationalism* results from discrimination or a negative experience of integration that migrants face in the host society. Therefore, a *positive* relationship between duration of residence, exclusion (negative integration) and transnationalism is assumed.

The research on the relationship between migrants' transnationalism and integration has found mixed findings rather than evidence conclusively pointing in any particular direction. Some studies support the idea that integration and transnational ties are not necessarily substitutes, but can be complements, in particular in the case of economic integration (Fokkema et al. 2012; Guarnizo, Portes, and Haller 2003; Itzigsohn and Giorguli Saucedo 2002; Landolt, Autler, and Baires 1999; Popkin 1999; Portes, Haller, and Guarnizo 2002; Sana 2005; Van Dalen, Groenewold, and Fokkema 2005). Other scholars do not agree with the assumed positive relation between migrants' integration and transnationalism (Basch, Glick Schiller, and Szanton Blanc 1994; Faist 2000; Portes 1997). Only a few studies have focused on 'how transnational practices change over time or the extent to which they remain salient beyond the first generation' (Levitt 2001, 196).

Despite the large number of studies investigating the transnational lives of migrants, there is still a dearth of research on migrants' strength of ties and types of transnational activities, and more particularly on links with duration of residence and the integration process into the host society. Firstly, the majority of existing studies on transnationalism have been qualitative in nature and mostly focused on specific aspects of transnational lives among a particular migrant group; there is a lack of quantitative studies analyzing the overall level of transnationalism across migrant groups and its links with factors like duration of residence and integration. Secondly, most of the previous studies have been conducted in the United States. Consequently, the transnational behaviour of migrants in Europe is less documented. Finally, as far as European studies are concerned, the attention is almost exclusively focused on the longer-established migration groups (e.g. Moroccans and Turks) rather than on the more recent ones, like those from Central and Eastern

Europe; and there are surprisingly few comparative empirical studies across different migrant groups (Fibbi and D'Amato 2008).

This study addresses these gaps by examining empirically the strength of transnational ties among Eastern European migrants in Italy and how these ties vary by duration of residence and level of integration into Italian society. As alternative and competing hypotheses are possible regarding the relationships between duration of residence, integration and transnationalism, the study will be explorative in nature; no specific hypotheses have been formulated beforehand.

Data, methods and measures

The data stem from the aforementioned Integrometro survey, administered in 32 provinces and towns across Italy, selected according to the high incidence of migrants and their diversification in relation to the socio-economic context. Respondents were selected using the 'aggregation center sampling technique' (Baio, Blangiardo, and Blangiardo 2001), which is a suitable method for taking into account both legal and illegal migrants. This methodology has two steps. The first one is a random selection of those places that are frequently visited by migrants from developing countries. The underlying assumption is that in each area migrants are considered as a set of statistical units, that for daily activities necessarily need a number of contacts with certain locales or 'aggregation places' that can be official or unofficial (hospital, church, café, associations, malls, phone centres, etc.). In the second step migrants were selected randomly for the face-to-face interview. Measures were taken in order to avoid distortion in the sampling caused by the probability of a migrant being present in more than one centre.

The aim of the survey was to gain insight into the degree of migrants' integration into Italian society (Cesareo and Blangiardo 2009). In all cities, an identical questionnaire was used, which made it possible to pool the datasets. The survey collected information on a total sample of 12,047 individuals aged between 18 and 71 years old, representing 128 different nationalities, with different religions and different types of migration, both in terms of socio-economic position and in terms of migration waves. For the purpose of our analyses, the dataset is reduced to $N = 3484$ individuals from Eastern European countries.

Dependent variable

The key dependent variable is *transnationalism*. The Integrometro survey contains various indicators that are generally used to measure migrants' level of transnationalism (e.g. Beauchemin, Lagrange, and Safi 2011; Fokkema et al. 2012; Kasinitz et al. 2008). As our focus is on transnational behaviour per se rather than on each transnational indicator individually, we carried out a Principal Components Analysis (PCA) with varimax rotation. This analysis extracted one factor, with an eigenvalue of 1.91 and explaining 48% of the total variance, using the following indicators: (1) *remitting*, based on the question 'Do you ever send money to your country of origin?' with the answer categories 0 = no never, 1 = yes, whenever I can and when there is a need, and 2 = yes, regularly; (2) *return intention*, proxied by the question 'Do you intend to settle in Italy?' with the answer categories 0 = forever, 1 = for a long period, 2 = don't know, and 3 = for a short period; (3) *feelings of belonging to the country of origin*, running from 0 = not at all to 3 = very much; and (4) *interest in the country of origin*, i.e. the extent to which one wants to know what happens in their home country, running from 0 = not at all to 3 = very much. Table 1 shows the factor loadings, i.e. the correlation of each of these four transnationalism indicators with the extracted factor. All factor loadings are above 0.50, indicating that our chosen indicators strongly determine transnational behaviour. Based on the factor loadings, each respondent was assigned a transnational score (regression scoring coefficients, see Table 1, were used to calculate the score). After standardizing this to mean 'zero' and standard deviation 'one', we use the transnational score as the dependent variable in the multivariate regression model. The interpretation of the transnational score is as follows: the higher the score, the higher the respondent's level of transnational behaviour.

Key independent variables

We operationalized two key independent variables: duration of residence and integration. The respondent's *duration of residence* refers to the length of time (in years) one lives in Italy, measured by the difference between the year of interview and the year at arrival. As regards *integration*, the Integrometro survey included a series of questions aimed at capturing respondents' integration into Italian society: (1) *educational attainment*, i.e. the highest level of education an individual has completed; (2) *employment status*, distinguishing between 0 = out of the labour force (retired, disabled, housewives, students), 1 = employed with an unstable labour market situation (temporary contract, irregular work), and 2 = employed with a stable labour market position (permanent contract, own business); (3) *perceived economic condition of the family*, with the answer categories 0 = 'we have difficulties to make ends meets', 1 = 'we spend everything we earn', and 2 = 'we manage to save something';[1] (4) *self-reported Italian-speaking proficiency*, running from 0 = not at all to 4 = very well; (5) *ethnic composition of respondent's friends*, with the answer categories 0 = only non-natives, 1 = more non-natives than Italians, 2 = both, and 3 = more Italians than non-natives; (6) *sympathy for the Italian life-style*, running from 0 = not at all to 1 = very much;[2] (7) *acceptance of exogamous marriage*, i.e. the level of agreement with the statement 'In case your daughter were to marry an Italian man, to what extent would you approve this marriage?', running from 0 = not at all to 3 = very much; (8) *feelings of belonging to Italy*, running from 0 = not at all to 3 = very strong; and (9) *interest in Italy*, i.e. the extent to which one wants to know what happens in Italy, running from 0 = not at all to 3 = very much. To obtain a reduced set of variables representing integration, we ran a PCA with

Table 1. Factor loadings and scoring coefficients for transnational behaviour (N-unweighted = 3484).

	Factor loadings	Scoring coefficients
Remitting	0.52	0.27
Return intention	0.56	0.29
Feelings of belonging to country of origin	0.82	0.43
Interest in country of origin	0.81	0.42

Source: Integrometro Survey.

varimax rotation on these indicators. The PCA identified two factors, with an eigenvalue of 2.51 and 1.29 and explaining 28 and 14% of the total variance, respectively (Table 2). The first factor mainly captures the non-economic indicators (4–9 in the above list) and is therefore referred to as 'socio-cultural integration'; whereas the second factor, labelled the 'economic integration', is highly loaded on the economic indicators 'employment status', 'perceived economic condition of the family' and, to a lesser extent, 'educational attainment'.[3] Following the same process as for the dependent variable transnationalism, two individual integration scores were calculated, on socio-cultural and economic integration respectively: the higher the score, the greater the respondent's degree of socio-cultural and economic integration respectively.

Control variables

Finally, we included the following control variables in the analyses: (1) respondent's *age at arrival* (measured in years); (2) *gender*, represented by the dummy variable man; (3) *partner status*, using two dummy variables comparing individuals with a same-ethnicity partner and those with a partner of a different ethnic background, respectively, to unpartnered individuals; (4) *parent status*, using two dummy variables comparing parents whose children are all living in Italy and parents with one or more children living abroad, respectively, to those without children; (5) *religion*, using a series of dummy-coded variables comparing Muslims, Orthodox Christians, Catholics and those with another religion, respectively, to non-religious individuals; and (6) *country of origin*, distinguishing the main emigration countries in the Integrometro survey (5% or more of the total Eastern European migrant population sample) – Romania, Albania, Ukraine, Moldova and Poland – from the other Eastern European countries. Table 3 provides descriptive information on all variables used in the analyses.

Table 2. Factor loadings and scoring coefficients for socio-cultural and economic integration (N-unweighted = 3484).

	Factor loadings		Scoring coefficients	
	Socio-cultural	Economic	Socio-cultural	Economic
Educational attainment	0.33	0.24	0.12	0.16
Employment status	0.03	0.76	−0.04	0.60
Perceived economic condition of the family	0.00	0.79	−0.06	0.62
Italian language proficiency	0.66	0.07	0.26	0.01
Ethnic composition of friends	0.72	−0.01	0.29	−0.06
Sympathy for Italian lifestyle	0.55	0.02	0.22	−0.02
Approval of exogamous marriage	0.55	−0.03	0.23	−0.07
Feelings of belonging to Italy	0.71	−0.01	0.29	−0.06
Interest in Italy	0.58	0.17	0.22	0.09

Source: Integrometro Survey.

DEVELOPMENT IN SOUTH-EAST EUROPE AND THE BLACK SEA REGION

Table 3. Descriptive statistics of the dependent and independent variables (N-unweighted = 3484).

	%	Mean	SD	Range	
				Min	Max
Transnationalism		0.00	1.00	−3.56	1.47
Integration					
Socio-cultural		0.00	1.00	−3.36	2.28
Economic		0.00	1.00	−2.31	1.90
Length of residence		7.35	4.65		
Control variables					
Age at arrival		29.85	10.85		
Man	41.5				
Partner status					
Partner, same ethnicity	74.1				
Partner, other ethnicity	14.5				
No partner	11.4				
Parent status					
Children, all in Italy	22.6				
Children, one or more abroad	36.3				
No children	41.2				
Religion					
Muslim	19.1				
Orthodox	47.0				
Catholic	22.7				
Other	3.5				
No religion	7.7				
Country of origin					
Romania	32.7				
Albania	31.1				
Ukraine	12.4				
Moldova	5.0				
Poland	6.4				
Other Eastern European country	12.4				

Source: Integrometro Survey.

Results

To examine the impact of duration of residence and integration on the transnational behaviour of first-generation Eastern European migrants, stepwise multiple regression analyses were carried out. Models 1, 2 and 3 sequentially include the control variables, the duration of residence variable, and the socio-cultural and economic integration factors. The results of these analyses are presented in Table 4.

Basic model

Looking first at the control variables in Model 1, age at arrival has the expected positive impact on transnationalism. The effect is linear; additional analysis showed a non-significant effect of the squared age at arrival. Thus, the younger the respondents were at the time of their move to Italy, the less they were oriented towards

DEVELOPMENT IN SOUTH-EAST EUROPE AND THE BLACK SEA REGION

Table 4. Determinants of the level of transnationalism among first-generation migrants from Eastern Europe (N-unweighted $= 3484$).

Model	1	2	3
Control variables			
Age at arrival	0.02***	0.01***	0.01**
Man	0.14**	0.16***	0.08
Partner status (Ref. no partner)			
Partner, same ethnicity	0.18**	0.12*	0.10
Partner, other ethnicity	−0.10	−0.10	0.02
Parent status (Ref. no children)			
Children, all in Italy	−0.23***	−0.12*	−0.07
Children, one or more abroad	0.38***	0.43***	0.35***
Religion (Ref. no religion)			
Muslim	0.32***	0.28***	0.18*
Orthodox	0.25**	0.22**	0.19**
Catholic	0.17*	0.16*	0.16*
Other	0.12	0.10	0.09
Country of origin (Ref. other Eastern European country)			
Romania	0.05	−0.02	−0.00
Albania	−0.09	−0.07	−0.03
Ukraine	0.17*	0.15*	0.09
Moldova	−0.04	−0.11	−0.11
Poland	0.20*	0.20*	0.13
Duration of residence		−0.03***	−0.02***
Integration			
Socio-cultural			−0.29***
Economic			0.14***
Adjusted R^2	0.156	0.174	0.254

***$p < 0.001$; **$p < 0.01$; *$p < 0.05$
Source: Integrometro Survey.

their country of birth at the time of the interview. Respondents' gender also emerges as a significant predictor: men report higher transnational scores than their female counterparts. With regard to the partner status, it is not so much the fact of having a partner that affects transnational behaviour, but the ethnicity of one's partner. Compared with their single counterparts, respondents whose partner is of the same ethnicity exhibit a higher intensity of transnational practices; no differences in transnationalism scores are found between those with an exogamous relationship and those without a partner. Being a parent coupled with the residence of one's children is significantly associated with the level of transnational engagement. Parents whose children are all living in Italy are less transnationally engaged than their childless counterparts, whereas transnational practices are more frequent among parents who have one or more children living abroad, presumably in the home country. The latter is likely to be an 'automatic' effect of exposure: migrants whose children are in the country of birth have more opportunities and responsibilities to be involved in transnational relations, to travel to the country of origin, and to maintain various linkages with the country of origin (Beauchemin, Lagrange, and Safi 2011). Respondents' denomination has an effect on transnationalism as well. Compared to those who identify themselves as non-religious, Muslims, Orthodox Christians and Catholics all report higher transnational scores (though with decreasing levels of statistical significance in that order); those with another religion do not diverge from the non-religious ones. Finally, the level of transnationalism is found to be linked with respondent's origin for those born in Poland and Ukraine.

Duration of residence

Model 2 shows that duration of residence has a significantly negative effect on transnationalism: the more years living in Italy, the lower the level of transnationalism. Additional analysis suggests that this effect is more or less linear: the coefficient of the square of the duration of residence is negative but not significant.

Introduction of the duration of residence variable leads to an increase of the explained variance from 15.6 to 17.4%, and hardly affects the direction and significance of the effect of the control variables. The only exception is that the previously observed strong effects of having a same-ethnicity partner (positive) and children living in Italy (negative) lose strength substantially, although both effects retain statistical significance.

Integration

Respondents' level of integration determines their engagement in transnational practices to a considerable extent, increasing the explained variance in Model 3 by a further 8.0%. The effect directions of socio-cultural and economic integration, however, are each other's opposite: the transnational score decreases significantly in proportion to level of socio-cultural integration, while a positive association is observed between level of economic integration and transnational engagement. Moreover, the strength of the positive impact of economic integration on transnational engagement, though significant, is modest compared to that of the negative influence of socio-cultural integration. All else equal, the transnational score decreases by about three-tenths of a standard deviation with each standard deviation increase in the socio-cultural integration factor score.

Once the economic and socio-cultural integration variables are taken into account, no significant differences are found anymore between the distinctive migrant groups. Additional analyses show that the relatively high transnational score of the Polish migrants is mainly the result of their low level of socio-cultural integration into Italian society, while both the high level of socio-cultural integration and the low level of economic integration are attributable to the relatively high level of transnational engagement among those born in Ukraine. Furthermore, the previously observed positive effects of being a man and having a same-ethnicity partner become insignificant, as do the negative effect of having children who all live in Italy. In addition, the above-average level of transnational engagement among Muslims reduces substantially once integration is taken into account, although the difference between Muslims and non-religious respondents is still significant. The most relevant finding, however, is the persistent negative effect of duration of residence on transnational behaviour, suggesting that the relation cannot be explained exclusively by a higher level of socio-cultural integration over time. Overall, the variables included in the regression analyses explain 25.4% of the variance in the level of transnational engagement.

Conclusions

The aim of our paper was to examine empirically the strength of transnational ties among Eastern European migrants in Italy, and more specifically how these ties vary by migrants' duration of residence and level of integration into Italian society. We pursued this goal through analyses of Integrometro survey data on migrants in Italy and focused on transnational behaviour in the round rather than on each transnational indicator individually. As alternative and competing hypotheses are possible regarding the relationships between duration of residence, integration and transnationalism, the study was explorative in nature.

Immigrants' transnationalism and integration are hot topics both in the political and academic debate. Although they represent two sides of one phenomenon – migration – maintaining transnational ties is sometimes considered either to impede the integration of migrants or to be a reaction to experiences of exclusion (negative integration) and discrimination. This was partly confirmed by our study: a strong negative association is observed between Eastern European migrants' level of socio-cultural integration and their transnational engagement. However, in accordance with several previous studies and the 'transnational circuits' and 'resource dependent' typologies of Faist (2000), and Itzigsohn and Giorguli Saucedo (2002), respectively, there was a clear positive relationship of transnationalism with economic integration. The opposite directions of the effects of socio-cultural and economic integration suggest that only economic resources (both in terms of human capital and income) are helpful in maintaining and developing transnational ties, while being socio-culturally integrated in the host society weakens the ongoing relations with the countries of origin.

As pointed out by Guarnizo, Portes, and Haller (2003) with regard to Colombians, Salvadorans and Dominicans in the US, the national origin and the context of exit and reception turned out to be relevant determinants of migrants' relations with home countries. This is the case of Poles and Ukrainians, although their effects on transnationalism are mediated by the level of integration.

Other individual characteristics that turned out to be associated with transnationalism, for a large part through the mediating role of integration, are gender and the ethnicity of the partner: males and those with a same-ethnicity partner are less integrated into Italian society, and hence more transnationally active. An explanation for the difference between men and women can be found in the different gender roles within their exit context: for many women migration represents both an escape route from patriarchal societies, unsuccessful marriages, domestic violence, etc. and an empowerment path, thanks to the economic independence achieved. This process contributes to transforming their migratory projects into definitive settlement and hence to weaken the ties with their country of origin.

The findings of our study also revealed a number of individual characteristics that are associated with a high level of transnational engagement, regardless of their level of integration: older age at arriving (which can be a proxy for a higher number of relatives and friends left behind), the presence of children living abroad (that implies close family contacts in the home country and responsibilities and obligations towards them), and being Muslim/Orthodox/Catholic. On the last point, religion probably acts as a transnational institution that helps to keep alive and strengthen the community bonds in and towards Italy, as found in the ethnographic study of Cingolani (2007) on Romanians in Italy. Perhaps the most striking finding is the persistent negative relation of length of residence with transnationalism, that is not entirely attributed to a higher level of socio-cultural integration over time.

Our study, however, has some limitations; one of the most important is the missing information about the composition of the family and friends left back home. Further explanation of migrants' transnational behaviour could be found through a multi-sited investigation, not only quantitative, but also qualitative, carried out both in destination and origin settings. More in general, we think that although the emergence of a transnational perspective has enriched the study of international migration, much remains to be done, since many shortcomings play along with this perspective. Contrary to the study of remittances, for example, where conceptual and quantitative studies abound, the more social dimensions of transnational behaviour are somewhat bereft of concrete assumptions and hypotheses derived from theoretical frameworks; instead there is only a huge variety of empirical (mainly qualitative) evidence. Accordingly, systematic research on specific types of transnationalism, their magnitude and determinants is still missing. Future research on transnationalism has to challenge questions like how transnationalism is related to the process of migrants' integration in the receiving societies and to the duration of residence. Why do studies repeatedly find a negative relationship between socio-cultural integration and transnationalism? And why is transnational engagement negatively associated with duration of residence, irrespective of one's level of integration? Probably the first step towards answering these kind of questions is to develop a theoretical framework and generate clear hypotheses that can act as a baseline for future studies.

Acknowledgment

We would like to thank the ISMU foundation for providing us with the Integrometro dataset.

Notes

1. Personal income, the objective measurement of income available in the survey, was not included for two reasons: respondents' personal income variable was categorical, thus impeding the calculation of an exact income, and included many missing values.
2. The respondents were asked to what extent they are in favour of six lifestyle aspects of the Italians, namely the way they (a) raise their children; (b) work; (c) go through the family relationships, (d) dress; (e) spend their leisure time; and (f) their food. The response categories ranged from 'don't like at all (including don't have information about it)' to 'like it very much'. The scores on these six items were converted into one summary scale, reflecting the degree of sympathy for the Italian lifestyle.
3. The rather low factor loading of educational attainment on economic integration is likely to be related to a severe mismatch between migrants' skills and jobs. This is a contextual factor due to the Italian legislation (and lack of bilateral agreements with origin countries) that does not recognize migrants' qualifications, resulting in their embeddedness in low-skilled and low-paid jobs without possibility of upward mobility. At the same time, the factor loading of educational attainment on socio-cultural integration is rather high, which is not surprising given that highly educated people generally have a more secular and open worldview and that highly skilled migrants are likely to experience fewer class and attitudinal differences with native-born populations and to face less discrimination (Fokkema and de Haas 2011).

References

Alba, R. 1985. *Italian Americans: Into the twilight of ethnicity.* Englewood Cliffs, NJ: Prentice-Hall.

Alba, R., and V. Nee. 1997. Rethinking assimilation theory for a new era of immigration. *International Migration Review* 31, no. 4: 826–75.

Ambrosini, M. 2005. Inside the invisible welfare: Immigrant helpers and elderly care [in Italian]. *Studi Emigrazione* 42, no. 159: 561–95.

Baio, G., G. Blangiardo, and M. Blangiardo. 2001. Center sampling technique in foreign migration surveys: A methodological note. *Journal of Official Statistics* 27, no. 4: 451–65.

Ban, C. 2009. Economic transnationalism and its ambiguities: The case of Romanian migration to Italy. *International Migration* 50, no. 6: 129–49.

Banfi, L., and P. Boccagni. 2011. Transnational family life and female migration in Italy: One or multiple patterns? In *Gender, generations and the family in international migration*, ed. A. Kraler, E. Kofman, M. Kohli, and C. Schmoll, 287–311. Amsterdam: Amsterdam University Press.

Basch, L., N. Glick Schiller, and C. Szanton Blanc. 1994. *Nations unbound: Transnational projects, postcolonial predicaments, and deterritorialized nation-states.* Langhorne, PA: Gordon and Breach.

Beauchemin, C., H. Lagrange, and M. Safi. 2011. Transnationalism and immigrant assimilation in France: Between here and there? Working Paper 172. Paris: Institut National D'Études Démographiques (INED).

Castagnone, E., M. Eve, E. Petrillo, F. Piperno, and J. Chaloff. 2007. Migrant mothers. Care migration from Romania and Ukraine to Italy: Paths and impact on countries of origin. Working Paper 34. Rome: Centro Studi di Politica Internazionale (CeSPI). http://www.cespi.it/WP/WP34%20Madri%20migranti.pdf (accessed June 10, 2011) [in Italian].

Catanzaro, R., and A. Colombo, eds. 2009. *Badanti and Co: Foreign domestic work in Italy.* Bologna: Il Mulino [in Italian].

Cela, E., and E. Moretti. 2011. Determinants of remittances: Evidence from Serbians and Albanians in Italy. In *Remittances and migration: Interpretive hypotheses and empirical testing*, ed. A. Arrighetti and A. Lasagni, 61–82. Milano: Franco Angeli [in Italian].

Cesareo, V., and G. Blangiardo. 2009. *Integration indices: An empirical study in the Italian migratory context.* Milan: Franco Angeli [in Italian].

Cingolani, P. 2007. Transnational communities in a globalized world: Romanians in Italy. FIERI Research Report. http://www.fieri.it/download.php?fileID=194 & lang=ita (accessed June 10, 2011).

Faist, T. 2000. Transnationalization in international migration: Implications for the study of citizenship and culture. *Ethnic and Racial Studies* 23, no. 2: 189–222.

Fibbi, R., and G. D'Amato. 2008. Transnationalism of migrants in Europe: Empirical evidence [in French]. *Revue Européenne des Migrations Internationales* 24, no. 2: 7–22.

Fokkema, T., and H. de Haas. 2011. Pre- and post-migration determinants of socio-cultural integration of African immigrants in Italy and Spain. *International Migration,* doi:10.1111/j.1468-2435.2011.00687.x.

Fokkema, T., L. Lessard-Phillips, J.D. Bachmeier, and S.K. Brown. 2012. The link between the transnational behaviour and integration of the second generation in European and American cities: Does the context of reception matter? *Nordic Journal of Migration Research* 2, no. 2: 111–23.

Glick Schiller, N., L. Basch, and C. Szanton Blanc, eds. 1992. *Towards a transnational perspective on migration: Race, class, ethnicity, and nationalism reconsidered.* New York, NY: New York Academy of Sciences.

Glick Schiller, N., L. Basch, and C. Szanton Blanc. 2006. Transnationalism: A new analytic framework for understanding migration. *Annals of the New York Academy of Sciences* 645: 1–24.

Gordon, M.M. 1964. *Assimilation in American life: The role of race, religion, and national origins.* New York, NY: Oxford University Press.

Guarnizo, L.E., A. Portes, and W. Haller. 2003. Assimilation and transnationalism: Determinants of transnational political action among contemporary migrants. *American Journal of Sociology* 108, no. 6: 1211–48.

Itzigsohn, J., C. Dore Cabral, E. Hernandez Medina, and O. Vazquez. 1999. Mapping Dominican transnationalism: Narrow and broad transnational practices. *Ethnic and Racial Studies* 22, no. 2: 316–39.

Itzigsohn, J., and S. Giorguli Saucedo. 2002. Immigrant incorporation and sociocultural transnationalism. *International Migration Review* 36, no. 3: 766–98.

Kasinitz, P., J.H. Mollenkopf, M.C. Waters, and J. Holdaway. 2008. *Inheriting the city: The children of immigrants come of age.* New York, NY and Cambridge, MA: Russell Sage Foundation and Harvard University Press.

King, R. 2000. Southern Europe in the changing global map of migration. In *Eldorado or fortress? Migration in Southern Europe,* ed. R. King, G. Lazaridis, and C. Tsardanidis, 3–26. London: Palgrave Macmillan.

King, R. 2002. Towards a new map of European migration. *International Journal of Population Geography* 8, no. 2: 89–106.

King, R., and N. Mai. 2008. *Out of Albania: From crisis migration to social inclusion in Italy.* Oxford: Berghahn.

Kivisto, P. 2001. Theorizing transnational immigration: A critical review of current efforts. *Ethnic and Racial Studies* 24, no. 4: 549–77.

Landolt, P., L. Autler, and S. Baires. 1999. From 'hermano lejano' to 'hermano mayor': The dialectics of Salvadoran transnationalism. *Ethnic and Racial Studies* 22, no. 2: 290–315.

Levitt, P. 2001. *The transnational villagers.* Berkeley, CA: University of California Press.

Popkin, E. 1999. Guatemalan Mayan migration to Los Angeles: Constructing transnational linkages in the context of the settlement process. *Ethnic and Racial Studies* 22, no. 2: 267–89.

Portes, A. 1997. Immigration theory for a new century: Some problems and opportunities. *International Migration Review* 31, no. 4: 799–825.

Portes, A., L.E. Guarnizo, and I. Landolt. 1999. Introduction: Pitfalls and promise of an emergent research field. *Ethnic and Racial Studies* 22, no. 2: 217–37.

Portes, A., W.J. Haller, and L.E. Guarnizo. 2002. Transnational entrepreneurs: An alternative form of immigrant economic adaptation. *American Sociological Review* 67, no. 2: 278–98.

Portes, A., and G.R. Rumbaut. 2001. *Legacies: The story of the immigrant second generation.* Berkeley, CA: University of California Press.

Portes, A., and M. Zhou. 1999. Entrepreneurship and economic progress in the 1990s: A comparative analysis of immigrants and African Americans. In *Immigration and opportunity: Race, ethnicity, and employment in the United States,* ed. F.D. Bean and S. Bell-Rose, 143–71. New York, NY: Russell Sage Foundation.

Sana, M. 2005. Buying membership in the transnational community: Migrant remittances, social status, and assimilation. *Population Research and Policy Review* 24, no. 3: 231–61.

Van Dalen, H.P., G. Groenewold, and T. Fokkema. 2005. The effect of remittances on emigration intentions in Egypt, Morocco, and Turkey. *Population Studies* 59, no. 3: 375–92.

Vlase, I. 2006. Romanian migrant women and housework in Italy [in Italian]. *Studi Emigrazione* 43, no. 161: 6–22.

The migration–development nexus in Bosnia and Herzegovina: Center for Local Development and Diaspora seen 'from below'

Bojana Babić

Faculty of Linguistics and Cultural Studies, University of Oldenburg, Oldenburg, Germany

The paper explores the migration–development nexus in Bosnia and Herzegovina (BiH) from the perspective of the development policies vis-à-vis returnees and refugee migrants from 1995 onwards. In order to understand the link between the two, the paper elaborates on the Center for Local Development and Diaspora (CLDD) model established between the City of Stockholm and six municipalities in BiH. The key question is how 'development' can be understood under the complexities of the economic and social transformation processes in BiH. The empirical evidence – based on interviews with individuals conducted in BiH and Sweden in 2012 – suggests that the meaning and implications of 'development' recommended by the CLDD model differ from how returnees and refugee migrants perceive these.

Introduction

This paper is motivated by the recent optimism over the positive causal relationship thought to exist between migration and development in the countries of migrants' origin. The viewpoint that migrants are able to facilitate development in their home countries is promoted by several European governments and by various international organizations. A country that has been undergoing transition from a centrally planned to a market economy, Bosnia and Herzegovina (BiH) represents a particularly interesting example for the study of the migration–development nexus due to the great number of refugee migrants – people who were displaced during the civil war in the 1990s.[1]

To that end, the paper focuses both on refugee migrants from BiH who stayed in Western European countries and on people returned to their homes upon the end of war in 1995. It presents a case study of a programme aimed at returnees' and refugee migrants' engagement in local development that sheds light on current issues of migration and development in BiH.

The 1995 Dayton Peace Agreement, which ended the war in BiH, addressed – through its Annex VII – the need of return for refugee migrants and internally displaced persons (IDP) to their pre-war place of residence. In addition, the integration of returnees and refugee migrants in BiH's post-1995 development processes was framed by the assumption that 'constructive disorders' caused by war might present a background for a new and better state to emerge (Mehler and Ribaux 2000, 107). This encouraged various international development aid initiatives to place returnees and refugee migrants at the centre of their programmes. In the beginning, the international development aid programmes implemented 'from above' involved first and foremost the returnees, as they financed the postwar reconstruction and recovery. Later on, development initiatives that tried to make use of the forces 'from below' positioned not only returnees, but also refugee migrants who remained abroad, as potential development agents in BiH. In practice, however, the challenges for development in BiH have been very complex. Returnees and refugee migrants are often confronted with structural constraints, such as unemployment, problems with housing and poor social protection, in ways that are not prescribed by development policies but rely on a number of individually carved livelihood strategies. This paper does not make any general claims. However, the interviewees' reflections quoted below give an insight into the ongoing economic, political and social processes in BiH from the perspective of returnees, refugee migrants and particular institutional development agents. They provide an apt illustration of the gaps between policy recommendations and the 'on-the-ground' reality of links between migrants and development.

The paper builds upon a case study of the Center for Local Development and Diaspora (CLDD), established in 2004 as a co-development initiative between the City of Stockholm and six municipalities in BiH.[2] The goal of this initiative was to stimulate development in BiH through empowerment and incorporation of the returnees and refugee migrants in the re-building of their local municipalities. The material presented in this paper is based on qualitative research conducted in BiH over four months in 2012. The fieldwork included visits to each of the 6 CLDD offices, participant observation in events (called 'Di-LoK' 2012) organized by the CLDD offices, interviews with employees of the City of Stockholm and employees of the CLDD in BiH, as well as with returnees and refugee migrants. In total, I interviewed 35 people: 7 employees of CLDD in BiH and 3 from the City of Stockholm, 15 returnees and 10 refugee migrants. The selection of interviewed returnees and refugee migrants was done on recommendation by the employees of the local CLDD offices. All interviews were conducted in the municipalities where the CLDD has its offices and translated from Bosnian/Serbian into English by the author.

The paper proceeds as follows. First, background information is provided on the initiatives of different international actors towards integrating the returnees and refugee migrants in BiH's development over the past two decades. The CLDD model that frames 'development' on the ground is then elaborated, pertaining to development at the local (CLDD model) and individual/household (returnees and refugee migrants) level. This section is followed by a comparative presentation of how development is understood among returnees and refugee migrants vis-à-vis the CLDD employees. The concluding section suggests how the insights provided in this paper might stimulate further discussion and research in this area in BiH.

Challenges to development in postwar BiH

From 1995 onwards, the processes of democratization in BiH (Kostovicova and Bojičić-Dželilović 2006) coincided with putting in place a liberal peace-building model (Duffield 2001) and a (neo)liberal formula of development through economic liberalization, deregulation of industry and privatization of public enterprises (Haque 1999). At the same time, as a consequence of the war, half the Bosnian population was forced to leave their homes. Only during the war period 1992–1995, some 2.2 million people were resettled both internally and internationally, with the expectation of international organizations such as the United Nations High Commissioner for Refugees (UNHCR) that they would return once the war ended.

Ever since then, returnees and refugee migrants have been placed on the development agenda of international organizations such as the World Bank and the United Nations Development Programme (UNDP), as well as some European countries. The post-1995 development policies advocated an active role for returnees and refugee migrants in promoting economic development in BiH. The idea was that offering development aid to help repair the destroyed housing and the devastated economy, along with social security and access to the labour market, would create the conditions necessary for development to emerge (Rajchel et al. 2010). For example, in 1997, the UNHCR implemented a programme called the 'Open City Initiative' which granted development aid to those municipalities whose leaders publicly expressed willingness to welcome returnees. However, for the resettled population, the physical security and access to housing provided through external financial support has rarely been accompanied by access to the labour market and other social rights, including education, health care and pensions necessary for the viability of return (Rajchel et al. 2010).

Previous studies have pointed at various difficulties associated with development aid policies, such as the inability of such aid to adequately respond to social and political factors as well as to economic needs over the long run for a country like Bosnia (Väyrynen 1997). Instead of economic recovery, political transformations coupled with a steady influx of development aid resulted in aid dependency, weak local ownership[3] and local elites who do not work towards the expansion of the formal economy, and an overall weak civil society in BiH (Chandler 1998; Fagan 2005; Sarajlić and Marko 2011).

Responding to such local circumstances as well as a relatively low number of returnees, the European countries involved in BiH's development designed a new policy regarding the engagement of returnees and refugee migrants in this process. The new development approach does not put the donors at the centre but other 'development actors' such as migrants themselves (Panizzon 2011, 187). While the earlier development aid policies attempted to overcome the structural constraints in BiH with financial resources coming 'from above', the introduction of 'new' development agents – more specifically the returnees and refugee migrants – implies and calls upon their ability to facilitate a 'development from below' (de Haas 2008, 49).

In BiH, however, the livelihood strategies of both returnees and refugee migrants are not easily related to the idea of their crucial engagement in the development processes mentioned above. On the contrary, households and their individual members employ a combination of atomistic and disconnected activities to maintain, secure and improve their livelihoods (de Haas 2010, 24). For the returnees, remittances received from family members and their own savings as well as pre-war personal networks within the local municipalities in BiH, are crucial for organizing their lives locally. Other authors have shown that remittances are an increasingly important and relatively stable source of external finance in countries affected by economic and political crises (Kapur 2004). They may enable households to invest in productive activities and improve their livelihoods, thereby contributing to poverty reduction in BiH (IOM 2007). Moreover, with shares of gross domestic product (GDP) at nearly 20% in some years, remittances continue to sustain people's livelihoods (World Bank 2011). At the same time, by changing their temporary protection status to permanent residency, half a million of the BiH refugee migrants have remained in their new country of settlement (Koser and Black 1999, 533). Instead of a permanent return, seasonal visits of family and friends in BiH, individually sent remittances and other forms of piecemeal engagement have become a norm for most of these refugee migrants (Al-Ali, Black, and Koser 2001; Dimova and Wolff 2009; Franz 2003; 2010; Valenta and Ramet 2011).

These complex realities on the ground suggest that the role of returnees and refugee migrants in BiH's development remains under-explored. First and foremost, the underlying understanding of 'development' itself needs to be illuminated. Questions to reflect on include 'what kind of development' (Van Hear 2011, 85) has been promoted so far; the way that 'development' has been understood by returnees and refugee migrants; and how this understanding differs from the CLDD development model in the context of the current transformation process in BiH. In the context of BiH, celebrating migrants as new development agents in a 'development from below' model (de Haas 2010) relies more on the (neo)liberal ideologies than on the empirical evidence.

A note on development

In a general sense, development is understood as a complex and multifaceted process. In its consideration as a fundamental or structural change it should be distinguished from development in the sense of improvement, positive change or as a platform for improvement (Gasper 2004). Furthermore, development as growth in GDP is differentiated from human development as human security, capability or freedom, and autonomy (Sen 1999).

Distinguishing between different definitions of development is crucial to the analysis of how policies aimed at stimulating development through migration have evolved over the past two decades. In the overall debate in conceptualizing the link between migration and development, the economic development paradigm initially predominated over other non-economic factors (Faist 2009). Today, the shift in contextualizing development often results in a neglect of underlying structural constraints due to its predominant focus on non-state actors. In particular, migrants are regarded as the new agents of development or providers of 'foreign aid' through remittances and transnational engagement in their countries of origin (Kapur 2004). However, in an unfavourable structural environment, individuals or households might achieve a certain level of human development[4] provided by various livelihood strategies, which can have little or no influence on further development at local or national level. The problem, therefore, is that 'development from below' policies have the unintended consequence of shifting attention away from structural constraints, and hence from the responsibility of national governments to pursue economic and political reforms (de Haas 2012).

The following section elaborates on these issues through the CLDD model. The model is analysed against the background of returnees' and refugee migrants' perceptions, in order to understand 'development' as observed at the local (municipality) level.

The CLDD model

From the perspective of most international actors, such as the World Bank, NGOs and EU governments, their recent development policies have promoted more participatory forms of development at the local level (Faist 2008). To that end, the City of Stockholm has established the Centers for Local Development and Diaspora in six municipalities located in both entities of BiH: in Republika Srpska – Teslić, Banja Luka and Srebrenica; and in the Federation of BiH – Ilijaš, Goražde and Ključ. As explained in *The CLDD Annual Bulletin 2012*:

> In 1997 the City of Stockholm established a department for voluntary return for all people interested to return to their country after having spent some time in Sweden. Later, in 2004, together with the EU we established a project with BiH, and that was the first project across our borders, city and the state. The programme was completed in 2008 but our work has continued in BiH. The goal of this project was stimulating development in BiH through empowerment and incorporation of returnees and refugee migrants in the re-building of their local municipalities. Today, in 2012, the CLDDs are in ownership of their municipalities whose work is supervised by the City of Stockholm. All services are in the hands of community development workers, educated to work according to and implement EU standards. (City of Stockholm 2012, 1)

According to the representatives of the City of Stockholm, empowerment of the returnees and refugee migrants with support from the CLDD should turn them into agents of development in their original municipalities in BiH. In practice, the CLDD work is organized around empowerment of returnees regarding their employment, housing and social protection in BiH, while for refugee migrants' empowerment this means their (re)integration in the local BiH municipalities through investments and various social activities accompanying their visits to BiH. Instead of the previously implemented conditional development aid policies, in this model development should be achieved by the returnees and refugee migrants themselves. As emphasized by the representative of the City of Stockholm I interviewed in Sarajevo in summer 2012, empowerment should be understood as 'help for self-help':

> We have to work on empowerment of the returnees and refugee migrants. This means help for self-help and that is our first and main task.

To achieve this goal, the CLDD model focuses on the following activities within the economic and civil-society sphere. First, it assists with access to local, national and international donations for home reparation and infrastructure. Second, it assists in obtaining micro-loans and education programmes to access the labour market as well as to establish associations, most of which are focused on gender and youth issues. And finally, it encourages the presence of refugee migrants in development in BiH. The CLDD organizes summer meetings known as 'Days of Local Development and Diaspora' or Di-LoK (*Dani lokalnog razvoja i dijaspore*). They include cultural and sports programmes as well as economic forums for the returnees, refugee migrants and the local population. The main aim of the Di-LoK events is to establish stronger connections between the returnees and refugee migrants and involve them in further investment and cooperation activities in BiH.

As explained by a representative of the City of Stockholm at the occasion of the Di-LoK event in Banja Luka in 2012, empowerment of the refugee migrants should be achieved by networking:

> The BiH population around the world needs to know what they can do for their country. They want to help and that is a way to create a strong base for economic prosperity in BiH. So our motto is networking, networking, networking!

Each CLDD office employs two persons as 'community development workers' (literally: community leaders – *društveni vodiči*), who are mostly themselves returnees from Western Europe. According to the CLDD model, they are the most important figures because they coordinate contacts between returnees, refugee migrants, local, national and international institutions. As noted in *The CLDD Annual Bulletin 2012*, their work is organized 'on the principles and procedures of the highest EU standards' (City of Stockholm 2012). In other words, the CLDD employees are trained by professionals from Sweden while their daily activities are supervised through email, phone calls and internal supervisions organized by representatives of the City of Stockholm who visit the local offices in BiH several times a year.

Consequently, each community development worker is expected to observe the CLDD principles and rules, yet to adjust the work of their office by taking into consideration a number of things such as whether the area is rural or urban, the opportunities and needs of their local municipality as well as the needs and capacities of returnees and refugee migrants from the municipality. They also need to follow the recommendations and requests coming from the representatives of the City of Stockholm. Although each CLDD office might prioritize different activities, like agricultural production in rural municipalities and small and middle-sized businesses in urban ones, their focus remains empowerment of returnees through employment, housing, social rights, and of the refugee migrants through networking. However, my empirical evidence shows that the situation on the ground is rather complex and creates divergent perceptions and opinions by returnees and refugee migrants as compared to those held by community development workers.

The returnees

For those who have returned, the obstacles to their establishment in the labour market and in obtaining other social rights have frequently been circumvented by livelihood strategies which comprise various capabilities, assets (both material and social) and activities (Carney 1998). This general statement applies in BiH, where most of the returnees whom I interviewed indicated the crucial importance of the remittances received from their families, as well as savings and pre-war personal networks. The returnees also indicated various hindrances which in their opinion prevent development at the municipality level, the most important being the lack of jobs and the corrupt local authorities. For example in Goražde, a municipality in the Federation of BiH where the majority of the 30,000 inhabitants are internal returnees and a high number of Goraždines live abroad, unemployment is one of the main problems. As pointed out in an analysis of the impact of return on south-east BiH by local development agencies (ALRIROPJ-BiH 2010), the examined sample of 295 returnee households, or 795 returnees aged between 15 and 64, had an unemployment rate of 73.5%, which is 12% higher than its equivalent amongst the local population in that part of the country. Although the majority of returnees have social insurance and their homes have been repaired through donations, these appear to have no influence on employment. Under these conditions, a married 50-year-old woman returned from Germany has relied on support and remittances from her family in Sweden and she considers leaving the country very soon:

> If there is no help from the diaspora this country will collapse tomorrow. I have been OK only thanks to my husband's family who kept sending me money all the time. His family took our children (both were in high school) with them to Sweden. I couldn't see any future for them here, and my daughter couldn't adjust to the education system. She suffered a lot here but now both of my children live in Sweden, and we visit them frequently. But, I would leave this country tomorrow if I could [she was forced to return]. Simply, this system is wrong!

According to her, the poor economic situation in Goražde, and in BiH generally, is a consequence of high levels of corruption at local and national level, as well as the non-adjustment of development aid policies to local development needs. She thinks that international donors' financial support should have been invested in industry (jobs) rather than housing:

> Just look at the health system, how much do you have to pay to the doctor to 'look at you'. And think how many donations came into this country, we could have a paradise. And for what were they used? The repair of houses. Now people sit in those houses hungry. That money should be invested in jobs, industry. If you have a job, you can simply get a credit to buy a house.

I recorded similar statements in Teslić, a municipality in Republika Srpska, where an estimated 60,000 inhabitants includes a high percentage of returnees and IDPs. Although the municipality is registered as one of the most successful in terms of (re)integration of returnees as well as one of the most economically successful municipalities in Republika Srpska, a high number of refugee migrants live abroad while unemployment has increased significantly since 2010. For example, a 64 year-old returnee from Sweden, a former primary school teacher, was able to maintain her standard of living thanks to the remittances from her family in Sweden, whom she frequently visits. According to her, the crucial problem of development in her municipality is unemployment:

> Honestly, the only help here is a job. Give people work and then you will strengthen their family and community – community is so important for people. But if there are no jobs, families are in difficult situations and there is no community, nothing.

Furthermore, she explains that local community ties have weakened due to the high number of displaced people and the social transformations that followed the war. In her opinion, the high level of corruption among local authorities is a consequence of displaced populations and a newly emerging social order:

> I must say that what really bothers me is that all urban people [*gradska raja*] left, and those primitives [*seljaci*, IDPs who moved in from rural areas]. They don't respect anything, and I think that influenced a lot the corruption. They all got jobs in the local

authorities, which are the most corrupt. If there is any help, it never gets to the right place; instead it always finishes in the hands of three or four people.

Besides corruption at the local level, which implies misuse of donations, this woman perceives the ruling positions of IDPs who are not part of the pre-war population of Teslić (*izbjeglice i došljaci*) as a main hindrance to development. In addition, the many returnees I interviewed point to the pre-war personal networks as crucial to their (re)integration.

After spending six years in Germany, a 57 year-old man returned to Teslić, where he lived before the war and to which he has a strong sense of belonging:

> I had some money I had earned in Germany to buy some machines and my old friend, who I know from before the war, hired me to work for his firm. Then step by step. Later, we opened a grill (*roštiljnica*) where all my family started to work. I don't complain, I feel good here and I don't want to go anywhere. I am happy here where I feel that I am somebody. All the people know me and respect me here!

However, he is still concerned for the future of his job and his family. According to him, nobody takes responsibility for the people in BiH:

> But the only problem for me is that all my property is under mortgage, and I am now thinking to take the loan for returnees offered by the Turkish Bank. I heard it is very good. But again, this bank also asked for interest, although they said it is without interest because it is devoted to the returnees ... But I am not surprised because there is no state here. Everybody does whatever he or she wants. That's why I understand young people who want to leave.

At the same time, the community development workers I interviewed shared the opinion that unemployment and the overall economic situation are the main obstacles for progress in their local municipalities, but not the only ones. They also complained about the returnees' passive attitude towards engagement in the labour market. According to them, one of the main reasons for a lack of interest in work is the returnees' habit to live on donations. For a female community development worker in Goražde, the efforts of her CLDD to influence local development still face problems with both returnees and the municipality:

> The main problem here is unemployment, and the aim of this centre is to improve working conditions and to prevent people from going abroad, and for that reason we are trying to open new workplaces. Well, we work mostly with women's associations. We financed one small business here – handicraft. But people are coming to the office to ask just for donations, if they can get some mechanization for free. Our municipality needs an office like this but I think they are not interested in doing anything for the community.

The situation is problematic also in Srebrenica, a municipality in Republika Srpska where international and local donors have contributed millions of dollars in the last 15 years. The lack of returnees' initiatives is perceived by a community development worker as one of the main obstacles for economic development to occur. Referring to a life with poor physical infrastructure, reliance on social welfare and unemployment reaching even 90%, the community development workers claim that donations have 'spoiled people'.

DEVELOPMENT IN SOUTH-EAST EUROPE AND THE BLACK SEA REGION

According to the words of a community development worker in Srebrenica, despite good relations with the local municipality and his daily contact with the beneficiaries, donations decrease the returnees' initiatives for work in rural areas as well:

> I am in touch with people every day. I talk to people, and I think about how to get some money to share with others. This centre focuses on infrastructure projects and on agricultural production, like fruit-growing, and apiculture. We work on concrete things. You cannot go and talk to a peasant about projects. The cooperation with the municipality is excellent, but the problem is usually in the selection of beneficiaries. For example, we had a big project donation from the Government of Japan for the production of raspberries. We selected twenty households and they just had to prepare the land for cultivation. I went there a day before donors came to visit – only one person had prepared the land. Others said 'I looked you in the eyes', meaning they promised to do something only because they know me and they wanted to do me a favour. I think that donations spoiled people. They got used to living on aid.

Also, the community development worker from Teslić pointed out that the CLDD's beneficiaries have to learn to live off their work. As she put it, 'We give them a hook but they must fish themselves'. She further explained:

> Our beneficiaries have already learned that they have to live from their work, and we are helping them. There were many great activities in the centre but I should mention one which was very successful. Recently, we had a good activity in cooperation with a bank from Turkey. They are giving very advantageous loans to returnees. We assisted in offering these loans to returnees, so that they can start a small business and employ more people. There are many of them [returnees] who have taken the loans.

In the majority of interviews with the returnees, the structural constraints and their overall lack of power in relation to the high number of IDPs who are 'new' to the municipality, emerged as important in their daily lives. Dealing with these constraints on a daily basis is something returnees do themselves by relying on their own personal or family networks and resources, rather than on the support provided by the CLDD programmes and activities. In order to access the labour market or obtain some social rights, such as housing, health care or their children's education, returnees combine their capabilities and access to material and social resources, such as remittances, savings and pre-war personal networks. Most returnees share the opinion that this situation is a consequence of the high level of corruption in BiH followed by a lack of state responsibility towards its citizens and the overall economic transition. At the same time, while some community development workers agree that personal interests at the local level, indeed, dominate over community interests, they claim that the main problem with the returnees originates from the previous development aid policies and the returnees' habit of simply receiving aid. In other words, they suggest that the majority of returnees prefer aid to work. But then again, community development workers depict the overall development processes in BiH as influenced by difficulties of the transformation processes in the country and by the lack of state initiatives regarding economic and political reforms which would enable individuals 'to make strategic life choices and to participate in the processes of decision making which helps to frame such a choice' (Kabeer 2003, 3).

The refugee migrants

The CLDD model also sees refugee migrants as important 'agents of development' and presumes their loyalty and engagement towards their country and localities of origin (see also Piper 2009, 94). As noted in the context of the human development paradigm, refugee migrants 'who primarily escape life-threatening circumstances, may end up remitting substantial amounts of money or becoming a transnational entrepreneur' (Lindley 2007). However, the lack of confidence in BiH institutions, along with the knowledge of better economic prospects gained by living abroad, prevent them from being involved in other relationships than with family or friends. In the case of a 38 year-old female refugee migrant in Sweden, the connection to BiH is still the most important one, and she even considers returning there one day. She visits Teslić every summer with her family and spends at least one month there. In the meantime, she regularly sends money to her family, and also to some friends. She thinks that people are interested in helping and doing something for BiH while hoping to go back there one day:

> I know that sometimes, like last week, there was an event organized for the New Year, for the people who wanted to send parcels to the children in Bosnia. A lot of people participated, and I think that all of us are nostalgic about Bosnia. We just dream to return there. I would start a small business there and return tomorrow, if I knew it would be successful. But then the economic situation is bad and I have family, so it is hard to take the risk. I am therefore staying here where my children have better living conditions. But myself, I am nowhere.

She explained that in the past, she also used to remit money through a religious organization, but stopped doing so because she lost trust in that organization:

> Before, there was a religious organization here through which we were sending money to Bosnia. Everybody would be assigned a child to take care of and then you would pay the money to her/his account every month. But later we heard that the money was not going to the right place, so I stopped giving anything. Since then I am sending money just to people I know, and I am not interested in any organization anymore.

I recorded similar stories of ambivalence and lack of trust in diasporic organizations in several other interviews with refugee migrants. After obtaining permanent residence in Sweden, a 55 year-old male refugee migrant and his family in Sweden have been helping their family and friends in Goražde by remitting money and visiting BiH every summer and winter holidays. In the past, they had also participated in both informal and organized activities among refugee migrants in Sweden, but they have stopped doing it now. The interviewee explains:

> Well, we don't have contacts with any institution or organization. I remember the period after the war, donations we sent never reached the people. We don't know where they ended up ... So we prefer to send the money to the accounts of our families so they can give to those who need it. Sometimes, we (a group of refugee migrants from Goražde) also collect money among ourselves in Sweden and send to Bosnia. Just now we brought the money for one man ... We heard from our families here, in Goražde, that one young man needs an urgent operation and we decided to collect some money among us. I hope it will help.

At the same time, the community development workers I interviewed believe that refugee migrants have great potential to help further development in BiH. The only thing that prevents them from investing in BiH is the current economic situation. The following statement by the community development worker in Goražde echoed what I was told by virtually all other CLDD employees in the six municipalities:

> We are in contact with the diaspora (refugee migrants); they are interested in what is happening here. I know for sure that there are people who would return, they ask what possibilities for investments there are, what they might do if they return. But that is still only informative due to the insecurity of the economic situation.

However, according to the community development worker in Teslić, investments by refugee migrants are already taking place in BiH:

> We work by following their initiative; they come to tell us what they need and we try to provide them with that. The diaspora (refugee migrants) are very much interested in what is going on here, they call us, they come to visit and they are waiting for a better moment to invest. Most of them repaired their houses and that is already a great help to the community. They used the materials and labour from here.

Furthermore, community development workers put a lot of hope in the 'Di-LoK' days. In their opinion, the obstacles to further investments by refugee migrant will be overcome through networking and stronger links between the returnees and refugee migrants.

However, the following quote of a successful 58 year-old businessman from Sweden, who has been regularly participating in the economic forums organized under the 'Di-LoK' days, suggests that the situation on the ground is rather different. He is considered as a promising transnational entrepreneur and responsible for the wider networking among entrepreneurs from BiH and Sweden. Yet, for him, starting a firm and investing in BiH are still impossible due to the corrupt local authorities and the lack of an adequate business environment:

> Although I started a firm in Croatia, with a lot of success, I am not even considering to do the same in BiH. Simply because to do so here you need one year and to pay [bribe] every administrative worker, or to know 'one key person'. There is simply no support from the state, just a circle of taking and giving … In any normal business world, like in Sweden, you need to have a guarantee from the state, but here what is a state? We are meeting here every year and we are always discussing the same problems. We are tired of talking. There is no confidence of the BiH population settled abroad when it comes to business in this country. The investment atmosphere is bad here, it takes too long to register your firm and even talking about potential subsidies or other kinds of support. Therefore, I am asking where the state is in all this.

Therefore, in the interviews above, but also in my interviews with other refugee migrants, the insecurity of the economic environment and the lack of trust in institutions clearly pointed to the low interest of refugee migrants to engage in investment activities in BiH. Despite the CLDD initiatives to incorporate them in their local municipalities through networking and events such as 'Di-LoK', refugee migrants remain involved with BiH mainly through informal relationships. The stories of refugee migrants demonstrate that the transnational household strategy, with remittances and return visits, is their most prominent characteristic. In addition, refugee migrants whom I interviewed pointed to the lack of trust in any form of network other than personal. The postwar experiences of donating and sending remittances through organized diasporic channels caused a lack of trust in the institutions and organizations in BiH and now prevent further cooperation. Finally, an observation from other studies reviewed by de Haas (2010, 30), namely that a positive turn in the development of the origin country is accompanied by an improving trust in government, and that this dynamic will encourage migrants to be among the first to join in and recognize new opportunities, has not been happening in BiH. The difficulties of the economic transformations and the high levels of corruption remind us of that. Yet, community development workers believe that refugee migrants' investments are already taking place in BiH indirectly through the reconstruction of their pre-war houses.

Conclusion

The material presented and analysed in this article suggests that defining the relationship between migration and development in BiH is anything but straightforward. According to the community development workers, local development in BiH should be stimulated by empowering and incorporating the returnees and refugee migrants in re-building their municipalities. As such, national development would occur 'from below'. However, opposite to what is promoted by the CLDD model, returnees tend to rely on different livelihood strategies based mostly on remittances, savings and networks, for their (re)integration in their local municipalities. Refugee migrants maintain contacts with BiH mostly through personal networks, while adopting transnational lives without any interest in investments or other formal economic engagement.

Taking into account people's stories, several reasons emerge for such a gap between expectations and realities on the ground. On the one hand, returnees and refugee migrants see unemployment and high levels of corruption as the main obstacles for development in their municipalities. They stress the lack of state responsibility for national reforms as well as the previous development aid policies and new social realities involving new populations in their municipalities. Development remains a contested issue as it requires that one's position is negotiated in new contexts of power and inequality under emerging social transformation processes (Ranger 1994). On the other hand, according to community development workers, the responsibility for the current situation in BiH does not only rest with the state but with the people themselves. They consider returnees as aid-dependent and lacking initiatives with regard to work. At the same time, they believe that refugee migrants' potential would be reached once their closer connection with their municipalities in BiH is established according to the CLDD model. They do not reflect on the fact that this model might shift attention away from a lack of the state responsibility for economic and social transformations in BiH.

Therefore, for further research, it might be important to approach the issues of the migration–development nexus in BiH by addressing the local-level social transformation processes and conceiving development as a part of an effort to change power structures. Local power structures, involving aid dependency but also corruption, are perceived by the locals as barriers that prevent people from participating in the issues that affect their lives. Therefore, a systematic comparison of the dynamics of migration and development in a number of local contexts is needed, that would provide a better understanding of locality as well as of the needs and opportunities of the returnees and refugee migrants and their relations with those who stayed behind.

Acknowledgements

I am grateful to all my research interviewees and to Julie Vullnetari, Russell King and workshop participants for their constructive feedback on an earlier version of this paper presented at the IMISCOE Annual Conference in Amsterdam in August 2012. Above all, I express my deep gratitude to Maja Povrzanović Frykman for giving me constant support to finalize this paper despite challenges I encountered along the way.

Notes

1. The civil war in BiH in 1992–1995 caused huge economic and human losses. UNHCR (1997) estimates that over a million refugees from BiH, constituting 23.9% of the pre-war population, live in about a hundred countries all over the world. I use the term 'refugee migrants' to reflect their now consolidated status, with citizenship, in many European and other countries, especially Sweden. Hence they no longer carry the 'categorizing' implications and potential stigmatization that the simple term 'refugees' connotes.
2. Out of some 2.2 million persons from BiH who were forcibly displaced during the war in the 1990s, some 800,000 left for Western Europe. The Swedish government decided to devote the entire refugee quota (1800 people) for the budget year 1992/93 to refugees from Former Yugoslavia (FY). For the budget year 1993/94, the refugee quota was extended to 6000, and 5500 out of those were reserved for people from the FY. Moreover, an *ad hoc* decision that took into consideration the massive plight of one particular group of people was made on 21 June 1993, when 42,000 asylum seekers from BiH were granted permanent residency. A third of some 400,000 individuals who sought asylum in Sweden between 1984 and 2007 originated from the FY. In connection to the war in 1992–1995 Sweden received 60,000 refugees from BiH. By 2008, some 80,000 people of Bosnian origin lived in Sweden, and some 50,000 have obtained Swedish citizenship (see Povrzanović Frykman 2012).
3. There has been a long discussion of the application and meaning of the concept of local ownership. In general, local ownership is regarded as a desirable outcome of international peace operations, which enables local populations to 'control reform and reconstruct processes, and internationals to eventually scale down or end their presence in a country' (Martin and Moser 2012, 1). In the case of BiH, the studies of Wittman and Bojičić-Dželilović (2012) and others show that local ownership is not a straightforward concept and the relationships between local and international actors are multi-faceted and present a particular case due to high levels of mistrust and the lack of constructive interaction between different actors. While local and international constituencies agree that international intervention in BiH was successful in ending the war, it has been less successful in building a functioning state. In addition, there are disagreements within and between local and international actors on how the international community can leave behind sustainable institutions, even when there is broad agreement on the overall goals of the intervention.
4. Human development is defined as the process of expanding people's choices and improving human capabilities (the range of things that they can do or be in life) and freedoms so they can live a long and healthy life, access education and a decent standard of living, participate in their community and the decisions that affect their lives (Sen 1999).

References

Al-Ali, N., R. Black, and K. Koser. 2001. The limits to 'transnationalism': Bosnian and Eritrean refugees in Europe as emerging transnational communities. *Ethnic and Racial Studies* 24, no. 4: 578–600.

ALRIROPJ-BiH. 2010. *Analysis of return in Southeastern BiH with recommendations for sustainable return.* Agency for Local Development Initiative and Regional Committee for Return to the Southeast (ALRIROPJ) BiH, http:// http://www.budzet.ba/files/ANAL-IZA_POVRATKA%20.pdf (accessed February 11, 2013).

Carney, D.E. 1998. Sustainable rural livelihoods: What contribution can we make? Papers presented at the Natural Resources Advisers' Conference organized by the UK's Department for International Development (DFID), July, London.

Chandler, D. 1998. Democratization in Bosnia: The limits of civil society building strategies. *Democratization* 5, no. 4: 78–102.

City of Stockholm. 2012. CLDD Annual Bulletin 2012. Stockholm: City of Stockholm, The Center for Local Development and Diaspora, Department for Voluntary Return, http:// cldd.org/bs/content/cldd-download-bih (accessed January 7, 2013) [in Bosnian].

de Haas, H. 2008. Migration and development: A theoretical perspective. Working Paper 9. Oxford: University of Oxford, International Migration Institute.

de Haas, H. 2010. Migration and development: A theoretical perspective. *International Migration Review* 44, no. 1: 227–64.

de Haas, H. 2012. The 'migration and development pendulum': A critical view on research and policy. *International Migration* 50, no. 3: 8–25.

Dimova, R., and F.C. Wolff. 2009. Remittances and chain migration: Longitudinal evidence from Bosnia and Herzegovina. Discussion Paper 4083. Bonn: Institute for the Study of Labor (IZA).

Duffield, M. 2001. *Global governance and the new wars: The merging of development and security.* London: Zed Books.

Fagan, A. 2005. Civil society in Bosnia ten years after Dayton. *International Peacekeeping* 12, no. 3: 406–19.

Faist, T. 2008. Migrants as transnational development agents: An inquiry into the newest round of the migration–development nexus. *Population, Space and Place* 14, no. 1: 21–42.

Faist, T. 2009. Transnationalization and development: Towards an alternative agenda. *Social Analysis* 53, no. 3: 38–59.

Franz, B. 2003. Bosnian refugees and political realities: Changes in asylum and residence laws in Austria and the United States. *Journal of Ethnic and Migration Studies* 29, no. 1: 5–25.

Franz, B. 2010. Returnees, remittances and reconstruction: International politics and local consequences in Bosnia. *Journal of Diplomacy and International Relations* 11, no. 1: 49–62.

Gasper, D. 2004. *The ethics of development.* Edinburgh: Edinburgh University Press.

Haque, S. 1999. The fate of sustainable development under neo-liberal regimes in developing countries. *International Political Science Review* 20, no. 2: 197–218.

IOM. 2007. *Migration profile of BiH 2007.* Ljubljana: Republic of Slovenia Ministry of Interior and International Organization for Migration.

Kabeer, N. 2003. *Gender mainstreaming in poverty eradication and the Millennium Development Goals: A handbook for policy-makers and other stakeholders.* Ottawa: Commonwealth Secretariat, International Development Research Center and the Canadian International Development Agency.

Kapur, D. 2004. Remittances: The new development mantra? Discussion Paper 29. New York, NY: United Nations Conference on Trade and Development and the Intergovernmental Group of Twenty-Four (G-24) on International Monetary Affairs.

Koser, K., and R. Black. 1999. Limits to harmonization: The temporary protection of refugees in the European Union. *International Migration* 37, no. 3: 522–43.

Kostovicova, D., and V. Bojičić-Dželilović. 2006. Europeanizing the Balkans: Rethinking the post-communist and post-conflict transition. *Ethnopolitics* 5, no. 3: 223–41.

Lindley, A. 2007. The early morning phone call: Remittances from a refugee diaspora perspective. Working Paper 47. Oxford: University of Oxford, Centre on Migration Policy and Society.

Martin, M., and S. Moser, eds. 2012. *Exiting conflict, owning the peace: Local ownership and peacebuilding relationships in the cases of Bosnia and Kosovo.* Berlin: Friedrich Ebert Stiftung.

Mehler, A., and C. Ribaux. 2000. Crisis prevention and conflict management in technical cooperation: An overview of the national and international debate. Working Paper 270. Wiesbaden: Deutsche Gesellschaft für Technische Zusammenarbeit [GTZ]).

Panizzon, M. 2011. France's co-development program: Financial and fiscal incentives to promote diaspora entrepreneurship and transfers. In *Diaspora for development in Africa*, ed. S. Plaza and D. Ratha, 183–229. Washington DC: World Bank.

Piper, N. 2009. The complex interconnections of the migration–development nexus: A social perspective. *Population, Space and Place* 15, no. 2: 93–101.

Povrzanović Frykman, M. 2012. Struggle for recognition: Bosnian refugees' employment experiences in Sweden. *Refugee Survey Quarterly* 31, no. 1: 54–79.

Rajchel, R., R. Esanu, A. MacBain, and B. Rohwerder. 2010. Bosnia and Herzegovina: Post-conflict reconstruction. Conflict mapping paper. Fife: St. Andrew's University, Centre for Peace and Conflict Studies.

Ranger, T. 1994. The invention of tradition revisited. In *Inventions and boundaries: Historical and anthropological approaches to the study of ethnicity and nationalism. Papers from the Researcher Training Course Held at Sandbjerg Manor, 23–29 May 1993*, ed. P. Kaarsholm and J. Hultin, 9–50. Occasional paper 11. Roskilde: Roskilde University, International Development Studies.

Sarajlić, E., and D. Marko, eds. 2011. *State or Nation: The challenges of political transition in Bosnia and Herzegovina.* Prepared in the framework of the Regional Research Promotion Programme in the Western Balkans (RRPP). Sarajevo: University of Sarajevo, Centre for Interdisciplinary Postgraduate Studies.

Sen, A. 1999. *Development as freedom.* New York: Anchor Books.

UNHCR. 1997. *Census of refugee and other war-affected persons in the Federal Republic of Yugoslavia.* Geneva: United Nations High Commissioner for Refugees (UNHCR) Repatriation and Return Operation in BiH.

Valenta, M., and S. Ramet, eds. 2011. *The Bosnian diaspora: Integration in transnational communities.* Farnham: Ashgate.

Van Hear, N. 2011. Diasporas, recovery and development in conflict-ridden societies. In *The migration–development nexus*, ed. T. Faist, M. Fauser, and P. Kivisto, 85–103. Basingstoke: Palgrave Macmillan.

Väyrynen, R. 1997. Economic incentives and the Bosnian peace process. In *The price of peace: Incentives and international conflict prevention*, ed. D. Cortright, 155–80. Oxford: Rowman and Littlefield.

Wittman, A., and V. Bojičić-Dželilović. 2012. Local ownership and peace building relationship in the case of BiH. In *Exiting conflict, owning the peace: Local ownership and peacebuilding relationships in the cases of Bosnia and Kosovo*, ed. M. Martin and S. Moser, 8–14. Berlin: Friedrich Ebert Stiftung.

World Bank. 2011. *Migration and remittances factbook.* Washington DC: World Bank.

Albanian-speaking transnational populations in Switzerland: continuities and shifts

Bashkim Iseni

Swiss Forum for Migration and Population Studies, University of Neuchâtel, Neuchâtel, Switzerland

For more than four decades, Switzerland has been a primary destination for the Albanian-speaking immigrants originating in Kosovo, Macedonia, southern Serbia and Montenegro. Throughout this time, migrants have continued to retain strong transnational links with their areas of origin, which until the end of the 1990s meant important economic and financial support, but also political mobilization. Today, however, the diaspora is increasingly focused on integration in Switzerland, a process which seems to be characterized by a redefinition of migrants' transnational relations at the crossroad between the culture of the country of origin and that of destination.

Introduction

The Albanian-speaking diaspora has been present in Switzerland for more than four decades. Switzerland was a key destination particularly for the unqualified Albanian immigrants from Former Yugoslavia (FY). They originated mainly from villages in Kosovo but also from Macedonia, southern Serbia and Montenegro, in other words the most underdeveloped regions in FY.[1] Consequently, migration became an important factor in improving living standards in these regions which faced high population pressures (Burri-Sharani et al. 2010; Dahinden 2010; Leuenberger and Maillard 1999; Roux 1992; von Aarburg and Gretler 2008). These immigrants were intensively engaged in the national issues in the Balkans and in the reconstruction of their areas of origin after the wars that engulfed the region since 1998. Today, the integration process of the numerous Albanian-speaking population in Switzerland seems to be characterized by a redefinition of migrants' identity as the intersection of the cultures of both the host and the origin country.

As Dahinden (2010, 63) emphasizes, the Albanian-speaking immigrants have developed different types of transnationality in Switzerland. Transnationalism in this article is understood as social fields in which migrants create links – imaginary or real – between the country of origin and that of destination (Bauböck and Faist 2010; Glick Schiller, Basch, and Szanton Blanc 1992; Levitt and Jaworsky 2007; Portes 1999).

This article's goals are as follows. First, I argue that in the earlier phases of Albanian immigration from FY to Switzerland, their transnational orientation was mostly towards the country of origin. Thus, the significant role of diasporas for development in countries of origin is emphasized. This impact is considered in terms of financial and social remittance transfers, including networking skills (Castles and Delgado Wise 2008; Glick Schiller 2009; Kapur 2004; Mercer, Page, and Evans 2011). The second aim of this article is to illustrate, through the case study of the Albanian-speaking immigrant population in Switzerland, how transnationality changes in parallel with the settlement process of an immigrant population in a host country.

As such, this migrant population offers a fruitful platform from where to examine how the reconfiguration of the diaspora's economic, cultural and political attitude vis-à-vis the country of origin and that of the destination is articulated on its transnational relations. It thus offers an opportunity for understanding the continuities and shifts that are produced over time among diasporas vis-à-vis both these countries. To pursue this understanding, a brief review of the historical phases of migration to Switzerland from regions of the FY is first necessary. The article then traces the historical role and impact of the Albanian diaspora on the socio-economic and political processes in the migrants' areas of origin. Next, it analyses the continuities and changes observed among Albanian-speaking migrants and how the latter impact the development of their areas of origin. Last, some generalizations are provided concerning the interactions of migrants' integration in the host country, the maintenance of the links with the culture of origin and the consequent shifts of their role for the development processes of the country of origin.

A methodological note

This paper draws on empirical research carried out over a period of many years and within the framework of a number of projects. Primary data collection rests on a qualitative methodology which involved participant observation, in-depth interviews and focus-group discussions. First, participant observation has been facilitated through the author's presence in the midst of the Albanian-speaking community in Switzerland since 1991. The author has participated in various community events and festivities related to the community's cultural, political, religious and sports life. Participant observation was also one of the methods employed in two consecutive studies conducted in Switzerland in 2005 and in 2006–2007, which this article draws on (Haener, Iseni, and Bougarel 2007; Iseni 2008).

Second, semi-structured in-depth interviews enabled data collection on changes occurring in the diaspora since the end of the wars in the origin countries, i.e. the period of the 2000s. Twelve interviews were conducted during 2005–2008 with first-generation Albanian-speaking community leaders in Switzerland, including representatives of associations, religious groups, sports clubs and experts from the community. Another 60 semi-structured interviews were carried out in 2011 with first- and second-generation Kosovar Albanians in Switzerland as part a research project jointly conducted with the University of Lugano.[2] These interviews are useful to understand recent evolution and the emergence of new structures within the Albanian-speaking community in Switzerland. The interviews were recorded and later transcribed, before proceeding with coding and thematic analysis.

Finally, five focus-group discussions were organized as part of another study, involving the main stakeholders of the Albanian-speaking diaspora in Switzerland, held in July 2008 and October 2010 in Zürich, Bern, Lausanne and Geneva (see Haxhikadrija 2009). Their aim was to understand the Kosovar diaspora in Switzerland, especially their needs and key concerns.

In addition, secondary data were also used to inform a background analysis and complete the macro-level picture. Swiss official statistics are the most important of these. Overall data analysis was grounded on a systematic critical review and discussion of the relevant academic as well as grey literature. The latter included community information, online publications, newspapers and television documentaries. All these sources were useful in understanding the evolving characteristics of this migrant community, its immigration waves, but also its socio-demographic evolution, remittances and transnational ties.

A brief profile of Albanian migration from FY to Switzerland

Phases and chronology

The emigration process of the Albanian-speaking population from FY to Switzerland has gone through three phases. The first started in the mid-1960s, was composed of low-skilled labourers and was primarily economic in nature.[3] Migrants originated from some of the most deprived areas of FY which were suffering from very high unemployment rates and low socio-economic prospects.

Economic stagnation in Yugoslavia during the 1980s caused a second wave of migration from Kosovo, Macedonia and southern Serbia to Switzerland. This stream was once again characterized by the movement of low-skilled men recruited to work mainly in construction, agriculture and industry. These push factors were interwoven with pull factors as, during the economic recovery in the 1980s following the oil-crisis recession of 1973, demand for labour among Swiss companies soared. A large foreign labour force came from the Balkans, thus infusing new 'blood' to the Swiss economy (Piguet 2004, 37–42). In the construction sector alone, more than 40,000 people from Kosovo were recruited in the 1980s (L'Hebdo 2004). This group of migrants was part of the working population in Switzerland, but at the same time they had their eyes and interests riveted on their places of origin, using their earnings in Switzerland to financially provide for their families in Kosovo and Macedonia, thus ensuring the maintenance of many households and family businesses there. This population was poorly qualified, with a low socio-economic profile and composed mainly of men. Most women emigrated later together with their children to join their husbands who had worked in Switzerland for years.

In the first years, Albanian migrants entering Switzerland received a seasonal status.[4] Under this regime, there was a provision which enabled migrants to apply for family reunification after having spent several years in the country.[5] This type of immigration, which considered the migrants' stay as temporary, was congruent with the objectives of the Swiss authorities, namely workforce rotation. In other words, foreign labourers who came to work in Switzerland without their families were welcomed for a number of years and were then replaced every few years by other seasonal workers (von Aarburg 2002; von Aarburg and Gretler 2008).

The third wave of Albanian immigration to Switzerland took place during the 1990s, leading to an increase of this immigrant community there, due primarily to two key reasons. First, an intensive process of family reunification took place, made possible by the transformation of the seasonal status into a residency permit for those migrant men who had been working in Switzerland for many years (Gross 2006). Second, there was the arrival of thousands of refugees and asylum seekers fleeing the political and socio-economic situation which prevailed in Kosovo at that time. The refugees and asylum seekers circumvented the policy of 'three circles' which was intended to prevent most non-EU country citizens, including those from FY, from immigrating to Switzerland.[6] Official statistics on this are very revealing: in 1999, nearing the end of the war in Kosovo, the total number of asylum applications from the republic of Serbia and Montenegro in Switzerland had reached a record of 52,360 people, a significant growth compared to previous years – 26,991 in 1998, 23,717 in 1997 and 21,382 in 1996. The majority of these applicants were Albanians from Kosovo.[7]

Numbers

It is currently difficult to give a precise figure of the actual number of Albanian-speaking immigrants from FY in Switzerland (Burri-Sharani et al. 2010). Four are the main reasons for this. First, until the disintegration of Yugoslavia, Kosovars were registered within Swiss statistics together with other national and ethnic groups of FY as Yugoslav citizens. Second, an important number of Kosovar Albanians held on to their Yugoslav/Serbian citizenship until 1999, due to practical reasons such as ease of travelling outside the country. Third, there are the changes in their current status through the naturalization process and the existence of a significant second generation which is born in Switzerland. Fourth, it is difficult to estimate the number of individuals residing there with an irregular status.

Despite these difficulties, the picture emerging from existing data is the following. Official Swiss statistics recorded 24,971 immigrants from Yugoslavia living in Switzerland in 1970. In 1980, the number had increased to 60,916 and then nearly tripled by 1990 to a total of 172,777 (SFOS 2004). By 2003, unofficial estimates suggested this figure to be around 351,960 individuals (L'Hebdo 2004), whereas by 2012 it is expected to be even higher.

As for the Albanian-speaking migrants within this community from FY, unofficial estimates suggest a figure of between 200,000 and 250,000 (Malaj 2009). The majority of them are from Kosovo, whereas approximately 55,000 come from Macedonia, and several thousands from the Presevo Valley (southern Serbia) and Montenegro (Akkaya and Soland 2009). According to the Swiss Federal Office for Migration, there were 155,000 Kosovars residing in Switzerland in 2007, the vast majority ethnic Albanians. Micheline Calmy-Rey, former President and Head of the Swiss Federal Department of Foreign Affairs, declared in an interview for the news agency <Albinfo.ch> that there were 170,000 Kosovars in Switzerland by 2011.[8] In addition, about 40,000 inhabitants of Kosovar origin are naturalized Swiss citizens (Malaj 2009).

Migrants' transnational ties

The Albanian-speaking diaspora in Switzerland has been strongly linked with its areas of origin. Until the end of the 1990s, this reality was reflected by way of an

DEVELOPMENT IN SOUTH-EAST EUROPE AND THE BLACK SEA REGION

important economic and financial support, but also through political mobilization, as discussed in more detail next.

Economic and financial support

As mentioned earlier, the vast majority of the Albanian-speaking diaspora in Switzerland until the early 1990s consisted of migrant men, whose point of reference was their country of origin where their families, in the broad sense of the word, lived and relied on their economic support. This economic support from the migrant population was an important factor in the reduction of poverty and the improvement of living standards among ethnic Albanians in Kosovo, Macedonia and the Presevo Valley, regions that faced high population pressures at the time (Roux 1992; von Aarburg 2002). As suggested by von Aarburg (2002) and von Aarburg and Gretler (2008), in the early stages of Kosovar emigration, seasonal migrants lived on the margins of the host country, leading a parallel social life to mainstream populations. This explains to some extent why, prior to 1990, Swiss citizens had little awareness of the presence of ethnic Albanians in Switzerland.

In these early years of migration, Kosovar immigrants lived in modest socio-economic conditions in order to save money to invest in their areas of origin. It was in Kosovo that they built family houses and bought land and agricultural technology, as well as fund relatives' (expensive) weddings.[9] As Dahinden (2010, 65) emphasizes:

> Albanian migrants built their houses in Kosovo, sent remittances and went there regularly on holidays and to fulfill family obligations towards their parents and siblings. This transnational field relied mainly on family relations and mutual support and reciprocity. This support turned into an obligation as the situation in Kosovo increasingly deteriorated after 1995.

Financial remittances continued to be sent throughout the 1990s and well into the 2000s. According to a recent study on the Kosovar diaspora (USAID-UNDP 2010), more than 30% of households in Kosovo have access to international remittances – in the form of money or goods. There are more beneficiaries of remittances in rural areas than in urban ones (33% as opposed to 26%). This is primarily explained by the higher numbers of migrants from rural areas, but also by the larger average size of the households in rural areas (6.9 as opposed to 5.5 persons per household in rural and urban areas, respectively). The major part of remittances comes from the Kosovar diaspora in Germany and Switzerland. The Kosovar diaspora has been and continues to be a crucial force in the socio-economic well-being of Kosovo: in 2009, some 422.7 million Euros, or 11% of Kosovo's GDP, came from the remittances of migrants living in Western countries. The Albanian-speaking diaspora has also been responsible for rebuilding the country after the devastating effects of the conflict that took place there in 1998–1999.

Like in Kosovo, the flow of diaspora remittances to Albanian communities in western Macedonia is also crucial in staving off poverty and sustaining families. Some of the most important remittance sums derive from the Albanian-speaking populations in Switzerland (Akkaya and Soland 2009). The World Bank (2011, 167) estimated the amount of remittances sent to Macedonia in 2010 as reaching 414 million USD, representing 4.5% of the country's GDP.[10]

However, a recent study on Kosovo's diaspora and its role in the country's development relativized the range of positive impacts that migration can have on the development of migrants' country of origin, such as reduction of poverty, promotion of employment, new economic activities, investments and trade, increased tourism and consumption (Haxhikadrija 2009). The study's main conclusions were that 'remittances from the Diaspora are used mainly for consumption and luxury goods', 'only a very small percentage of remittances are used for educational purposes' and 'the level of Diaspora investment in Kosovo remains lower than expected'. This study, however, emphasized the fact that the 'support received from the Diaspora for starting up a new business is twelvefold higher than that received from international development agencies' in Kosovo.

A similar perspective has been put forward in an earlier study by the European Stability Initiative (ESI 2006) which emphasized Kosovo's dependency on remittances and its counter-productive effects. For the authors of this study, remittances and migration 'have simply substituted for the lack of any effective development policies. In doing so, they have helped to preserve one of Europe's oldest and most conservative institutions: the traditional, patriarchal household'.

It is true that the contribution of the diaspora has also its dark sides, such as a potential structural dependency of the economy or the development of a culture of laziness amongst those receiving remittances, especially the younger generation. Nevertheless, without its economic and financial support, the Albanian-speaking regions in FY would have been in relative autarchy. Due to socio-political reasons, these areas were for long characterized by chronic underdevelopment and institutionalized cultural stagnation. The latter was a result of repressive measured taken by the Serbian and Macedonian authorities such as the closure of primary and secondary schools as well as universities and a lack of political will to support the socio-cultural development of the Albanian population (Iseni 2013). These factors (and others) in turn explain the reasons behind the emigration of significant numbers of Albanians from FY to Western Europe and the USA. Hence, the contribution of the diaspora for the socio-economic development can only be adequately understood by taking a historical perspective.

Political activism

The majority of the Albanian-speaking diaspora in Switzerland chose to support *political activism* in favour of Kosovo's status in order to oppose the political and military domination of Belgrade. Additionally, in Macedonia and the Presevo Valley, it supported the cause for the improvement of the socio-political status of the ethnic Albanian populations living there.

The socio-political tensions in Kosovo as well as in Macedonia have undoubtedly influenced the evolution of Albanian immigration in Switzerland. Since 1981, due to the escalation of the Albanian political resistance in both Kosovo and Macedonia and the pursuit and persecution of Albanian political activists by the Yugoslav regime, some individuals and groups sought refuge in Switzerland, but also in other Western European countries such as Germany and Belgium, and as far as North America and Australia. Subsequently, they were given refugee status which enabled them to establish themselves in these countries and follow their political aims from there. In the absence of a democratic political space in their origin areas and heavy persecution from the Yugoslav and later Serbian authorities, the Albanian migrant activists continued their struggle for the resolution of the Albanian question in FY from various Western capitals, especially in the USA, where they could undertake lobbying activities (Hockenos 2003; Kandel 2010). Thus, they conducted intense activities from abroad and remotely pursued numerous underground political activities in the Balkans.

Under the leadership of political figures, and following the development of events in the origin country and the persistent activism of political refugees, the majority of the Albanians in Switzerland became highly politicized. Their political activities irritated politicians in their areas of origin. Thus, migrants were accused by the FY regime of 'anti-revolutionary' propaganda and were described as an enemy by the FY's official press (cited in Torche 1989, 129). In addition, ethnic polarization between Albanians and Serbs or Macedonians in Kosovo and Macedonia, respectively, was reflected in Switzerland by the structuring of groups and cultural associations along these ethnic lines.

In the beginning of the 1990s, there was a particularly active political mobilization among the Albanian-speaking diaspora in Switzerland regarding Albanian national issues in FY. This was reflected in a number of ways. First, an active political and community life was developed in order to support political militants in the country of origin. Second, the diaspora created very active cells of the political parties from Kosovo and Macedonia.[11] Third, it was strongly involved in political lobbying of Western countries in order to influence public opinion there, especially through the arrangement of extensive meetings with political leaders from the home countries. Finally, it sought to raise the public profile of the situation through publications, organized public demonstrations, petitions and fundraising campaigns.

This dynamic led to the creation of militant networks in support of Kosovo's independence and towards the organization of a powerful political mobilization for the resolution of the Albanian national issue in Macedonia and the Presevo Valley. In turn, this set of activities had direct implications in the political development of the Albanian communities of FY. During the 1990s, the internationalization of the question of Kosovo and the non-violent Albanian resistance there led by the charismatic leader Ibrahim Rugova were in large part funded by the diaspora through a voluntary tax (3% of individual income). The key founders of the Kosovo Liberation Army (KLA) emerged from the Kosovar diaspora in Switzerland. Moreover, this diaspora strongly supported the KLA through financial contributions and by supplying volunteers in the fight against the Serbian army from 1998 to 1999 (Hockenos 2003; Kandel 2010). These patterns of support were replicated later on for the conflict in Macedonia in 2001 and to a certain extent for those concurrent in the Presevo Valley (2000–2001).

At this point, it is safe to argue that the economic contribution of the Albanian diaspora vis-à-vis the origin areas was closely linked with its political influence in these areas. It would be a mistake to underestimate the political activism of the diaspora only as aiding the operations or financing nationalist conflicts. In addition, migrants' presence in Western democracies increased awareness – in a sense internationalized the case – of the violations of human rights and repression of ethnic minorities in FY.

Settlement process

The Albanian diaspora in Switzerland had invested heavily in their country of origin because the migrant labourers had not planned a long-term stay in Switzerland. In addition, their mobilization for the political cause of Kosovo, Macedonia and the Presevo Valley kept them in a limbo – neither returning to these areas nor integrating in Switzerland. According to Torche (1989), mobilization over the Kosovo issue even impeded the integration process into the host society during the 1980s. Overall, the political situation that prevailed in the country of origin seems to have had a direct impact on the transnational activities of the Albanian-speaking diaspora in Switzerland. The Albanian-speaking media produced and consumed in Switzerland were devised with the objective of maintaining and strengthening ties with the country of origin.

After the end of the conflicts in the Albanian-inhabited areas of FY, a deflation of diasporic activity was observed within the community of Albanians in Switzerland, especially in regard to formal transnational events towards areas of origin. A number of socio-cultural and political structures which had been very active in the activities discussed earlier were put to sleep and diasporic activities became less and less visible.

Thus, the end of wars and conflicts in their areas of origin and the 'stabilization' of Kosovo and Macedonia marked the beginning of a new era for the Albanian diaspora in Switzerland in terms of the nature of the links with both the host and the origin country. More specifically, this was the beginning of the process of 'settling down' in Switzerland. Although family reunion had been ongoing since the late 1980s, migrants continued to support the idea of returning to their country of origin until the late 1990s. They educated their children with the idea of going back to the country of origin after the resolution of the national issues there. However, this return will not happen for the vast majority of them.

With the improvement of the overall political situation in Kosovo following the NATO intervention, and in particular following the arrival of a third influx of immigrants from Kosovo, the project of settling in Switzerland on a long-term basis started to become a reality. Already in 1999 while the war in Kosovo had not come to a conclusion, IOM (1999) recorded a negative attitude towards the idea of returning to Kosovo among Kosovar families living in Switzerland.

Different indicators of the process of settling in Switzerland can be observed. These include the strong propensity for naturalization; the acquisition of real estate in Switzerland; a decrease in investments in real estate in areas of origin; an abundance of Albanian-owned small and medium-sized enterprises in Switzerland; and the investment in the education of children there.

Among the key changes in this orientation is the decrease of remittances sent to areas of origin. This is mainly the result of family reunification which, in turn, affects the socio-economic position of migrant families in Switzerland as there are now increased living costs. A study on the Albanian migrants from Tetovo (Macedonia) in Switzerland emphasized that after family reunification 'many immigrants have hardly any money left over for remittances to [send to] further relatives in Tetovo' (Akkaya and Soland 2009, 8). Similarly, a recent study on the Kosovar community in Switzerland argued that this population is exposed to socio-economic precarity. This is mainly due to deficiencies in terms of schooling and training, but also because of discrimination (Burri-Sharani et al. 2010; Dahinden 2010; Fibbi,

Kaya, and Piguet 2003). Economic marginalization has become the sociological reality for the Albanian community in Switzerland, especially discrimination in the labour market for both the first and the second generation; some even live in precarious circumstances.

Our interviews with a group of first- and second-generation Kosovar migrants living in Switzerland reveal some of the key reasons behind the settlement of the Albanian-speaking community in this country.[12] The first is clearly related to the lack of prospects in the areas of origin due to chronic underdevelopment, continued political instability and institutional corruption. The second factor reflects the new dynamics of integration and acculturation in the host country which are leading to a redefinition of the relationships of the Albanian-speaking diaspora vis-à-vis both the origin and host societies.

Shifts in transnational activities

Since the end of the Balkan conflicts, we can see a transformation in terms of the living conditions of the Albanian diaspora in Switzerland. Yet the integration process is also characterized by the renegotiation of migrants' identity as a cultural meeting point between the host and origin society. The changes currently taking place undeniably influence the terms under which the diaspora impacts development in the origin country.

The recent study conducted by the author of this article and colleagues from the University of Lugano on the Kosovar community in Switzerland has allowed us to gain a better understanding of these complex processes. The relations with the country of origin are mediated through several factors, including the frequency and motivation to travel there, the existence or abandonment of the return project and the perception of 'home' and belonging. These changes are in turn reflected at the level of community organization and hence, the nature of the contribution that the diaspora makes to the areas of origin.

Return: visits, plans and myths

The evolution of the frequency of trips and of the motivation to travel to origin areas reveals elements of continuity and change. More specifically, whereas in the past the trips to the 'homeland' were part of the ongoing process of one day returning 'home', today these visits are related to migrants' identity, i.e. maintaining an emotional bridge with relatives in Kosovo and the culture of origin.

For the vast majority of the first generation, visiting the country of origin, at least once a year, appears to have become a rule. For those who were born and raised in Kosovo, travelling there means going back 'home'. This carries an emotional weight because it is a way to reconnect with one's roots. In other words, nostalgia for the country of origin has a strong presence among the first generation of immigrants, both for women and men. The following two quotes from such interviews are typical in this context:

> Kosovo is where I feel good, from the sentimental or spiritual point of view, because I'll be there for myself, but as long as the basic living conditions there do not seem to improve, I will disagree with the policy we have in place [in Kosovo], which does nothing. (F, 27, arrived in Switzerland at the age of 20)

For us who are born there, it is very simple. It is this patriotism that motivates us. Even if we do not necessarily have easy holidays because of the stifling heat and different conditions to those in Switzerland, I always have a pleasant stay. Not that Kosovo offers living standards up to those in Switzerland, but to us, to me, it is a perfect place. This is my land. (M, 39, arrived in Switzerland at the age of 17)

Some first-generation migrants, in their construction of a hypothetical return, have developed an idealized relationship with the country of origin. However, since the political resolution of the Kosovo issue, the meeting between the dream and the reality of the country has disillusioned some of them:

At first, I did not dare go back, I could not do so for 11 years and I had not been able to return. Nostalgia and missing my country was great and for 11 years I had not seen my homeland. But when I returned, I did not find my country; it wasn't as I had left it. It was completely different. There was an air of disappointment in comparison to the nostalgia that I had and what I had expected. Now sometimes I go back, because I feel the need, a huge need, but every time I go, I'm disappointed. I see nothing good. It seems to me that people have also changed, and even my environment has changed … (M, 66, arrived in Switzerland at the age of 43)

Most of our first-generation migrant interviewees are men and women who left the country for economic reasons, which is the case for the majority of such migrants. Their discourse on return is linked to the lack of opportunities and economic prospects for themselves and their offspring in the country of origin. The following quote refers to the conflicting possibilities offered by different life-stages and family formations: a possible return upon retirement, but also the 'blocking effect' of children, grandchildren and other relatives in Switzerland.

My generation and I are torn on both sides. We are not in a position to decide on whether we will end up here or there … I think my generation is very nostalgic for our country, it was part of my youth, the time of study, school, work, many memories of life there. So when the question of employment is no longer a concern, the period of life of retirement, I think the individual will spend most of his time there … But people who create their family here, and their descendants who are born, their nephews, their nieces, are forced to stay here because of the members of their family. (M, 54, arrived in Switzerland at the age of 32)

If the hypothetical project of return rests an undecided issue for men, as in the quote above, women of the same generation tend to exclude this option; they remain oriented towards their families abroad and fear a return to a more 'traditional' way of life in the 'homeland'.

The change that occurs among first generation migrants in the direction of structural, cultural and juridical integration in the host country is also reflected in their sharply critical views towards the country of origin. These views are often used to justify inaction or abandonment of the proposed return. The comparison between Switzerland and Kosovo, in terms of levels of development, is certainly a cause for frustration among the Kosovar migrants, as the following quote reveals.

This does not mean a lot to me, to go to Kosovo. I like Kosovo of course, but I cannot spend quality time there because some things bother me, such as unemployment, especially among young people, and these things bring forth a lot of stress. (M, 45, arrived in Switzerland at the age of 23)

On the other hand, the disequilibrium in the levels of development between the areas of origin and Switzerland is also a source for status enhancement. Clearly, the quality of life in Switzerland is in many aspects incomparable to that of the migrants' country of origin. Albanian migrants realize the opportunities they have by living in a prosperous and stable country like Switzerland. This gives them a better social and material status compared to those still living in their areas of origin. Despite the low status of their employment in Switzerland, the 'status paradox of migration' (Nieswand 2011) means an enhanced status in their home country. It is not difficult to observe the change of behaviour and the evident manifestation of material wealth of people from the diaspora when they return to their origin areas during the holiday seasons (for similar accounts see Hemming 2009; Markov this issue). These events are also the source of mutual prejudices between Albanians still living there and those visiting from the diaspora. In fact, it is not uncommon to see it as an emerging rhetoric of self-differentiation and cultural identity. The terminology 'them' (those in the country of origin) and 'us' has recently appeared in the vocabulary of the Albanian diaspora in Switzerland.

While the economic disequilibrium – and perhaps even the status paradox of migration (Nieswand 2011) – are strong influencing factors in the frequency of travel to the country of origin, currently, for migrants from Kosovo, the return issue is more dependent on the natural transformation of the family situation in Switzerland. In the past, migrant families could not afford to visit Kosovo more than once a year on their modest budget. Nowadays, this is more affordable due to low-cost flights operated by companies such as Easyjet. However, the family situation in Switzerland does not allow them to go as often as they would wish.

> No I can't afford it because I have children and maybe sometimes for economic reasons. Generally speaking, the appearance of the Easyjet flights has given the Albanians the opportunity to go back home more often. I wish I could go there more often, but the fact is that I work, I have my children, and they are in school. These are my reasons. (M, 36, arrived in Switzerland at the age of 29)

To sum up at this point, the abandonment of the return project in the short to medium term is strongly influenced by the lack of socio-economic prospects and policies in Kosovo, Macedonia and the Presevo Valley. Migrants are very critical about their countries of origin and the political elites there. The long period of structural underdevelopment of these regions has contributed towards the alteration of the perception afforded to the origin country and has led migrants to refocus on more personal concerns. Thus, the idea of return has been sacrificed on the altar of priorities and needs of their nuclear families in Switzerland, at the expense of the extended family in the place of origin.

Return visits and the second generation

The theme of return appears to have strongly conditioned the socialization process of Kosovars in Switzerland, including the second generation. In the past, children were brought up with the idea of returning to their country of origin, but this return has not happened, nor is it likely to happen any time soon. This has undoubtedly had an impact among the young people of the second generation. For this group, going to their countries of origin (or that of their parents) represents a different set of symbols from those of their parents: not so much showing off wealth and status but a period of school breaks, memories of encounters with the extended family, weddings, etc. It is more of a vision of a 'host' country than one of origin, as elaborated in this quote by a 22-year-old woman who arrived in Switzerland at the age of six:

> Because I like it, if I don't go there once a year I feel bad. Simply because I see my relatives, I see my grandfather, who is a smart 102 year old man. Then, I see my cousins. It will not be as good as here in Switzerland but it's still nice to go there.

> […]

> All who are abroad go to Kosovo in the summer on holiday and then we find ourselves a bit, including relatives, then maybe there are some weddings. So we are among friends, you spend (…) the evenings. So it is nice that you find these pleasant and warm gatherings.

Yet, for some second-generation migrants, travelling to Kosovo is considered less as a trip of leisure and vacation and more as a certain constraint or a standard to follow the parents, at least during childhood. As they grow up and reach adulthood, the second generation adopts two types of attitudes: those who continue to travel to Kosovo with an annual frequency (for professional or personal reasons such as relatives or marriage) and the others for whom the frequency of such trips declines. The latter would clearly prefer a holiday outside of Kosovo, as the following interviewee explains:

> I am sorry to say but honestly if I have two weeks of holiday I prefer to use those days somewhere else instead of going back home. Certainly nothing to take away from my relatives and a year ago when I last saw them they were all using all [the new] technology and social networks such as Facebook, messenger, etc … (F, 20, born in Switzerland)

Some second-generation individuals are adverse to the idea of returning to the country of their parents, but for different reasons. For women, the mentality seems the most problematic. In other words, if they were to return, then, according to their perceptions, they would be facing restrictions in terms of individual freedoms, considering the fact that Kosovar society is more conservative than the Swiss one, especially in the villages from which their parents originate.

> Switzerland, this is my country, even if I am originally from Kosovo. I have Swiss nationality, it's not for nothing. So that's why for me I consider it my country. I mean, it's true that my roots are from Kosovo, but I mean, it's not really … I don't see myself ever living there. (F, 31, born in Switzerland)

For men, this return is likewise unthinkable, probably due to the fact that Switzerland is the country where they were born or grew up, but also because of conditions in Kosovo:

> It is unthinkable to return to […] Maybe my parents will go back but I do not think I will. (M, 30, arrived in Switzerland at the age of 10)

Home, belonging and questions of integration

From the patterns of settlement in Switzerland, we have observed that the cultural characteristics and transnational practices of ethnic Albanians in Switzerland of all generations have gradually metamorphosed. There is clearly a redefinition of ties with the customs and traditions of the country of origin and their reinterpretation in the context of diaspora. The use of new technology, especially the internet, has truly revolutionized many aspects of life for Albanian migrants in Switzerland. For first-generation migrants, messaging and telephone internet applications such as MSN and Skype have reduced the distance with their families or elsewhere. In this sense, opening the MSN or Skype on their computer has become a 'new need' for them.

In parallel, there is the advent of a hybrid process of belonging within the everyday context of the diasporic family and the predominant values of the host country. This affects the perceptions and feelings of 'home'. In this regard, there exists a clear generational gap about 'feeling at home' in Kosovo and in Switzerland; the second generation express feelings of in-betweenness.

However, despite distancing oneself from the countries of origin, paradoxically, a section of this population continues to maintain a strong sense or link with their ethnic Albanian identity.[13] They continue to maintain close ties with the culture of origin while soaking in the Swiss cultural modernity characterized by the centrality of the individual. For example, marriage is still largely endogamous, including many of the second generation; and Albanian values and family traditions continue to occupy a leading position, despite the time spent in a diasporic context.

Yet, beyond the rhetoric, the second generation is undoubtedly more attached to the way of life in the host country. Several indicators point in this direction: the lack of interest in current affairs of the origin country which results in the media consumption almost exclusively of that of the host country, fewer trips to areas of origin, food and eating habits, symbolic celebrations and so on.

As mentioned earlier, the Albanian migrant population has been subject to situations of discrimination in the host country. For example, young Albanians who are in search of an apprenticeship may face discrimination when prospective employers notice their Albanian surname. The negative image of especially Kosovar migrants, associated with crime by populist tabloids in Switzerland, further contributes towards the discrimination and negative perception of Albanians in this country.[14] This image is also affected by the increase of the immigrant population because it influences the process of integration and acceptance by the host-country population and institutions. Some success stories, on the other hand, help break the chain. For example, the remarkable breakthrough of football players from Albanian immigrant families in the Swiss national team has contributed to a strong symbolic fight against clichés and stereotypes directed at the Albanian-speaking immigrant population in Switzerland.[15] In other cases, perhaps as a reaction to this discrimination, second-generation elite groups have mobilized in a process of renewal of Albanian transnational activities in Switzerland, this time oriented also towards the home country. Their increased mobilization in support of new community structures has resulted in new and vibrant migrant associations such as the Assembly of Albanians in Switzerland, the web platform Albinfo.ch, the League of Albanian Parents and Children in Switzerland, the Albanian People's University in Geneva, the Albanian Section of the Demo-Christian Party of Switzerland, the Albanian activists of the main labour Union (Unia). These structures, but also the public statements of new

Swiss political actors originating from this community, are used as vehicles for the community's voice to be heard both in their country of origin and in Switzerland. This is a significant change which often meets with some resistance from the first generation. These elite second-generation individuals who are leading the emerging community structures are often educated in Swiss universities, are engaged in the socio-political life of Switzerland and articulate a new philosophy vis-à-vis the countries of origin and destination. Their cultural and symbolic hybridity and engagement represent a synonym of a new generation of Albanian-speaking immigrants. These new actors are critical about the political and economic developments in both countries.

It is true that other diasporas, such as the Croatian or the Romanian ones (Nedelcu 2008), are characterized by a scientific community abroad. In the case of Albanians in Switzerland whose first generation was lower skilled for the vast majority, the challenge is to promote the upward social mobility of its second and third generation and build up a more solid professional layer, which would in turn get formally organized at an institutional level. A further challenge is to be able to keep links and relations with the country of origin over time as the new generations emerge.

Conclusions

The Albanian population in Switzerland offers a particularly revealing case study towards the understanding of continuities and ruptures that often characterize an immigrant community and its transnational activities.

In the past, this particular migrant community had developed strong economic, political and social transnational practices towards its areas of origin. These relationships seem to have had undeniable development impacts there, whether in terms of poverty reduction, or in the domains of investment in infrastructure and overall economic development. While the role of the diaspora may be subject to criticism, the Albanian diaspora has been a real beacon for FY countries which were (and still are) confronted with chronic socio-economic underdevelopment. However, in parallel with the end of war experienced by the country of origin, but also the beginning of a reoriented projection of the population with a view to settling in Switzerland, gradually new types of transnational relations have emerged. This time they are directed not only to the origin areas, but also to the host country.

This change is based mainly on the duration of immigration, but reflects also the evolution of the socio-political situation in the country of origin. Orientation towards the areas of origin, and in particular the long-drawn conflicts of the 1980s and 1990s, have, to some extent, slowed down the diaspora's investment in favour of it own integration in the host country. As a result, the process of integration really started to consolidate only after the end of conflicts in the respective countries of origin and after a long period of physical presence in Switzerland.

Integration and development are complementary and can lead to maintain, but also to redefine and develop, new transnational practices adapted to the evolution of diasporic realities. The stability and the impact of these transnational practices in the integration process in the host country, but also in the development of the home country, involve necessary preconditions, both from the country of origin (in order to attract the diaspora's capital, networks and expertise), the host country (to promote and support resources of the diaspora) and the diaspora itself. However, the diaspora must organize itself in order to be audible throughout the country of origin and destination.

Acknowledgement
I would like to thank Julie Vullnetari and Russell King for their useful comments on earlier versions of the paper.

Notes
1. To understand the structural factors that led to this underdevelopment, see Roux (1992). Albanian-speaking migrants from FY living in Switzerland are the subject of my analysis in this article and they are interchangeably referred to as the 'Albanian-speaking diaspora', 'Albanians in Switzerland', 'Albanian immigrants' and 'Albanian-speaking community in Switzerland'. This article does not deal with migration from the Republic of Albania, although inevitably some macro-statistics on migrants' numbers in Switzerland may include them; in any case, their numbers are negligible (see Dahinden 2005).
2. Marta Cola and Manuel Mauri Brusa were the partners from the University of Lugano, as part of the project 'The construction of identities between media use and diasporic traits: The Kosovar migrants in Switzerland', commissioned by the Swiss National Research Fund, Project 2010–2012 (see Cola, Iseni, and Brusa 2012).
3. The boundary between economic and other types of migration is not always clear. In fact, the economic category can mask another type. For instance, political factors may be the source of underdevelopment and socio-economic insecurity of a region or population, and therefore, a major cause of migration.
4. This consisted of a permit which allowed the holder to work in Switzerland for nine months in a year; for the other three months, the person was obliged to leave the country.
5. They could do this once they obtained an annual residence permit, which was issued after several seasonal stays.
6. The 'three-circle' model proposed by the Federal Council in its 1991 report on the policy towards foreigners and refugees set criteria for recruitment of the foreign labour force based on considerations of geography and culture, politics and national economy. The inner circle (or the first circle, namely states of the EU and EFTA) allows for the free movement of persons. In the middle circle (or the second circle, including the US, Canada, Australia and New Zealand, with the potential subsequent addition of the states of Central and Eastern Europe), a limited number of foreign persons can be recruited. In the outer circle (or third circle, i.e. the 'rest of the world'), there is normally no recruitment possible, except in a few specific cases of highly qualified specialists. This policy was officially abandoned in 1998. On this topic see Leuenberger and Maillard (1999) and Burri-Sharani et al. (2010).
7. Swiss Federal Office for Migration database, http://www.bfm.admin.ch/content/bfm/fr/home/dokumentation/zahlen_und_fakten/asylstatistik/jahresstatistiken.html (accessed February 14, 2013) [in German]. After the end of the Kosovo conflict and the beginning of the administration of the country by the United Nations Mission in Kosovo, most of these asylum seekers were repatriated to Kosovo and have benefited from assistance programmes supported by the Swiss authorities in order to reintegrate them there.
8. 'In & Out' www.albinfo.ch, transmitted to the Radio-Television of Kosovo, http://www.albinfo.ch/inout/intervist%C3%AB-ekskluzive-me-micheline-calmy-rey-44749, 11.11.2011 (accessed August 1, 2012) [in Albanian].
9. Financial help and solidarity were not limited to close relatives, but included the extended family and distant cousins as well.
10. These estimates should be higher due to the transfer of money through informal channels. See Ivaylo Markov's paper in this special issue for a detailed study of the impact of remittances on Macedonia's ethnic Albanian communities.

DEVELOPMENT IN SOUTH-EAST EUROPE AND THE BLACK SEA REGION

11. Initially, cells were based in the political movement in Germany. However, after the murder there of the Gervalla brothers as well as of Kadri Zeka in 1982 by the Yugoslav intelligence services, the epicentre of Albanian diasporic political activism gradually moved from Germany to Switzerland.
12. Conducted in March–June 2011 as part of the project mentioned in Note 2.
13. Drawing on my participant observation, as well as focus group discussions conducted in 2006 and 2009, and in-depth qualitative interviews of 2011. Most participants were Albanians from Kosovo.
14. Several populist and xenophobic campaigns of the Democratic Union of the Centre have targeted people originating from Kosovo and living in Switzerland. The last stage in 2011 put in a sentence that was explicitly aimed at Kosovars through the generalization of individual cases of violence.
15. The Swiss national team often counts four or five players of Albanian origin in its midst. Some of the most renowned are Xherdan Shaqiri, Granit Xhaka, Admir Mehmedi, Valon Behrami and Blerim Xhemajli. Shaqiri was recently awarded the 'medal' of Albanian diaspora in Switzerland for his contribution towards integration and improving the image of the Albanian diaspora there.

References

Akkaya, G., and B. Soland. 2009. *The impact of the emigration of Albanian migrants on their home region of Tetovo: A qualitative exploratory research study in the region of Tetovo, Macedonia.* Luzern: University of Applied Sciences and Arts.

Bauböck, R., and T. Faist, eds. 2010. *Diaspora and transnationalism: Concepts, theories and methods.* Amsterdam: Amsterdam University Press.

Burri-Sharani, B., D. Effionayi-Mäder, S. Hammer, M. Pecoraro, B. Soland, A. Tsaka, and C. Wysmüller. 2010. *Kosovar population in Switzerland.* Berne-Wabern: Office Fédéral des Migrations (ODM) [in French].

Castles, S., and R. Delgado Wise, eds. 2008. *Migration and development: Perspectives from the South.* Geneva: IOM.

Cola, M., B. Iseni, and M. Mauri Brusa. 2012. The Kosovar diaspora in Switzerland: Construction of identities between media use and diasporic traits. *Romanian Journal of Communication and Public Relations* 14, no. 4: 47-63. http://journalofcommunication.ro/archive2/028/28/cola_iseni_brusa_28.pdf.

Dahinden, J. 2005. Contesting transnationalism? Lessons from the study of Albanian migration networks from former Yugoslavia. *Global Networks* 5, no. 2: 191–208.

Dahinden, J. 2010. The dynamics of migrants' transnational formations: Between mobility and locality. In *Diaspora and transnationalism: Concepts, theories and methods*, ed. R. Bauböck and T. Faist, 51–71. Amsterdam: Amsterdam University Press.

ESI. 2006. *Cutting the lifeline: Migration, families and the future of Kosovo.* Berlin: European Stability Initiative.

Fibbi, R., B. Kaya, and E. Piguet. 2003. *Nomen est omen: When being called Pierre, Afrim or Mehmet makes a difference.* Berne: Directorate of the National Research Programme 43 – National Fund for Scientific Research (PNR43 – FNRS) [in French].

Glick Schiller, N., L. Basch, and C. Szanton Blanc, eds. 1992. *Towards a transnational perspective on migration: Race, class, ethnicity, and nationalism reconsidered.* New York, NY: New York Academy of Sciences.

Glick Schiller, N. 2009. A global perspective on migration and development. *Social Analysis* 53, no. 3: 14–37.

Gross, D. 2006. Immigration to Switzerland: The case of the Former Republic of Yugoslavia. Policy Research Working Paper 3880. Washington DC: World Bank.

Haener, O., B. Iseni, and X. Bougarel. 2007. Islam and politics in Western Balkans [in French]. *Politorbis: Revue de Politique Étrangère* 43, no. 2. Berne: Swiss Federal Department of Foreign Affairs.

Haxhikadrija, A. 2009. *Diaspora as a driving force for development in Kosovo: Myth or reality?* Prishtina: Forum for Democratic Initiatives with the Swiss Agency for Development and Cooperation.

Hemming, A. 2009. Migrant identity on display: The *xhiro* in Rrëshen. *Southeast European and Black Sea Studies* 9, no. 4: 575–88.

Hockenos, P. 2003. *Homeland calling: Exile patriotism and Balkan wars*. Ithaca, NY: Cornell University Press.

IOM. 1999. *Survey among Swiss residents of Kosovar origin: March–June 1999*. Berne: IOM Bern Mission [in French].

Iseni, B. 2008. *The national question in Southeastern Europe: The origins, emergence and development of Albanian national identity in Kosovo and Macedonia*. Bern: Peter Lang [in French].

Iseni, B. 2013. Same state, divided society: The Albanians in Macedonia. In *Civic and uncivic values in Macedonia*, ed. P.S. Ramet, O. Listhaug, and A. Simkus, 175–92. Basingstoke: Palgrave.

Kandel, M. 2010. Diaspora diplomacy? Mobilization of the 'Yugoslav' diasporas in the USA and their influence on American foreign policy during the Balkan wars of the 1990s [in French]. *Relations Internationales* 1, no. 141: 83–97.

Kapur, D. 2004. Remittances: The new development mantra? Discussion Paper 29. New York, NY and Geneva: United Nations Conference on Trade and Development and the Intergovernmental Group of Twenty-Four (G-24) on International Monetary Affairs.

L'Hebdo. 2004. 370,000 Former Yugoslavs in Switzerland: Who are they really? Swiss weekly published in Lausanne, September, no. 37/9 [in French].

Leuenberger, U., and A. Maillard. 1999. *The condemned of the third circle: The Kosovars in Switzerland, 1965–1999*. Genève: Editions Metropolis [in French].

Levitt, P., and N.B. Jaworsky. 2007. Transnational migration studies: Past developments and future trends. *Annual Review of Sociology* 33: 129–56.

Malaj, N. 2009. Press conference of the Ambassador of the Republic of Kosovo to Switzerland, University of Lausanne, February 19, Lausanne.

Markov, I. 2013. Migration, remittances and socio-cultural dynamics: The case of Albanians from the Republic of Macedonia. *Southeast European and Black Sea Studies* 13, no. 2: this issue.

Mercer, C., B. Page, and M. Evans. 2011. *Global migration governance*. Oxford: Oxford University Press.

Nedelcu, M. 2008. Internet diaspora: How Romanian scholars abroad connect home. Working Paper 17. Florence: European University Institute, Research Network 1989.

Nieswand, B. 2011. *Theorising transnational migration: The status paradox of migration*. London: Routledge.

Piguet, E. 2004. *Immigration in Switzerland: 50 years of semi-openness*. Lausanne: Presses Polytechniques et Universitaires Romandes [in French].

Portes, A. 1999. Conclusion: Towards a new world? The origins and effects of transnational activities. *Ethnic and Racial Studies* 22, no. 2: 463–77.

Roux, M. 1992. *Albanians in Yugoslavia: National minority, territory and development*. Paris: Editions de la Maison des Sciences de l'Homme [in French].

SFOS. 2004. *Foreign population resident in Switzerland*. Neuchâtel: Swiss Federal Office for Statistics (SFOS) [in French].

Torche, D. 1989. Links between national identity and migration: The case of Albanians of Yugoslavia [in French]. *Revue Suisse de Sociologie* 15, no. 1: 115–38.

USAID-UNDP. 2010. *Kosovo remittance study*. Prishtina: UBO Consulting for USAID-UNDP.

von Aarburg, H.P. 2002. Albanian migration from Kosovo to Switzerland: The unpredictable evolution of migratory projects [in French]. *Ethnologie Française* 32, no. 2: 271–82.

von Aarburg, H.P., and S. Gretler. 2008. *Kosovo-Switzerland: Albanian labour and asylum migration between Kosovo and Switzerland (1964–2000)*. Zürich: Lit Verlag [in German].

World Bank. 2011. *Migration and remittances factbook 2011*. Washington DC: World Bank.

Migration, remittances and socio-cultural dynamics: the case of Albanians from the Republic of Macedonia

Ivaylo Markov

Institute of Ethnology and Folklore Studies with Ethnographical Museum, Bulgarian Academy of Sciences, Sofia, Bulgaria

This article examines the patterns of contemporary labour mobility and migrations in search of better living conditions and livelihoods amongst the Albanian population in the Republic of Macedonia. Effects of migration are studied in the context of the social and cultural practices and connections which individuals and groups carry and develop, and their reflections on the places of origin. Special attention is paid to the effects of financial and social remittances upon living conditions, infrastructure and architecture in home places; the changes in local social organization and family–kin relationships; and the ways connections and relationships between migrants and non-migrants affect individuals' roles and social status.

Introduction

The history of the Balkans offers numerous examples of seasonal and temporary labour migration to different destinations as well as at different times. The mountainous regions in the western part of the Republic of Macedonia are known for their migratory traditions in search of a better livelihood. The Albanians are one of the main ethnic groups living in this ethnically and religiously diverse area. As citizens of socialist Yugoslavia (1945–1991) and, after 1991, of the Republic of Macedonia, many ethnic Albanians settled as workers in a number of Western European countries (primarily in Germany, Austria and Switzerland), temporarily or for a long time. Yet, their patterns of labour migration continue to be under-researched.

The aim of this article is to examine contemporary labour mobility and migrations amongst Albanians from Macedonia. I focus especially on the dynamics of social and cultural practices and connections which migrants develop, and their reflections on migrants' places of origin. The main research questions concern the effects of financial and social remittances upon living conditions, village infrastructure and architecture in the migrants' places of origin; the changes in social organization and family–kin relationships affected by migration; and the ways in which connections and relationships between migrants and non-migrants affect people's social status and roles.

The article starts with brief discussions of the theories and methodology framing my study. Next, the historical dynamics and changing practices of migration amongst Albanians from Macedonia are examined. Then, in the second half of the paper, the effects of migrations on local community and development in areas of origin are described and analysed.

Theoretical framework

The effects of migration and remittances on development in migrant areas of origin have been the subject of more or less continuous debate since the 1950s, with opposing optimistic or pessimistic perspectives replacing each other over the decades (Castles 2009; de Haas 2010). In this article, I endorse de Haas' (2010, 240) position that neither the pessimists nor the optimists were right or wrong, as 'the heterogeneity of real-life migration–development interactions is too high to fit them into deterministic theoretical schemes'. The extant literature has demonstrated that migration *can* have positive impacts on individuals and households, but evidence that migration and remittances stimulate development on a macro-scale is rather thin. Moreover, effects have different meanings for migrants, non-migrants and policymakers. As such, my examination of 'development' in this article is understood as part of a dynamic set of transformative processes which can be either positive or negative.

In addition, in studying the impacts of migration on development in these areas of origin, I seek to go beyond the economic effects, often related to the spending and investment of monies earned abroad. Instead, I aim to pay equal attention to what are called 'social remittances' (Levitt 1998) and the resulting transformations in patterns of consumption, social ranking, interpersonal attitudes and behaviours in migrants' areas of origin. For this reason, the concept of 'culture of migration' plays a key role in my analysis as it allows us to capture how migration changes values and cultural perceptions and becomes deeply ingrained into people's everyday life (Massey et al. 1993, 452).

Drawing on anthropological epistemology, this research focuses on labour migration dynamics at the micro level by examining the motivations, actions and practices of individuals and groups. The family household is the main unit of analysis, mediating between individuals and the larger structural setting and conditions (Boyd 1989, 645). However, I also take into account processes at the macro level by paying attention to the structural and historical context in which such dynamics operate.

My analysis is framed by two theoretical frameworks that allow for a deeper understanding of migrants' lifeworlds and their connections across time and space. First, I employ social networks theory in order to grasp the relations between departed migrants, returnees and non-migrants, all of whom are engaged in a set of complex social and interpersonal relations through kinship, friendship and feelings of affection towards the shared place of origin (Massey et al. 1993, 448). These networks – of information, assistance and obligations – allow us to understand why migratory movements are not necessarily limited in time, unidirectional or permanent (Boyd 1989, 641).

The second framework is the transnational migration paradigm which had its origins in the 1990s (Glick Schiller, Basch, and Szanton Blanc 1992; Vertovec 2009). Transnationalism has been defined as 'the processes by which immigrants forge and sustain multi-stranded social relations that link together their societies of origin and settlement' (Glick Schiller, Basch, and Szanton Blanc 1995, 48). 'Transmigrants' differ from emigrants and immigrants, and from returnees, because by the act of moving back and forth between different places they 'develop their social spaces of everyday life, their work trajectories and biographical projects' in configurations of 'special practices, symbols and artefacts' across space (Pries 2001, 21). They move and interact within 'transnational social fields', which Levitt and Glick Schiller (2004, 1009) define as 'a set of multiple interlocking networks of social relationships through which ideas, practices, and resources are unequally exchanged, organized, and transformed'. Such a conceptualization of migration moves the analysis beyond those who actually migrate to those who do not necessarily move but are connected to migrants through the networks of social relations they sustain across borders. This insight is very important because it reveals that the impact of migration is not solely related to return; indeed those who stay behind are connected to migrants through social networks, thus being exposed to a constant flow of economic and social remittances on a regular basis (Levitt and Nyberg Sørensen 2004, 3).

The multiplicity of involvements that migrants sustain in both origin and host places is a key element of daily experiences, activities and practices of Albanian migrants. However, applying the term 'transnationalism' to the Balkan – and hence the Albanian – context is problematic, not least because here it appears as vague and misleading. For instance, Pichler (2009, 215) criticizes it as a construct closely linked to the 'Western' concept of nation state, according to which 'state' and 'nation', as well as 'nationality' and 'citizenship' are generally used synonymously. The Balkan countries, however, follow the model of ethnic rather than civic nationalism. 'National' in the Balkans can refer both to nation state and to an ethno-national community, dispersed also within neighbouring countries (Čapo Žmegač 2003, 119). As Pichler (2009, 215) notes '… to consider oneself Albanian in Austria or in Switzerland is to understand oneself as belonging to the Albanian ethno-cultural nation, which encompasses persons with different citizenships living in different states that might be far away from the imagined ethnic territory'.

Instead, two substituting terms are offered. Čapo Žmegač (2003, 120) applies the term 'inter-state translocality' in her study of Croatian migrants in Munich, considering it more accurate since it preserves the notion of locality that is crucial for migrants and avoids the ambiguity of the term 'transnationalism'. In turn, Pichler (2009, 215), in his research on Albanian migration from Macedonia to German-speaking countries, suggests the term 'transterritorial'. He finds 'translocal' to be 'too confined a concept to understand the relationship that the migrants have with their home (land)'. In contrast, 'territorial' conveys the double meaning of the idea of an Albanian ethnic space, as well as of the strong links between different places of migration and origin, rather than 'country of origin' as often implied in migration studies. Although the transnational paradigm remains significant, I seek to understand the practices and networks in a specific and transterritorial context.

Methodological notes

The research for this article is based on ethnographic fieldwork conducted in the western municipalities of Macedonia, namely Skopje, Tetovo, Teartse, Struga and Debar, where the Albanian population is concentrated. The 2002 census enumerated a total population of just below 700,000 in all five municipalities, around a third of whom were of Albanian ethnicity (SSO 2005).

Four field research sessions of 10–15 days each were carried out in this area in 2008–2010, as well as several shorter occasional field trips. Furthermore, as an Erasmus student in Ljubljana (November 2009–February 2010), I had the chance to talk to Albanian restaurant workers, confectioners and bakers, most of whom were born in Tetovo and its surroundings but lived and worked in Slovenia.

Most of the ethnographic interviews I conducted were a combination of semi-structured and biographical (life history) narratives. The life-history approach is very valuable in studying processes, social changes and everyday life, especially in cases when the archives are incomplete or missing (Thompson 1978). Life histories allow us to observe the changes in the cultural and social experience of the individuals, their points of view and daily cultural practices, and in the meanings people invest in their actions (Roberts 2002, 21). This approach takes into consideration the fact that life histories are subjective, but finds them valuable as they reveal the respondents' opinions, dispositions and attitudes (Lieblick, Tuval-Maschiach, and Zilber 1998).

A set of 54 interviews with 75 respondents was conducted in both rural and urban locations.[1] Respondents were former migrants, migrants who at the time of the interview were on return visits in their places of origin, and local people who had never migrated but had relatives abroad. Conversations with members of the local administrative authority at research sites in Macedonia were also carried out. All these narratives were recorded and then transcribed. In addition, the research benefited from several informal conversations in the study locations.

Most of the interviewees were Albanians ($N=41$) whilst others were Slavic Orthodox Macedonians ($N=10$), Muslim Macedonians (Torbeshes, $N-19$) and Turks ($N=5$). This mixed ethnic and religious background enabled me to place the migratory experiences of Albanians in the context of a more general picture of labour mobility in the area.

The age range of my respondents was from 18 to 75 years, with most having attended primary and secondary school, and a few having higher education. Almost all my interviewees were men, with the exception of three Albanian women. This reflected very much the patriarchal context of society in western Macedonia, within which young unmarried men such as myself are only allowed to access male spaces. Even the three interviews with the women were conducted in the presence of their male companions – either husband or friend – with whom I had established close relationships of trust.

Labour migration amongst the Albanians from western Macedonia: historical dynamics and changing practices

Emigrations with the aim of earning for a living (so-called '*kurbet*') have been practised for centuries amongst the population inhabiting the mountainous western regions of today's Macedonia. Populations from different ethnic and religious communities, including Albanians, participated in these migratory flows. *Kurbet*, however, was a typically male occupation and was usually seasonal: men left in the spring and returned home in the fall. They were engaged in different types of economic activities, either agrarian such as harvesting and sheep breeding or craft industry such as construction, confectionery and pottery (Palairet 1987, 25–37).

Statistics on early Albanian migrants are difficult to come by, due to the lack of historical sources for the pre-1945 period.

The socialist period

The Second World War and its aftermath proved to be a turning-point in the process of labour migration from Macedonia. The foundations of socialist Yugoslavia were laid in late 1943 and included large territories inhabited by Albanians. A part of them were organized in the autonomous Kosovo and Metohija region within the Socialist Republic of Serbia, whilst another significant part was under the administrative authority of the newly created Socialist Republic of Macedonia. Modernization and industrialization were key elements of socialist Yugoslavia (Rossos 2008, 244–5). Equal job opportunities were proclaimed for all Yugoslav citizens within the boundaries of the federation (Janeska 2001, 166). In the early post-war years, emigration abroad was seen as political and social disloyalty to the country and socialist ideals. As a result, during the 1950s and 1960s, a sizable part of seasonal emigrant workers turned into 'socialist workers', by moving from rural areas to work in state factories and enterprises (Hristov 2008, 225). A significant section of the Macedonian population left their villages and settled in closer or more distant towns with their families.

However, Albanians were a different case for a number of reasons. First, they are ethnically different from the Slavic people in the federation. Second, they differ in terms of religion, as most of them are Muslims. Third, their Albanian language is also disparate and does not belong to the South Slavic group. For these and other historical reasons, the proclaimed idea of Yugoslav identity had not gained a foothold amongst them. In turn, the attitude of the Yugoslav authorities towards Albanians, especially during the 1950s and until the mid-1960s, was extremely harsh and they were put under strong economic and political pressure.[2] According to my research participants, it was a time of discrimination as they were not given the opportunity to work in the state and local administration and in the new state enterprises – whether in Macedonia or elsewhere in Former Yugoslavia. Furthermore, the level of education amongst the Albanian population was poor and access to education was hampered (Brunnbauer 2004, 582–3).

As a result, Albanians did not have equal opportunities to participate in this Yugoslavian project of socialist modernization, but they were also less eager to become part of it (Pichler 2009, 217–8). In contrast to the intense rural-urban migrations of Macedonians, the majority of Albanians remained in their native villages. Even when some of them moved to towns in Macedonia and in other parts of the Yugoslav federation, Albanians were not involved in the same way and to the same extent in these internal migrations as the Macedonians. Theirs was a short-distance shuttle or seasonal migration: an Albanian worker usually travelled to and back from the town on a daily basis or came back to the village on the weekends or even at the end of the working season when he worked in more distant places (Mirchevska 2010, 213).

In the mid-1960s, the position of the Yugoslav government towards Albanians softened. With authorities trying to ease tensions which had been flaring up due to the oppressive conditions, Albanians obtained more cultural and social rights, guaranteed by the Constitutions of 1963 and 1974 (Milosavlevski and Tomovski 1997, 16–19). Around this time (mid-1960s), the Yugoslav international migration policy also changed, resulting in active participation in the guest-worker programmes of the time. Because Kosovo, Macedonia and Bosnia and Herzegovina remained the most economically underdeveloped areas in Yugoslavia, the government directed this new, more open migration policy especially to these regions (Dimova 2007, 2–3). At the same time, Western Europe was still enjoying its post-war economic boom and migrant labour was very much in demand. The Yugoslav government signed official agreements with, amongst others, the Federal Republic of Germany, Austria, Switzerland, France and Sweden, which became important destinations for migrant workers from the underdeveloped regions of the federation.

As such, different migration patterns emerged: whilst ethnic Macedonians were mostly involved in large-scale rural-urban migration within the Republic of Macedonia and Yugoslavia more widely, ethnic Albanians aimed to make a living by seeking work abroad – in Germany, Austria and Switzerland (Dimova 2007, 5). In the next two decades, the number of Albanian migrants who went to Western European countries increased. All of them were men and mainly low skilled.

A change occurred in the structural conditions of Yugoslav labour mobility in the mid-1970s. The oil crisis of 1973 and the subsequent economic recession affected the host European countries so that they needed fewer foreign workers. Yet, contrary to expectations and in spite of restrictions put in place, migration continued. This time it was structured not around work but kinship ties. Given the circumstances, migrant workers feared that returning to their native country would render their re-migration to the West impossible. Therefore, paradoxically, the freeze on recruitment of new guest-workers stimulated settlement. During the following decades, the process of 'family reunion' gradually gained speed (Castles and Miller 2003, 79–80).

Reflecting this trend, relatively few Albanian migrants returned to Macedonia, and many ended up settling in their host countries. There were also a few cases of clandestine departures for European countries. Some of the young men left to join their fathers abroad. Gradually, the number of women who joined their husbands also increased, and consequently, also the number of children born and raised abroad.[3]

The first post-Yugoslav decade

The disintegration of Yugoslavia in 1991 is the turning point in the history of the study region. In this year, the independent Republic of Macedonia appeared on the political map. This was a period of deep political, economic and social change in this new state.[4] The companies established in socialist Yugoslavia turned out to be too large and not suitable for the new market-oriented economy. Many of them began to dismiss their employees or even collapsed (Janeska 2001, 238–9; Xhaferi 2005, 14–17). Ethnic Macedonians employed in these companies saw their living standards fall.

For the Albanian population in Macedonia, the situation was different as most of them lived in the countryside and only a small percentage worked in the public industry and state enterprises. A very large section of them provided for their families by working in Western Europe. The close networks which had tied together Albanian migrants and their villages of origin during the previous three decades allowed Albanian households to make a living. The established culture of migration played a crucial role during the 1990s and 2000s so that migrations continued with high intensity,[5] despite the limited opportunities for going abroad due to the strong visa restrictions for all former Yugoslav citizens. The strong endogamous tradition amongst Albanians played an important role as marriage became a way of overcoming these restrictions. Hence, the main source of the new Albanian migration from Macedonia during these post-socialist decades has been the so-called 'family formation'. As a result, contemporary migration is not exclusively a man's territory, as it was in the traditional *kurbet*, but it involves women and children as well.

The ethnographic data collected for this study clearly illustrate these migration trajectories. Emigration, settlement abroad, return and re-migration to a different country coexist in the Albanian context under study. Thereby different types of migrants (also in the sense of gender and age) living or only temporarily working in different countries are interconnected economically and emotionally through kinship and friendship ties, in turn also connected to relatives and household members in the places of origin. The dynamics of relations within such transterritorial networks have a specific influence over the economic, social and cultural life of the researched communities in Macedonia. This is the basis of a peculiar 'culture of migration', as the next section further explains.

Effects of migrations on local community and development in areas of origin

Remitting, building, investing

Precise data about the means that Albanian migrants use to remit to their relatives in Macedonia are lacking. The channels of sending money in most cases are informal, the key ones being self-delivery and via friends and relatives. Only 22% of the migrants responding to a recent survey sent money through formal banking channels (Mughal, Cipusheva, and Abazi 2009, 64–70).

As for their uses, the majority of my Albanian respondents confirmed that remittances are spent first and foremost to meet essential needs locally – food, medicines, clothing, different taxes and fees. However, the most visible are the funds invested in the reconstruction or construction of houses, as well as in their furnishing. Entering an Albanian village one might be impressed by the number and the size of the houses created by such remittances, with varied planning and architectural features from Alpine-style houses to colourful Mediterranean-type homes, each reflecting the influence on migrants' culture and aesthetics from their host countries (see Figure 1).[6] Most of these houses have been built in the last 20–30 years and differ significantly from their more 'traditional' counterparts built earlier. Many are still under construction.

> We Albanians have a different mentality – if you have a house, you have everything! The house has the first place of importance. If you are five brothers, five houses are built (Figure 2). If there is not so much money, the building goes upwards – a separate floor is built for every son. (M, born in 1963, worked in Germany [1985–1998], living in rural Tetovo)

Expensive construction materials and many decorative architectural elements (columns, parapets and cornices) are used with the aim of demonstrating richness and wealth (for similar findings amongst other migrant groups see Smith and Mazzucato 2009). Sizable financial resources are spent for furnishing and modern

Figure 1. Albanian migrants' houses near Struga, 2010.

Figure 2. New Albanian houses in the same plot of land, village near Struga, 2009. Each of the three brothers (working abroad) has built a separate house for their nuclear families. Two of them live with their families in Switzerland and Austria respectively. The youngest brother works seasonally in Austria and Italy, leaving his family in Macedonia.

household equipment – a washing machine, a dishwasher, an electric cooker etc. A computer, a plasma TV and a video camera typically complement technical equipment of the household. One of my respondents told me with great satisfaction about the expensive fireplace with its steam heating installation which he had ordered from Germany.

In addition to these expenditures, some remitted funds are invested in production activities. The majority of first-generation migrants want to invest their savings in small businesses in their native place, aiming to provide a regular income for their families. Some fail, others only partially achieve this goal.

> I opened a shop. But our people here, they get used to buying on tick. For three months I lost 70,000 marks. I closed the shop and I began to work in parks and landscaping in Tetovo [...]. (M, born in 1955, worked in Switzerland [1988–1999], living in Tetovo)

Other respondents have had better luck, for example several owners of small cafés, grocery stores, small family hotels and transport companies. Some of these initiatives are sustainable due to periodical money transfers by the owner's brothers who continue to work abroad. In the last decade or so remittance-funded successful business activities have become increasingly visible, gradually changing the business environment in areas inhabited by Albanians. Examples that stand out include a textile mill near the village of Slatino, a juice-production plant near Tetovo and a shopping mall in Struga (Figure 3). Some of these companies employ hundreds of people. Here is how an employee (M, born in 1975) in the local administration of the municipality of Teartse explained the changing attitudes brought about by financial remittances:

> Till now we have mainly invested in houses. Big houses have been built. But people have already started to think otherwise, they know that you can build a house, but you must maintain it. Each year at least 1000 Euros are needed [for this]. And now some have started, we can say, ten good businesses have started since I have worked here [in the municipality], since 2005. And all of them are investments with capital gained abroad.

Besides individual remittances, the villages of origin are transformed by an injection of collective funds in public infrastructure and services (for more on such remittances see Goldring 2004). Respondents in all research villages explained the existence of a special fund to which each village household must pay a certain contribution according to how many members they have working abroad and their income. The money has been invested in asphalting streets, building bridges and fountains, renovating schools and religious sites (Figure 4) or supporting vulnerable households such as those seriously ill or hit by some disaster.

At this point, it is important to turn to the question of what constitutes productive and unproductive activities. De Haas (2005, 1274–5) argues that labelling expenditure on housing, food, health care and education as unproductive is inaccurate as such funds are also 'invested', except this time in wellbeing and human capital. They are important as they have a long-term potential to increase people's productivity, freedom of choice and capacity to participate in public debate, thus making them a key element in the broad process of development. In the words of my respondents, these remittances go beyond material expression in

Figure 3. A hotel and a trade centre in Struga built by Albanian returnees, 2009.

Figure 4. New mosque built by Albanian migrants near Struga, 2010.

infrastructure and economic development. The benefits they provide have broader significance: unemployment falls as jobs are created through infrastructure projects; new social and cultural assets are developed such as school computer rooms, sport halls and playgrounds, modern medical and community centres; people acquire new knowledge and skills and their self-confidence increases.

> After we went abroad, we realized what civilization is. Here everything was primitive. There was no equipment or technology. Abroad people learn know-how, get to know other cultures. Migrants did so much. If they didn't work abroad, it would be misery here. Nowadays people know to operate machinery, to drive a car. Children go to colleges and universities. Thus through the work in Europe we have come close to Europe. (M, born in 1941, worked in Australia [1966–1973], Germany [1977, six months] and USA [since 1979], living as a pensioner in rural Struga)

The family and kinship ties are key to structuring individual remittance transfers in the research context by providing channels for their physical transfer and social structures for their investment in the form of everyday needs or family-run local businesses. Even larger businesses are run along family and kinship ties. Such social networks that tie together Albanian migrants, returnees, young people wishing to migrate and those who stay in their native villages are thus very important in individuals' everyday actions and practices. However, kinship relations and family structure are not static. They are also strongly influenced by intensive and ongoing migration.

Migration, family structures and relations

During the initial migratory phase (mid-1960s to mid-1980s), Albanian labour migrants from the region were solely men, and migration was temporary. These trips followed the familiar patterns of *kurbet*: young and middle-aged men left in search of earnings, whilst older men, women and children stayed behind in the villages. Before leaving their birthplaces, almost all first-generation migrants had lived in extended households. Many of them were already married, some even had children. However, their wives and children stayed behind and were taken care of by the husband's parents, unmarried brothers or sisters. Ideally, when an Albanian went abroad to work, he did not go 'for himself', but to improve the living conditions of his entire family (Reineck 1991, 143). Money earned abroad was sent to the male head of the household who was in charge of controlling the finances and not to one's own wife or children.[7] One of my respondents shared his memories of the 1970s:

> Then there was a huge family, probably about 30 people. Uncle, cousins, brothers – all of them under the same roof [...] We, my brothers and I, went abroad in order to earn money. And when we were coming back each of us was giving his earnings to the father. The oldest man held the money. It didn't matter that I was the one earning it – he was the one taking it. He was taking care of our children – whether to go to school or work. He was the chief, he kept the business accounts. (M, born in 1944, worked in Germany, living as a pensioner in rural Struga)

Although these migrants were physically away from the family, they were active members in the household and their efforts were orientated towards meeting the needs of the entire household unit. This began to change in the 1980s when family reunion and family formation caused the number of women and children abroad to increase, affecting in turn the structure of the Albanian transnational household and relationships amongst its members. As a result, conflicts – related to individual interests or gender – started to emerge, bringing about splits within many of the extended family households. Often my respondents pointed out that migration had certainly contributed to the emergence of nuclear families and their gradual endorsement as a dominant form of family life. The previous interviewee explained:

> No matter whether you liked it or not – you had to obey your father, because he was the oldest man. Such was our tradition. And actually we respected each other much more. [This lasted] probably until 20 years ago. And after that you take your family abroad and you don't need to be obedient any more. The old people don't have that influence any more. The children are independent of their parents and do not pay much attention to them, as they used to. They also do not give money to the oldest men.

Since the 1980s, the biggest dilemma all Albanian men working abroad were faced with was whether to take their nuclear family along with them to the foreign country or not (cf. Reineck 1991, 128–30). At its root stood a combination of material and socio-cultural factors. From a material point of view, remittances have enabled women and children left behind to live in much better conditions than their neighbours who cannot rely on such resources. At the same time, this is also a less expensive option than taking them along abroad, a process which would incur higher expenses, especially when this extra money can be saved for the future return home. On the other hand, when abroad women too can take up wage work and contribute financially to the nuclear family unit.

> Earlier, until the 1950s and 1960s, women were not working, but then they began [to work]. The costs are very large, the husband cannot make good money and the wife began working to help him. Thus they can have a better life. (M, born in 1963, worked in Switzerland [1988–2001], living in Tetovo)

The second set of factors behind the aforementioned dilemma is socio-cultural in nature. Many migrants still think that wives and children should stay in their motherland. Fear of assimilation in host societies is presented as the strongest reason when it comes to children who are thought to be at risk of losing their Albanian identity, language and culture.

> While I was in Austria, I met some people who had been there since 1968. Until 1980 they had been alone. Then they had decided to take their family with them. I saw their grandchildren – they spoke German, even among themselves. They did not speak their mother tongue. That's why I did not want to take my children along with me. All the time you communicate only with Austrians and little by little you lose your mother tongue. So, the second or the third generation is already assimilated. (M, born in 1968, worked in Germany [1988–1990] and Austria [1991–1998], living in Skopje)

On the other hand, migrants recognize the strain caused by their physical absence in relations with their left-behind children. As de Haas and Fokkema (2010, 550–1) point out in their study on Moroccan migration, the prolonged absence of fathers changes intra-family and inter-generational relations. Having grown up without a father's observation, sons are used to being unrestricted and enjoy more liberty, all of which changes after the father's return. On the other hand, it is difficult for the father himself to regain the leading role he traditionally plays in such patriarchal societies. A similar situation was encountered in my Albanian case study. Many of the respondents who have been working abroad felt that they did not want to let their children choose this hard path of living and working far away from the native home. Feelings run high especially concerning daughters. But such attitudes become a cause for inter-generational conflict as these left-behind children consider themselves underprivileged in comparison with those who could join their fathers abroad. Thus, influenced by a surrounding 'culture of migration' and protesting against hegemonic patriarchal authority, many of my young interviewees manifested a strong wish to go abroad. For many of them, marrying an Albanian spouse who lives abroad is a way to accomplish their goal.

> I would like to become an investigative journalist. Last year I finished secondary school. Now my wish is to go to study journalism in England. But here, you know, the things are changing, but many norms are still strong and very traditional. I don't like this, but ... My father thinks the possibility to go abroad is completely inadmissible and beyond discussion, if I am not married. Maybe I can find in future some Albanian boy, who lives in England and get married to him. (F, born in 1989, living in Struga)

Growing up during the 1970s in families with absent migrant fathers had influenced many of my respondents to take their families with them when they themselves migrated abroad during the 1990s, giving their own children what they saw as a better family life.

> But since 1990 they have started getting the families abroad. Over the years another mentality has been developed. The old father came back here after 30 years of work in Germany and Austria, but he had already lost his life. People have begun to think otherwise – so, why should I maltreat my woman and children leaving them on their own? Thereby they have started taking them abroad. (M, born in 1965, from rural Struga but living with his family in Austria)

Dilemmas abounded on whether women should join their husbands and other male folk abroad or not. Concerns related to morality and honour, especially as women's honour was construed as having immediate repercussions on that of their closest male family members such as the husband (see Backer 2003, 94). The Western world was considered corrupt; keeping women away from it supposedly guaranteed preservation of their honour. Whilst men were abroad other members of the family ensured that the wife's honour back home was preserved. These attitudes changed gradually as households split as a result of conflict over property and personal interests, and women joined husbands abroad. Some change does take place to the benefit of women when they are abroad, as they enjoy more freedom and are not under the constant surveillance of the local village community. Many also work outside their home, as we saw earlier, which gives them a greater say in the household. Yet, some stereotypes persist even when they live abroad, reflected by the remarks of some male interviewees who still thought women's place was in the home to take care of the housekeeping and children. Overall, however, women's position in the family has strengthened as a result of their own emigration.

Perhaps the most important change has happened for women who grew up and completed their education abroad. Their position, in turn, has an important influence on changing patriarchal attitudes about women's role amongst people around them, including men. A young interviewee presented one such example:

> My wife was there, her father had been working in Italy for many years and he had taken her there as a child. When we married I also went there [...] I barely speak Italian. But my wife speaks [Italian], she is fluent. What I do not know, my wife knows. She is working in a pasta factory and she found the first job position for me. (M, born in 1990, from rural Tetovo but working in Italy)

But family reunification was not the only motive for migrant men to take their families to the country they worked in. Economic prosperity and individual independence from patriarchal and collective authority played a key role too. In the past, every man's contribution to the household's wealth was considered equal, no matter how much he had actually earned. But making good money could change this established status quo. The indisputable prestige of the household head was put to the test. It became more usual that he was increasingly dependent on the migrants' money to pay household bills or other taxes. Gradually, these resources became so important that prestige shifted to the provider away from the household head. In addition, Albanian migrants are faced with the choice between the traditional Albanian ideal of subordination to the common family interests or providing a better life only for their own wife and children, often abroad (Reineck 1991, 143). Since the mid-1980s and especially in the 1990s, the most frequent choice has been the second one.

Living abroad with the family changes migrants' priorities: the focus turns towards earning to provide for the nuclear family abroad, whilst remitting to villages of origin takes second place. As children grow up abroad, and create their own families and lives, return to the homeland for the first generation, even upon retirement, looks an increasingly remote option:

> It is very difficult for me to return. Because my whole family is there and if I come back with my wife here, all of my children will stay there. What are we going to do here, two old people? It is hard ... (M, born in 1954, from rural Struga, went to Switzerland in 1980 and took his family there in 1986)

Return is even less desirable for women who, as a result of living abroad, enjoy more freedom, especially as regards constant compliance with other members of the extended household and surveillance and supervision by the local community. They fear that return will restrict these freedoms, even in older age.

> The young bride left here does not dare to dress as young. Because her husband is not here. She must be dressed as some old woman. If she puts on new clothes, she would be laughed at, she would be told she is unfaithful, she is a prostitute. Even now those women are put under strong observation and in a very difficult position. (F, born 1973, from rural Struga, living with her husband in Austria)

Similarly, the idea of return does not appeal much to the second- and third-generation offspring of migrants. For them, Macedonia is a place to spend the summer vacations, but not to live in. They fear integration and adaptation problems were they to 'return', as well as a lack of the opportunities they are now so accustomed to (for similar findings see Vathi 2011b).

It is clear that the family structure and relationships, as well as the typical Albanian kinship solidarity, are changing, but retain their importance. Migrants tend to maintain kin relations and to invest economically and emotionally in their places of origin. Thus, their relatives in the native village receive economic aid and financial security, whilst migrants have the opportunity to acquire new social status and prestige.

Migration, social status and prestige

Social status is a specific form of social identity, which reflects the socio-economic positioning of an individual in a social field (Nieswand 2011, 125). In the study villages prior to the 1970s when mass migration had not begun, few people had significant wealth. The demonstration of this wealth was considered as immoral and ostentation was strongly condemned by the local community. According to traditional Albanian ethics, personal status derived not from material wealth, but from moral reputation, from the degree to which a family has collectively upheld the community's moral code (for a detailed analysis of the traditional Albanian household see Backer 2003). Changes in values and social relations caused by mass migration have affected the system by which Albanians rank each other in terms of social status. Today social status is based on a combination of moral reputation and material prosperity, with different weight accorded to each by generation. However, the importance of material wealth to achieve social position and prestige has increased over the years.

Nieswand (2011) points to the specific status paradox that can emerge in the context of contemporary mass migration. Most migrants are employed as unskilled workers, often illegally, in host societies and are thus unable to gain a high position there. On the other hand, the economic inequalities between the receiving and the sending country create incentives for migrants to transfer resources earned in richer countries to poorer countries in order to increase their purchasing power. In this way, regardless of their low social position abroad, they have a chance to become socially prestigious in their origin village or town and, thereby, to raise their status there. In general, a migrant's success depends not so much on their status abroad, but on the remittances sent to origin areas. For that reason, the results of migration must be made visible to the community.

The large multi-storey houses in Albanian villages are an obvious mark demonstrating well-being and enhanced social prestige. They are, indeed, visible for the local community.

> There is a contest – to build a larger house than others. There are such people, many people. For instance, if he has an old house, he will demolish it and erect a new one. And it should be larger than the neighbour's house. In order to demonstrate himself he would even build a swimming pool. (M, born in 1955, worked in Switzerland [1988–1999], living in Tetovo)

Another visible expression of prestige and an improved social position is the manifestation of well-being to the native village when migrants return during the summer. For several weeks, the villages are buzzing with people and expensive cars with foreign registration number plates – from Austria, Switzerland, Germany, USA etc. The cafés, pubs and restaurants are overcrowded during the entire day. Every returnee from abroad is expected to treat relatives and friends, showing the amount of his earnings. Young people show off the latest mobile phone models or walk along the main street of the village wearing designer clothes. When it comes to non-material markers of migrant's prestige, using German, Italian or English words and phrases, in the public sphere is especially significant. In this respect, my findings correspond to Hemming's (2009) study of migration status paradox and display of wealth from young Albanian migrant men during their visits to their hometown in northern Albania. Such a situation is not unique to the Albanian context, however, as shown by Nieswand's (2011) research amongst Ghanaians and Bielenin-Lenczowska's (2010) amongst Muslim Macedonians in the Struga region.

In the Albanian context, the grand weddings can be also noted. It is typical not only for the Albanian community, but also for other migrants from western Macedonia such as Torbeshes and Turks, that weddings are organized between July and August, the period in which most migrants have their annual holidays and return to their origin villages. Every day there are two, three, sometimes more weddings. The bride is often from the same village as the groom. Even after several decades of emigration, mixed marriages with host-country spouses such as Austrians or Germans are an exception. The wedding is a luxurious and lavish ceremony. All relatives and friends are invited – those living permanently in the village, as well as migrants arriving from various countries around the world. Nowadays, the number of guests usually reaches a few hundred. A noisy procession with expensive cars, loud Albanian music, blaring horns and Albanian flags passes through the village, so as to stress the wealth of the migrants and especially their identity. Evening festivities continue in the home of the groom, but during recent years this part of the ceremony has begun to shift to local restaurant halls. According to my respondents, such weddings can cost between 5000 and 10,000 Euros. The number of guests, the luxury cars in the procession and the expensive gifts are important symbols of well-being and social positioning of the household.

> The man brings many pieces of gold jewelry for the bride – necklaces, rings, bracelets. He also wants to demonstrate in this way how strong he is, how big the family is. (M, born in 1964, non-migrant in rural Struga)

The expressions of well-being and economic power easily translate into prestige and social status within the local village community. As Bielenin-Lenczowska (2010, 520) notes, organizing such events is possible and rational only in the place of origin, since only the local people can comment on their customs and only for them can the material and social aspects of weddings be observed and valued. But wedding rituals are also important as they refer to origins, ethnic unity and community consciousness (Pichler 2010, 225–6).

Conclusions

The specific position of the Albanians from Macedonia within the Yugoslav federation has determined labour migration abroad as a very important occupation for a large section of this Albanian population. The institutional conditions for work abroad created within the guest-worker system were also significant factors. Nevertheless, the existence of such conditions is not sufficient to explain the high rates of migratory activity and the various migratory practices amongst the Albanians, especially when the initial institutional frameworks changed. In the course of time, the migrants were moving between different places and were forming multiple transterritorial networks connecting with their relatives and friends in origin and host places (see also Dahinden 2010). They were an essential resource for overcoming the limitations of the respective migratory policies. Nowadays, we can observe two main patterns of migration: when entire families go abroad and live there; and when only men work abroad, coming back home at regular intervals. However, both types exist simultaneously and this contributes to the networks' multiplicity.

The relations within these networks have determined a number of characteristics and changes of community socio-cultural patterns. The intensive migration since the 1970s has significantly changed the area of origin and local communities. Its effects on socio-cultural development go beyond financial impacts such as meeting daily needs, improving the material conditions of life, building a house or starting business activities. Migration affects the general process of social and cultural transformation through changing traditional rules, behaviours, social structures and relations. In recent years, under the influence of increasingly accelerating family migration, the traditionally conservative Albanian family–kin structure and relationships have been modified. However, different tendencies can be observed: on the one hand, a loosening of the conservative patriarchal order and practices towards more individualization; on the other, considerable resources are invested in housebuilding, family rituals and community-based projects which underline the strong sense of communality and ethnic affiliation.

What future directions will migration amongst Albanians from the Republic of Macedonia take? What changes will occur in the overall migration patterns in the coming years? These questions leave the topic open for future research, especially if we consider the aspirations of Macedonia for EU accession.

Notes

1. Almost all interviews were conducted in the Macedonian language, which I am fluent in. This is also the official language of the Republic of Macedonia, which is taught at all primary schools there, hence my respondents' fluency in this language. Only in three cases I used verbal interpretation from the local Albanian dialect to Macedonian. In addition, I conducted one interview in English with a 20-year-old man who was a third-generation migrant living in the USA. He felt more comfortable speaking in English (for similar features amongst second-generation Albanians in Europe, see Vathi 2011a).
2. The split between the Yugoslav leader Tito and Stalin in 1948 and the subsequent close ties developed between Moscow and Tirana were of great importance in influencing the negative attitudes towards Albanians within the Yugoslav federation. Most Albanian-language schools at this time were closed, and measures were taken against the Albanian intelligentsia and teachers of history and the Albanian language. The commemoration of national holidays and the display of Albanian national symbols were banned. Simultaneously, the authorities took measures to encourage expression of a Turkish identity amongst all Muslims within the federation. In accordance with an agreement signed with Turkey in 1953, Yugoslavia allowed – and even 'encouraged' – large-scale emigration of Yugoslav 'Turks' to Turkey (Babuna 2000, 69–70; Blumi 2003). However, many of them were in fact Albanians from Macedonia and Kosovo who had claimed to be Turks in order to take advantage of the agreement. Around 250,000 left for Turkey at this time, half of whom were from Macedonia (Malcolm 1998, 323).
3. Between 1971 and 1981, the number of migrants (all ethnic groups) living outside Macedonia increased, the most significant growth being women and children. In 1971, the number of migrants' wives and children living with them was barely 2016, but in 1981 it grew to 42,958. Amongst the Albanians, women and children were around 30% in 1981; in 1994 this share rose to 49% (Janeska 2001, 201–3).

4. In the new 1991 constitution of the Republic of Macedonia, the state was pronounced as a 'country of Macedonian nation' without mentioning Albanian nationality, which was the case in the 1974 constitution. Consequently, Albanians were deprived of the right to use their native language in public and the use of the national flag was also banned. Thus, a struggle began between Albanian and Macedonian political elites in order to change the situation. Ethnic tensions increased leading to the armed conflict in 2001. The signing of the Ohrid Agreement was an attempt to overcome this situation, but ethnic clashes continued and Albanian and Macedonian populations remain strongly divided in their public life along ethnic lines.
5. Drawing on population censuses Janeska (2001, 202), estimates the number of Macedonian citizens of Albanian origin living abroad to have been 22,340 in 1981 and 51,685 in 1994.
6. All photographs were taken by the author during fieldwork.
7. Such strongly gendered remittance patterns continue to persist in other Albanian migratory settings. See, for example, King, Dalipaj, and Mai (2006) and Smith (2009).

References

Babuna, A. 2000. The Albanians of Kosovo and Macedonia: Ethnic identity superceding religion. *Nationalities Papers* 28, no. 1: 67–92.

Backer, B. 2003. *Behind stone walls: Changing household organization among the Albanians of Kosova.* Dukagjin: Dukagjini Balkan Books.

Bielenin-Lenczowska, K. 2010. Transnational ties among migrants and their families: The case of labour migrants (*pechalbari*) from the republic of Macedonia to Italy. *Kultura Polisa* 13–14: 509–34.

Blumi, I. 2003. Defining social spaces by way of deletion: The untold story of Albanian migration in the post-war period. *Journal of Ethnic and Migration Studies* 29, no. 6: 949–65.

Boyd, M. 1989. Family and social networks in international migration: Recent developments and new agendas. *International Migration Review* 23, no. 3: 638–70.

Brunnbauer, U. 2004. Fertility, families and ethnic conflict: Macedonians and Albanians in the Republic of Macedonia, 1944–2002. *Nationalities Papers* 32, no. 3: 565–98.

Čapo Žmegač, J. 2003. Two localities, two nation-states, two homes: Transmigration of Croatian labour migrants in Munich [in Croatian]. *Narodna Umjetnost* 40, no. 2: 117–30.

Castles, S. 2009. Development and migration – migration and development: What comes first? Global perspectives and African experiences. *Theoria* 56, no. 121: 1–31.

Castles, S., and M. Miller. 2003. *The age of migration: International population movements in the modern world.* 3rd ed. New York, NY: Palgrave Macmillan.

Dahinden, J. 2010. 'Are you who you know?' A network perspective on ethnicity, gender and transnationalism: Albanian-speaking migrants in Switzerland and returnees in Kosovo. In *Identity processes and dynamics in multi-ethnic Europe,* ed. Ch. Westin, J. Bastos, J. Dahinden, and P. Góis, 127–47. Amsterdam: Amsterdam University Press.

de Haas, H. 2005. International migration, remittances and development: Myths and facts. *Third World Quarterly* 26, no. 8: 1269–84.

de Haas, H. 2010. Migration and development: A theoretical perspective. *International Migration Review* 44, no. 1: 227–64.

de Haas, H., and T. Fokkema. 2010. Intra-household conflicts in migration decision-making: Return and pendulum migration in Morocco. *Population and Development Review* 36, no. 3: 541–56.

Dimova, R. 2007. From past necessity to contemporary friction: Migration, class and ethnicity in Macedonia. Working Paper 94. Halle: Max Planck Institute for Social Anthropology. http://eth.mpg.de/cms/en/publications/working_papers/pdf/mpi-eth-working-paper-0094.pdf (accessed October 24, 2012).

Glick Schiller, N., L. Basch, and C. Szanton Blanc. 1992. Transnationalism: A new analytic framework for understanding migration. In *Towards a transnational perspective on migration: Race, class, ethnicity, and nationalism reconsidered*, ed. N. Glick Schiller, L. Basch, and C. Szanton Blanc, 1–24. New York, NY: New York Academy of Sciences.

Glick Schiller, N., L. Basch, and C. Szanton Blanc. 1995. From immigrant to transmigrant: Theorizing transnational migration. *Anthropological Quarterly* 68, no. 1: 48–63.

Goldring, L. 2004. Family and collective remittances in Mexico: A multi-dimensional typology. *Development and Change* 35, no. 4: 799–840.

Hemming, A. 2009. Migrant identity on display: The xhiro in Rrëshen. *Southeast European and Black Sea Studies* 12, no. 9: 575–88.

Hristov, P. 2008. Trans-border exchange of seasonal workers in the central regions of the Balkans (19th–20th century). *Ethnologia Balkanica* 12: 215–30.

Janeska, V. 2001. *Contemporary international migrations: Emigration from the Republic of Macedonia and socio-economic development*. Skopje: Ekonomski Institut [in Macedonian].

King, R., M. Dalipaj, and N. Mai. 2006. Gendering migration and remittances: Evidence from London and Northern Albania. *Population, Space and Place* 12, no. 6: 409–34.

Levitt, P. 1998. Social remittances: migration driven local-level forms of cultural diffusion. *International Migration Review* 32, no. 4: 926–48.

Levitt, P., and N. Nyberg Sørensen. 2004. The transnational turn in migration studies. Working Paper 6. Geneva: Global Commission on International Migration. http://www.unhcr.org/refworld/docid/42ce48754.html (accessed October 24, 2012).

Levitt, P., and N. Glick Schiller. 2004. Conceptualizing simultaneity: A transnational social field perspective on society. *International Migration Review* 38, no. 3: 1002–39.

Lieblick, A., R. Tuval-Maschiach, and T. Zilber. 1998. *Narrative research: Reading, analysis and interpretation*. London: Sage.

Malcolm, N. 1998. *A short history of Kosovo*. New York, NY: New York University Press.

Massey, D.S., J. Arango, G. Hugo, A. Kouaouci, A. Pellegrino, and J.E. Taylor. 1993. Theories of international migration: A review and appraisal. *Population and Development Review* 19, no. 3: 431–66.

Milosavlevski, S., and M. Tomovski. 1997. *The Albanians in Macedonia 1945–95: Legislation, policy documents, statistics*. Skopje: Studentski Zbor [in Macedonian].

Mirchevska, M. 2010. Macedonian farmers between the tradition, transition and European regulations. In *Modern and post-modern etudes in ethnology and anthropology*, ed. V. Tepavicharov, 187–218. Sofia: Gutenberg.

Mughal, A.G., H. Cipusheva, and H. Abazi. 2009. *Migration, remittances and the standards of living in the Republic of Macedonia: A report based on the 2008 quality of life survey*. Tetovo: South East European University. http://.seeu.edu.mk/files/research/magchah-report-final.pdf (accessed October 24, 2012).

Nieswand, B. 2011. *Theorising transnational migration: The status paradox of migration*. London: Routledge.

Palairet, M. 1987. The migrant workers of the Balkans and their villages (18th century – World War II). In *Crafts in Central and Southeast Europe: Mobility, mediation and change in the crafts during the 18th and 20th century*, ed. K. Roth, 23–46. Munich: Südosteuropa-Gesellschaft [in German].

Pichler, R. 2009. Migration, architecture and the imagination of home(land): An Albanian-Macedonian case study. In *Transnational societies, transterritorial politics: Migrations in the (post-) Yugoslav region 19th–20th century*, ed. U. Brunnbauer, 213–35. Munich: Oldenbourg Verlag.

Pichler, R. 2010. Migration, ritual and ethnic conflict: A study of wedding ceremonies of Albanian transmigrants from the Republic of Macedonia. *Ethnologia Balkanica* 13: 211–29.

Pries, L. 2001. The approach of transnational social spaces: Responding to new configurations of the social and the spatial. In *New transnational social spaces: International migration and transnational communities in the early 21st century*, ed. L. Pries, 3–33. London: Routledge.

Reineck, J. 1991. The past as refuge: Gender, migration, and ideology among the Kosova Albanians. PhD diss., University of California.

Roberts, B. 2002. *Biographical research*. Buckingham: Open University Press.

Rossos, A. 2008. *Macedonia and the Macedonians: A history*. Stanford, CA: Hoover Institution Press.

Smith, E. 2009. 'Gap-fillers' or 'clan-destroyers'? Transnational female solidarity towards kin in the region of Fier. *Southeast European and Black Sea Studies* 9, no. 4: 555–73.

Smith, L., and V. Mazzucato. 2009. Constructing homes, building relationships: Migrant investments in houses. *Tijdschrift voor Economische en Sociale Geographie* 100, no. 5: 662–73.

SSO. 2005. *Census of population, households and dwellings in the Republic of Macedonia, 2002: Book XIII*. Skopje: State Statistical Office (SSO) of the Republic of Macedonia. http://www.stat.gov.mk/pdf/kniga_13.pdf (accessed October 24, 2012) [in Macedonian].

Thompson, P. 1978. *The voice of the past: Oral history*. Oxford: Oxford University Press.

Vathi, Z. 2011a. The children of Albanian migrants in Europe: Ethnic identity, transnational ties, and pathways of integration. PhD diss., University of Sussex.

Vathi, Z. 2011b. A context issue? Comparing the attitude towards return of the Albanian first and second generation in Europe. *Journal of Mediterranean Studies* 20, no. 2: 343–64.

Vertovec, S. 2009. *Transnationalism*. London: Routledge.

Xhaferi, S. 2005. *Migrants' financial capital and its involvement in the economy of the Republic of Macedonia*. Skopje: Interlingua [in Albanian].

Social development and transnational households: resilience and motivation for Albanian immigrants in Greece in the era of economic crisis

Domna Michail

Department of Pre-Primary Education, University of Western Macedonia, Florina, Greece

> This paper examines the ways in which the Greek economic crisis has affected the social development of Albanian immigrants in both the sending and the host country. It focuses on transnational households and family development projects and examines the degree of resilience and the power of motivation that drives people's reactions during the crisis, comparing first- and second-generation immigrants. My research focuses mainly on those Albanian immigrants who by the third year of the economic crisis still live in Greece. The empirical analysis is based on primary data derived from participant observation, a semi-structured questionnaire with second-generation migrants and in-depth interviews amongst first- and second-generation Albanian immigrants residing in both urban and rural areas in Greece.

Introduction

Albanian immigration to Greece started in the early 1990s and was initially characterized as basically male non-permanent immigration (Hatziprokopiou 2003; Korovilas 1999; Vullnetari 2007). In the course of time, however, it has taken on a more permanent character and, during the last decade, it has developed into permanent family settlement (King and Vullnetari 2012). According to the latest data (2010), registered Albanian immigrants number 485,000, whilst the undocumented are estimated at 390,000.[1] The National Centre for Social Research (EKKE) reports that Greeks, amongst all the other Europeans, present the most negative perceptions and attitudes about immigrants, related to economic, ethnic, cultural and quality-of-life reasons (National Centre for Social Research 2003). This is what Castles (2004, 867) refers to as 'the strength of nationalist and ethnocentric ideologies in immigration countries [that makes] it easy to mobilize public opinion against immigration'.

The need to overcome a marginalized status and at the same time achieve personal and family goals has led Albanian immigrants to adopt integrating strategies on two levels: a private and a public one. On the private level, they seem to develop a rather more 'co-operative model' within the nuclear family where gender roles become less bounded and more functional (Zachou and Kalerante 2009). The experience of migration has led in some cases to a retreat from traditional values (King and Vullnetari 2009; Smith 2009) since very often women provide the family with more stable income than men. This has become especially apparent during the last two-three years, when the economic crisis has left many male immigrants unemployed.

On the public level, the main integrating strategies are the patterns of baptism and name-changing (Doja 2000; Hart 1999; Hatziprokopiou 2003; Michail 2008a; 2008b; 2009; Nitsiakos 2003). Furthermore, the practices of name-changing and hiding religious affiliation entail a certain blurring of the ethnic boundary between Greek and Albanian identity (Kokkali 2011; Michail 2010a; Pratsinakis 2005).

Previous research in a community bordering Albania carried out by the author revealed that, at the time that the fieldwork was conducted (2005–2008), first-generation immigrants were enforcing transnational investment activities and mobility in both Greece and Albania (Michail 2009). I observed both capital and non-capital investment forms as strategies of integration, due to the economic and political instability in Albania, on the one hand, and the problematic migration policies in Greece, on the other. Proximity with Albania facilitated the first-generation immigrants' transnational investment practices and kept their connection with family members and places of origin quite strong. However, the second generation seemed to be taking recourse in building their future in Greece and being integrated within the Greek community (Michail 2010b).

Building upon this previous research, the present article aims to examine the multiple ways in which the economic crisis has affected Albanian immigrants, their well-being and relationships within their own community, as well as with the extended Greek community. I aim to gain insight into issues related to the economic and social development of the Albanian transnational households in Greece in the era of uncertainty that the economic crisis has generated. More specifically, I look at issues of legal and social status, honour and prestige, intra- and inter-community relations, identity and return.

The Greek economic crisis: an introduction

There have been various studies on the economic crisis in Greece.[2] One common view claims that the Greek crisis that followed the global economic recession in 2008 became more visible in late 2009 and was connected not only to structural weaknesses, which means the defects of the Greek state, economy and society, but also to Greece's joining 'a flawed monetary union'. Three Greek governments from 2010 to 2012 adopted two bail-out programmes accompanied by harsh austerity measures to reduce state exposure to debt and, second, structural adjustment to improve competitiveness, according to the policies dictated by the 'troika' (the EU, the IMF and the European Central Bank). Both have failed and exacerbated the crisis across Europe. A third bail-out programme has been prepared and agreed with the 'troika' but has not yet been voted by the Greek Parliament at the time of writing.

The damage that austerity has brought is material as well as non-material. Most people's livelihoods have been overturned, and their psychological state of being has been drastically affected. Consumption has decreased dramatically; families have further reduced any possible expenditure including vacations, eating out, even their children's after-school activities (Triandafyllidou 2012). The construction sector has been receding to an extreme point, since people stopped buying houses.[3] Leisure activities have become much restricted, unemployment has increased especially amongst young people, and suicides have increased by 40% during the last three years. Most of these suicides have been reported as a result of the people's inability to cope with their debts and lack of control over their lives.[4]

The crisis has particularly hit the main sector where immigrants have been employed: construction. The real estate market is in deep crisis and public works have almost stopped.[5] Other sectors like tourism or catering have also been severely affected.[6] Additionally, the crisis has affected women immigrants who work as cleaners since many families have reduced their household expenses. The majority of the Albanian immigrants who lost their jobs have been facing the risk of losing their legal stay status since they are not able to renew their stay permits. Stay permits in Greece are renewed every one or two years for the first 10 years with the condition that immigrants are legally employed and insured. Under the present economic situation this condition cannot be fulfilled since the existing work positions are unstable and cannot guarantee the required minimum of 25 working days per month for five months a year. Besides, the tax system has changed and requires the amount of €10,200 minimum yearly income (instead of €5000 that it used to be) to renew working permits. Greek employers are unable to insure and declare their employees for such an amount and most immigrants are facing the possibility of being forced to leave the country as soon as their existing permits expire. The alternative is to remain in the country in a status of illegality. So far those immigrants who return are mostly Albanians who have planned their return after many years of emigration, or those who have lost their jobs and legal status.[7]

Methodological reflections

This paper considers the social development process, in parallel to the economic development of the households of Albanian immigrants in Greece. I examine the ways in which these two processes are interlinked and how they have contributed to the well-being of immigrant families and individuals. I also focus on the first- and second-generation's resilience to the effects of the economic crisis on the transnational households as well as individual reactions according to personal motivation. The issue of return migration to Albania is becoming very relevant nowadays under the pressure of the economic crisis. First-generation Albanian immigrants seem to be stuck in limbo, hoping that something might happen to help them decide whether it is better for them to stay in Greece or to return to their home country. Meanwhile, second- generation Albanians seem not to share this state of limbo, but rather be more resilient and motivated to remain in Greece.

My approach in this paper broadly reflects the post-1990s 'transnational turn' in the anthropological study of migration. In anthropology, this means the study of human groups *in motion* and not as traditionally static entities (Mintz 1998). However, transnationalism is by no means the exclusive preserve of anthropologists. As Vertovec points out, 'the prominence of this topic goes far beyond anthropology ... [and] in recent years transnationalism has become one of the fundamental ways of understanding contemporary migrant practices across the multidisciplinary field of migration studies' (2010, 3–4). Migration and transnationalism are both complex interlinked fields and as such need to be approached by mixing different methods, theories and disciplines.

In this paper, I combine a mixed-method design applying both quantitative and qualitative methods as well as a mix of approaches drawing from anthropology, migration studies and social geography. My main focus was on the second generation but I also interviewed first-generation participants to get a dual insight into the issues under examination by comparing the ways in which members of the two generations experience transnationalism and social development in the era of the economic crisis. Definitions of the second generation are particularly important in comparative studies in fields like anthropology of education, anthropology of migration or sociolinguistics, based on quantitative data (Michail 2010b). Generally, there is no consensus amongst scholars in both the US as well as Europe regarding the definition of 'second generation' (Andall 2002, 390–1). King and Christou (2010, 106) suggest that the discussion about the second generation amongst scholars in the US 'is always framed with reference to an expected trajectory of assimilation into the host society', whilst more recent revisionist theories challenge the 'classical' assimilation trajectory; however, even the notion of alternative pathways or 'segmented assimilation' (Portes and Zhou 1993) still reflects 'the hegemonic assimilationist rhetoric characteristic of US immigration history and national self-identity'(King and Christou 2010, 106). A different approach to integration emphasizes the way in which immigrants negotiate their integration and participation in the wider community according to the political, social and economic environment of the host country (Levitt and Waters 2002). In Greece we do not observe much evidence of segmented assimilation during the process of integration of Albanian immigrants; rather, we find the existence of a segmentary model of identity construction within their own community where we observe social, economic, religious and ethnic variations (Chrysanthopoulou 2004; Michail 2010b). In the present study, I consider as belonging to the second generation the individuals of Albanian origin who were either born in Greece or came to Greece before the age of 12.

The study took place in 2010 and 2011. It was designed by the author and was carried out by the author and a group of graduate students from the Pre-Primary Education Department of the University of Western Macedonia who conducted interviews amongst second-generation informants. The student research team consisted of 15 individuals between the ages of 21–25 years old who participated in a research-methods seminar which formed part of their studies. The quantitative and qualitative analysis was carried out by the author and the results were presented and discussed at the end of the seminar.

Two research instruments were used: a questionnaire and in-depth interviews. The questionnaire was divided into two parts: the first consisted of several questions to be answered on a Likert scale, and the second included several open questions that took the form of semi-structured face-to-face-interviews. The respondents were contacted through the personal acquaintances of the members of the research team. In order to achieve as greater demographic coverage as possible, the research team members traced respondents to different parts of Greece, urban as well as rural (mainly Athens, Thessaloniki, Western Thrace, Epirus, the Ionian islands, the Dodecanese islands, the Peloponnese, Western and Central Macedonia and Thessaly). The questionnaire respondents ($N = 217$) are adult second-generation Albanian immigrants (18–32 years old) born to two Albanian parents. The respondents were either born in Greece ($N = 29$) or came to Greece before the age of 12 ($N = 188$). Amongst them there are 116 women and 101 men. The majority originate from southern Albania, mainly Korçë, Bilisht and Fier ($N = 80$), whilst 78 are from central Albania (Tirana, Elbasan), and a few from the northern areas (Shkodër, Peshkopi, Burrel, Bulqizë). Given that the respondent group was made up of second-generation Albanians, the language was Greek.

The in-depth interviews were conducted amongst a smaller group ($N=35$) of both first- and second-generation individuals – 20 men ($N=15$ first and $N=5$ second generation) and 15 women ($N=11$ first and $N=4$ second generation). Again, the majority originate from central and southern Albania. All these interviews were conducted by the author. The first-generation interviewees fulfilled the condition of having been in Greece for over eight years and knowing enough Greek to be able to carry out a conversation. The interviews were recorded and then transcribed. The Statistical Package for Social Sciences (SPSS) 19 for Windows was used to analyse the quantitative data that were collected via the first part of the questionnaire. From the responses to the open questions of the questionnaire and the in-depth interviews, I have selected the most reflective and revealing amongst the narratives of the themes I examine. After each narrative extract, I make a note for each participant in a parenthesis: 'M' for 'male' and 'F' for 'Female', then his/her age and the location of the interview. The study across generations provides a valuable insight into the issues of social integration and development, identity and return, as the findings reveal different identification processes, notions of home and belonging, as well as plans for the future articulated through the first- and second-generation participants' narratives.

Research questions and theoretical implications

The questionnaires provide feedback on demographic data and the second generation's attitudes on the issues under study whilst the interviews with members of both generations give a follow-up and more insight on the research questions. The two generations are examined comparatively in terms of their views and attitudes towards these perspectives. More specifically, I sought to address the following research questions:

- How far has the economic crisis affected the legal and social status and prestige of the immigrants and their families in Greece and Albania?
- How has the crisis affected immigrants' livelihoods, transnational households and family development projects? What are the material and psychological implications involved?
- What is the second-generation's positionality with regard to the issues of identity, belonging and return to the homeland?

Brettell (2003, 2; see also Massey et al. 1993) holds that through the migration process, where sending as well as host communities are transformed, a 'culture of migration' is created. Brettell proposes a typology of the migration process distinguishing a micro, meso and macro level of discussion. She states that 'an anthropological approach to migration should emphasize both structure and agency; it should look at macro-level contextual issues, micro-level strategies and decision-making, and the meso-level relational structures within which individuals operate' (2003, 7). At the micro level the focus of discussion is on the individual as the basic agent weighing the costs against the benefits involved in the decision to migrate (or not). Criticism on the part of some anthropologists has pointed out the social and cultural contexts that may shape and affect migration decision-making (Brettell 2003, 4). The meso level of discussion refers to the households and extended families and suggests that individuals do not act in isolation. My approach will remain at the micro-level strategies and decision-making and the meso-level relational structures within which Albanian immigrants operate. By situating individuals in relation to social groups, I can get an insight on the social and economic development process of transnational households (Faist 1997).

Albanian immigration to Greece has been fundamentally transnational in character (Michail 2009). Immigrants maintain their ties to their home country in various ways (paying regular visits, establishing transnational businesses, building houses, sending remittances), making 'home and host society a single arena of social action' (Margolis 1995, 29). Kearney (1995, 559) proposes that 'transnational communities commonly refer to migrant communities spanning two nations'. Along these lines Levitt (1998, 929) in her study of the Dominican-origin Mirafloreños in the US city of Boston points out that 'both migrants and non-migrants expressed a sense of consciously belonging to a group that spanned two settings'. If seen from a transnational perspective, migrants are not 'uprooted' 'but rather move freely back and forth across international borders and between different cultures and social systems' (Brettell 2008, 120). Changes to home communities are not only brought about through economic remittances but are also affected by social factors. Along these lines Levitt (1998, 926) suggests that 'social remittances are the ideas, behaviours, identities, and social capital that flow from receiving- to sending-country communities. The role that these resources play in promoting immigrant entrepreneurship, community and family formation, and political integration is widely acknowledged'. For anthropologists, the transnational approach reflects a more general move 'away from bounded units of analysis and localized community studies' (Brettell 2008, 121). The present study is set in a transnational framework where geographic and cultural borders are being transgressed by the migrants in the process of migration.

The economic crisis: social and economic development in transnational households

In the 1990s emigration to Greece was seen by many Albanians as a strategy for acquiring short-term financial capital, or as the 'key' to enter the 'door' of Italy (Hatziprokopiou 2003). The majority of the respondents in the survey ($N = 198$) mentioned economic and quality-of-life reasons ('better life', 'better conditions of living', 'security', 'more material goods', 'better education') as the main driving forces for their parents' decision to emigrate. Also, the majority amongst them ($N = 112$) declared that their parents came to Greece illegally, with no 'papers' and managed to regularize later. Regarding their parents' current residence, 163 respondents said that their parents still live in Greece, 19 that their parents had returned to Albania and the rest that they are considering the possibility of returning to their country of origin and for this reason they are trying to establish transnational business activities.

During the 2000s, Albanian migration in Greece matured into permanent family settlement (Michail 2010b). Greek governments, nevertheless, have been reluctant to accept immigration as a long-term feature of the modern Greek society, basically due to the 'ethnocultural definition of Greek nationality and citizenship' (Triandafyllidou and Veikou 2002, 191). The third decade – the 2010s – has started with the deepening of the ongoing economic crisis. The data provided by official Greek institutions such as the National Welfare Institute (IKA) and the Labour Force Survey clearly depict how the economic crisis has affected the immigrant population in general; unemployment and underemployment of third-country nationals and EU migrants has risen, surpassing that of natives for the first time in the last 20 years (Triandafyllidou 2012).

Moving now to some questionnaire results, the respondents, all belonging to the second generation, have a quite good educational background. This is mainly due to the fact that second-generation immigrants have been encouraged by their first-generation parents to achieve social mobility and integration in Greece through education (Table 1). Table 2 shows that, regarding their occupation, the majority worked in the private sector, mainly in the field of construction.

The survey data show that 65.3% of the respondents' parents had stable work before the crisis, and 29.2% of them had stable work right from the beginning. However, the economic crisis in Greece resulted in changes in the legal status of Albanian immigrants. Being unable to have stable work and welfare contributions, many immigrants cannot apply for the renewal of their residence permits. Work opportunities have become scarce and insecurity has brought most immigrants to a 'state of limbo'. One of our interviewees stated this clearly:

I have been in Greece for almost 20 years. I work as a construction worker. Two of my three children were born here. My sons are 21 and 19 and my daughter 16 years old. I opened this coffee-shop recently. The license of the shop is in the name of a Greek friend of mine who is the godfather of my youngest son. I could not open it myself, because my residence permit has recently expired and I can't renew it. There are no jobs. My elder son works in the coffee-shop and he has got insurance. If I put the youngest son in the shop I need 400 Euros per month for his insurance. As a family we are in a half legal, half illegal situation and that's because of the crisis. We were well settled before but now we don't know what to expect. There is neither back nor forth for us. Neither stay nor return. There is no way that our children will go to Albania. For us also it is going to be very difficult there. As difficult as it was when we first came here. It's too late for us to start all over again. (M, 48, Argos Orestiko)

The economic crisis seems to have resulted in a marked increase of antagonism over work availability amongst immigrants, leading to an escalation of tension between Albanians and Greeks affecting their collective well-being and their relationships. It has resulted in the revival of ethnic rivalry amongst the two communities. Albanian entrepreneurs in the construction sector compete with the Greek ones since the former have dropped the prices almost to half whilst the latter

Table 1. Educational background of the questionnaire respondents ($N = 217$).

Education	f	%
Primary	25	11.5
Junior High School	42	19.4
Senior High School	17	7.8
Technical/professional	90	41.5
University	43	19.8
Total	217	100.0

Source: Author's survey.

DEVELOPMENT IN SOUTH-EAST EUROPE AND THE BLACK SEA REGION

Table 2. Current employment of survey respondents ($N=217$).

Current occupation	f	%
Teacher	1	0.5
Public servant	1	0.5
Businessman	2	0.9
Private sector worker	86	39.6
Professional	7	3.2
Technician	27	12.4
Housewife	3	1.4
Unemployed	29	13.4
Student	61	28.1
Total	217	100.0

Source: Author's survey.

still keep prices high. Thus, at present, those Albanians who manage to undertake some construction projects are seen as the foreigners who 'steal the bread' from the locals at a period that 'there is not enough bread not even for the Greeks in Greece', to use the interviewees' words. A few female informants reported that, because of the crisis, personal and friendly relations have changed through envy and jealousy. One of the informants stated it as follows:

> The other Albanian women envy me very much because I have very good relations with the Greeks. They say: 'Why is it that V. has more than us and they do not prefer us?' Those who envy are those who want to make money and go back to Albania. [...] Before it wasn't like this, we had good relations with each other in general but now with the crisis and the scarcity of money jealousy came into the relations...who will earn more, who will manage to build a house. They want the money but they also want to show off who has good relations with the Greeks. If a Greek says a good word for someone [an Albanian], the others will find something bad to say. (F, 35, Argos Orestiko)

My ethnographic observations justify these views. It seems that antagonism amongst female immigrants is much more intense and more overtly expressed than amongst male ones. One of my key female informants pointed out that now, because of the crisis, very few women manage to earn as much as before and these are usually envied by others. She added that for this reason she avoids contacts with Albanians and socialises only with Greeks. In another case, three women married to three brothers do not communicate to each other information about the wages they take in order not to provoke each other's envy. Most of my male informants, on the other hand, seem to be more concerned about and supportive towards their non-relative compatriots and share with them information about work demand, than to their own relatives to whom they are more antagonistic. Men rely a lot on female labour but do not interfere with 'women's jobs'. Ethnic entrepreneurs are still powerful within their own community since they are the ones who decide whom they will hire to work for them.

Households have cut expenses to the minimum possible and most of our respondents and interviewees emphasized that they had also limited visits to Albania, remittances and any other expenses related to investments in the home country. One informant stated it as follows:

It's costly to go to Albania, it's not only the travel expenses but also the money you have to spend there and all the presents they expect you to bring from Greece. They are used to us carrying lots of things as presents all these years, and giving money. How can one go now empty-handed? It's a shame. So we don't go that often, only for very serious family reasons, like funerals, weddings. Even these if possible we avoid or we don't go the whole family all together like before, just one or two of us. (M, 35, Athens)

The migrant's prestige and status are measured by the generosity exhibited through remitting and through the treats and presents offered to one's family and relatives back in Albania. A successful migrant should also show his wealth and well-being through material achievements. 'Making' a house in Albania has been a way of maintaining connection with the homeland, 'a good reason for sending money to relatives who live in Albania, thus taking care of them' (Dalakoglou 2010, 766), whilst at the same time it keeps open the option of returning. Beyond this purpose, as Vullnetari and King observe, 'often migrants sacrifice a great deal while abroad — where they are often placed in the lower ranks of host societies performing the least qualified jobs and facing social exclusion — in order to retain or gain higher social status in origin communities' (2011, 127). Along these same lines, Hemming (2009) suggests that immigrants display wealth in order to counterbalance the reality of their life in the host country and create a new inflated persona in their own country that can give them status and prestige. The economic crisis has made such investments non-feasible and the flow of money, part of which was meant to support close relatives back home, has stopped or decreased. An interviewee refers to how the crisis has had an impact on real estate in Albania since many immigrants decided to return and invest their savings instead of using them to prolong their stay in Greece:

Most of the people I know have 'made' or bought a house in Albania. In my village now you cannot find a house to buy. They are all sold. I got mine for 6,000 Euros three years ago and I could sell it for 20,000 Euros now. There are people [Albanian immigrants] who had saved money here in Greece all these years and go back now because they don't have work. These have bought all the houses in my village but also in Fier and other places. And the prices have gone up. (M, 42, Kastoria)

The economic crisis might have precipitated the return of those who have completed their 'house-making project' and have to some extent satisfied the image of the successful emigrant. Those who have not managed to either make or finish off their house know that by going back they will not be able to save money and will be obliged to stay with their elderly parents or other close family, a return which does not add to the immigrant's prestige and status.

Our second-generation interviewees expressed some distance from their parents' 'house-making projects'. Many amongst them noted that they are not willing to follow their parents if they decide to return. One of them said:

Now we have our own house but still I don't like going as much, the village is too small and there isn't much to do. Besides I have no friends there. My cousins left the village when they grew up. [...] I don't know what I'll do if my parents decide to return. I definitely don't want to go to Albania. If Greece does not recover from the crisis I might leave for another country. Maybe to Italy to find my cousins. (M, 22, Kozani)

Status and prestige do not have the same significance for the first- and second-generation Albanian immigrants in Greece. First-generation individuals are more attached to the homeland and to social relations in Albania (with family, kin members and friends), and although they are interested in their immigrant legal and social status in Greece, they are also interested in constructing a positive image of the emigrant back home. The disruption of the construction of such an image as a result of the economic crisis has had both a practical as well as an emotional impact on them. The second generation, on the other hand, seems to be detached from this 'model' of the successful emigrant's self-realization. They perceive themselves through a different process, that of shifting adaptation and identification in a way different to that presented by Christou (2006) for the Greek-American second generation, where the 'imagining' of the ancestral homeland is framed by nostalgia, ethnic pride and national sentiments of belonging to a great nation with a great past. Of the second-generation respondents, 186 declared that the economic crisis has affected their life and plans for the future, but that they still want to remain in the host country. Greece, as the country where they were born, grew up and matured, constitutes for them a socio-spatial environment very different to the one they have experienced as 'temporary visitors' in Albania. Many are very critical in their judgments of the Albanian traditional customs and roles that they find too old-fashioned and incompatible with their standards as young people who have grown up in a European country.

Modernization theory suggests that migrants, through their savings and investments, become agents of change in their home communities. However, Brettell points out that studies on emigrant remittances, development and return demonstrate that such population movements often result in 'migration-dependent communities and the generation of further migration through the diffusion of consumerism' (2008, 119). I suggest that the Albanian second generation in Greece, unlike what Christou (2006, 1045) has described for the Greek-American second generation, does not form any dynamic distinct ethno-cultural group, and far less, an ethno-religious group characterized by 'a sense of peoplehood and ethnic consciousness'. The Albanian migrant identification process presents its own characteristics which will be analysed in the next section.

Identity and belonging through the looking glass of the crisis: the second generation

Anthropologists' interest in the study of identity, and by extension ethnicity, in migration studies has been mostly attracted by either the situational approach introduced by Barth (1969) or the instrumentalist approach that 'focuses on ethnicity as a political strategy that is pursued for pragmatic interests' (Brettell 2008, 131). Both these approaches emphasize the interactive understanding of culture, the shifting basis of self-identification and the creation and negotiation of boundaries that migration causes by bringing different populations into contact. As Gupta and Ferguson (1992, 7) suggest, when we refer to migrants, nomads and members of transnational business and professional elites there is no isomorphism of space, place and culture, and cultures are not 'discrete, object-like phenomena occupying discrete spaces'. They further state that 'people have undoubtedly always been more mobile and identities less fixed than the static and typologizing approaches of classical anthropology would suggest' (1992, 9). Binder and Tošić (2005, 607) have stated that: 'when groups migrate, they recompose in new settings, they reconstruct their histories and their ethnic concepts. In this way, the "ethnic" in the group context is endowed with a non-localized, harder to define quality, which ethnographic praxis needs to tune into'. And Christou (2006) suggests that migrant 'belonging works two ways, as an embodiment of psychological agonies as well as the political construction of collective symbols for identification'. She further points out that in the case of Greek-Americans, the second generation's 'belongingness and alienation, the idyllic and exilic spaces of return, resulting from interactions on both community and nation-state level [...] are acts of identification' (2006, 1045).

Along these lines, I suggest that Albanian second-generation immigrants also identify through manifesting their belongingness or alienation to either the host or the home country. I observed that there are significant differences in the process of identification amongst first- and second-generation Albanian immigrants influencing not only their integration and settlement experiences in the host country but also the perspective of 'remigration' or return. Notions of home and belonging for second-generation immigrants embody personal trajectories and aspirations built through an integration process chosen by their parents in the host country. The mode of incorporation and migration experiences of the first generation have had an impact on second-generation identity formation and led to a general trajectory of integration in the Greek community (Michail 2009). Vathi (2011, 121–2) suggests that parental and migrant identities are interwoven in the first generation and are in general experienced as the most important identity traits; the importance of the family and parenthood is emphasized in contrast to the insignificance of ethnic labels. Quite on the other side, in her study on Turkish returnees from Germany, Ruth Mandel (1989) implies the creation of a new ethnic category for the repatriated Turks, that of the *Alananyali,* or 'German-like'. Also, Caroline Brettell, in her study on the Portuguese emigrants in Brazil, suggests that her informants have stated that once a person emigrates he/she no longer has a country. For the Brazilians they are *Galegos* (Spanish Galician), a term generally applied to the Portuguese in Brazil, whilst for the Portuguese in Portugal they are 'Brasileiros' (2003, 18). Similarly, those emigrants in Greece when visiting Albania are usually named *'Grecos'* in a rather teasing way. Ethnic labels are articulated in various instances through my participants' narrations. The following statement is characteristic:

> In Albania I have nothing for myself. I'm used to the Greek ways and when I visit my relatives there [Albania] they call me *'Greco'*. Here *'Alvanós'*, there *'Greco'*. It is like having two identities but none makes me feel complete. (M, 20, Thessaloniki)

The quote above summarizes the main issue that the second generation faces in terms of self-identification. As Tseng (2002, 386) suggests, ethnic identification is 'dialogic, in the sense that it is created, preserved, reaffirmed, and even rejected through a continuous set of contrasts between one's own group and others'. The first-generation's efforts and expectations for integration into the Greek community by applying several strategies, as mentioned above, seem to have been effective mainly for their children. Parents see their return as a possible prospect for their lives, but their own children prefer to remain in Greece or re-migrate elsewhere. The following statement of a first-generation woman in a three-generation household is very characteristic:

> We have to consider returning because of the crisis. This time we take our parents back to Albania and leave our children behind in Greece. They don't want to come to

Albania. Our children are like Greeks. They don't feel Albania is like their home. They speak better Greek than Albanian. For them Greece is home. (F, 38, Argos Orestiko)

Hence the first- and the second-generation's routes seem to split. The issues of 'identity' and 'belonging' to either community arise as prominent for second-generation participants. Parents often express their anxiety in relation to their children's unwillingness to go to Albania. In the context of the economic crisis, they see the option of return open for them but not for their children.

Concluding remarks

The third decade of the Albanian immigration to Greece has started with the worsening of the economic crisis. Those amongst the Albanian immigrants who are still able to renew residence permits are seen to be in a state of limbo, not being able to judge whether it is better for them to stay in Greece or return to Albania. The image of the successful emigrant that the Albanians have been constructing over the years through material and social remittances has been disrupted and their status and prestige back home, and in the host country, is currently threatened. The crisis has affected not only their legal but also their social status; it has interrupted their life plans and social development in the host country and cancelled transnational household activities for most amongst them. My ethnographic observations show that the economic crisis has brought antagonism over work availability within the Albanian community, but also tension and rivalry between the Greek and the Albanian community, often expressed in ethnic terms mainly from the Greek part. Intimate and family relations have also been affected and female immigrants often suggest that personal and friendly relations have changed out of envy and jealousy expressed by Albanians at those amongst their compatriots who have been more successfully integrated in the host community and culture, thus exhibiting more resilience to the crisis.

I have suggested that the second generation does not seem to share with their parents the 'model' of the successful emigrant's self-realization, nor the same degree of connection with their home country. First- and second-generation Albanian immigrants exhibit different degrees of resilience to the crisis due to the fact that they have not followed the same process of integration. Although, as I have argued, they do not constitute a dynamic distinct ethno-cultural group with a sense of peoplehood and ethnic consciousness, they seem to perceive themselves through a diversified process of shifting adaptation and identification. The crisis has affected both generations but the second one's motivation to remain in Greece is stronger and their demonstration of resilience and persistence in staying in the host country is largely declared.

A new cycle seems to open for most of the immigrants' households. First-generation informants view the possibility for another family separation within their life cycle in the near future. This time first-generation and elderly people seem more likely to return to and regroup in Albania, whilst the second generation wants to either stay in Greece or re-migrate to another country. The migration cycle that opened for so many Albanian families over two decades ago is continued with its agents having to take decisions as important for their households as their initial one to emigrate to Greece.

Notes

1. National Statistical Service of Greece, Labour Force Survey, 4th trimester 2010, and Ministry of Interior, Valid Stay Permits, 31 December 2010.
2. See for instance Lapavitsas, notably his article in The Guardian: 'Costas Lapavitsas answers your questions on Greece and the eurozone crisis', http://www.guardian.co.uk/world/greek-election-blog-2012/2012/jun/13/costas-lapavitsas-greece-eurozone-crisis (accessed June 19, 2012); an interview given by Costas Lapavitsas for MONO 5, 7 April 2012 'There is no way-out for Greece without a cost', http://monopressgr.wordpress.com/2012/04/07/lapavitsas-mono/ (accessed June 19, 2012); also by the same author, 'Eurozone crisis: Beggar thyself and thy neighbour', RMF Occasional Report March 2010, http://researchonmoneyandfinance.org/media/reports/eurocrisis/fullreport.pdf (accessed June 22, 2012). See also Y. Varoufakis: for a compilation of some of his numerous articles, interviews and publications on the Economic Crisis see: http://gkdata.gr/category/βαρουφάκης/page/4/; also Varoufakis (2012).
3. See Institute for Education and Training of the Technical Chamber of Greece, 7 October 2011, http://www.iekemtee.gr/el/ (accessed June 19, 2012).
4. See Ta Nea [The News] 25 June 2012, http://www.tanea.gr/ellada/article/?aid=4638861 (accessed June 23, 2012); C. Lolis, Economic crisis and suicides in Greece, 01 March 2011, http://www.psychology-blog.gr/uncategorized/oikonomikh-krish-kai-autoktonies-sthn-ellada.html (accessed June 23, 2012).
5. See The Greek Construction Sector, B/2011, Half-Yearly Report, Issue 6, http://www.sate.gr/nea/press/FINAL_6–2011.pdf (accessed June 25, 2012).
6. Biannual Report Analysis of the Greek Tourism Activity Under the Auspices of the Academy of Tourism Research and Studies (ATEM) and The Tourism Research Unit of the Athens Institute for Education and Research (ATINER), 2, No. 4, July 2010, http://www.atiner.gr/atem/ATEM-01.pdf (accessed June 25, 2012).
7. See the article 'Immigrants on the threshold of migrating', Kathimerini, 22 August 2010, http://news.kathimerini.gr/4dcgi/_w_articles_ell_1_22/08/2010_412279 (accessed June 27, 2012).

References

Andall, J. 2002. Second-generation attitude? African-Italians in Milan. *Journal of Ethnic and Migration Studies* 28, no. 3: 389–407.

Barth, F. 1969. *Ethnic groups and boundaries: The social organization of culture and difference.* London: Allen and Unwin.

Binder, S., and J. Tošić. 2005. Refugees as a particular form of transnational migrations and social transformations: Socio-anthropological and gender aspects. *Current Sociology* 53, no. 4: 607–24.

Brettell, B.C. 2003. *Anthropology and migration: Essays on transnationalism, ethnicity and identity.* Walnut Creek, CA: Altamira Press.

Brettell, B.C. 2008. Theorizing migration in anthropology. In *Migration theory*, ed. C. Brettell and J. Hollifield, 113–59. London: Routledge.

Castles, S. 2004. The factors that make and unmake migration policies. *International Migration Review* 38, no. 3: 852–84.

Christou, A. 2006. Deciphering diaspora – translating transnationalism: Family dynamics, identity constructions and the legacy of 'home' in second-generation Greek-American return migration. *Ethnic and Racial Studies* 29, no. 6: 1040–56.

Chrysanthopoulou, V. 2004. The Albanian immigrants of Porto Rafti Mesogaias through their personal narratives. *Proceedings of the 11th Scientific Meeting of Southeast Attica*, November 11–14, in Spata, Greece.

Dalakoglou, D. 2010. Migrating-remitting-'building'-dwelling: House-making as 'proxy' presence in postsocialist Albania. *Journal of the Royal Anthropological Institute* 16, no. 4: 761–77.

Doja, A. 2000. The politics of religion in the reconstruction of identities: The Albanian situation. *Critique of Anthropology* 20, no. 4: 421–38.

Faist, T. 1997. The crucial meso level. In *International migration, immobility and development*, ed. T. Hammar, G. Brochmann, K. Tamas, and T. Faist, 187–217. New York, NY: Berg Publishers.

Gupta, A., and J. Ferguson. 1992. Beyond 'culture': Space, identity, and the politics of difference. *Cultural Anthropology* 7, no. 1: 6–23.

Hart, L.K. 1999. Culture, civilization and demarcation at the northwest borders of Greece. *American Ethnologist* 26, no. 1: 196–220.

Hatziprokopiou, P. 2003. Albanian immigrants in Thessaloniki Greece: Processes of economic and social incorporation. *Journal of Ethnic and Migration Studies* 29, no. 6: 1033–57.

Hemming, A. 2009. Migrant identity on display: The *xhiro* in Rrëshen. *Southeast European and Black Sea Studies* 9, no. 4: 575–88.

Kearney, M. 1995. The local and the global: The anthropology of globalization and transnationalism. *Annual Review of Anthropology* 24: 547–65.

King, R., and A. Christou. 2010. Cultural geographies of counter-diasporic migration: Perspectives from the study of second-generation 'returnees' to Greece. *Population, Space and Place* 16, no. 2: 103–19.

King, R., and J. Vullnetari. 2009. The intersections of gender and generation in Albanian migration, remittances and transnational care. *Geografiska Annaler: Series B, Human Geography* 91, no. 1: 19–38.

King, R., and J. Vullnetari. 2012. A population on the move: Migration and gender relations in Albania. *Cambridge Journal of Regions, Economy and Society* 5, no. 2: 207–20.

Kokkali, I. 2011. Strategies of integration and forms of adaptation of the Albanian immigrants in the Greek society: The case study of Thessaloniki. In *The social integration of immigrants in Greece*, ed. A. Moisidis and D. Papadopoulou, 211–65. Athens: Kritiki [in Greek].

Korovilas, J. 1999. The Albanian economy in transition: The role of remittances and pyramid investment schemes. *Post-Communist Economies* 11, no. 3: 399–415.

Levitt, P. 1998. Social remittances: Migration driven local-level forms of cultural diffusion. *International Migration Review* 32, no. 4: 926–48.

Levitt, P., and M.C. Waters, eds. 2002. *The changing face of home: The transnational lives of the second generation*. New York, NY: Russell Sage Foundation.

Mandel, R. 1989. Ethnicity and identity among guest workers in West Berlin. In *Conflict, migration and the expression of ethnicity*, ed. N.L. Gonzalez and C.S. McCommon, 60–74. Boulder, CO: Westview Press.

Margolis, M. 1995. Transnationalism and popular culture: The case of Brazilian immigrants in the United States. *Journal of Popular Culture* 29, no. 1: 29–41.

Massey, D., J. Arango, G. Hugo, A. Kouaouci, A. Pellegrino, and J.E. Taylor. 1993. Theories of international migration: A review and appraisal. *Population and Development Review* 20, no. 3: 699–751.

Michail, D. 2008a. Constructing identity among the Albanian immigrant students in Western Macedonia – Kastoria Greece. Paper presented at the 2008 Convention of the Association for the Study of Nationalities, April 10–12, Columbia University, New York.

Michail, D. 2008b. Albanian immigrants in Western Macedonia – Kastoria Greece: A challenge for rethinking Greek nationalism. In *Dynamics of national identity and transnational identities in the process of European integration*, ed. E. Marushiakova, 138–53. Newcastle-upon-Tyne: Cambridge Scholars Publishing.

Michail, D. 2009. Working here, investing here and there: Present economic practices, strategies of social inclusion and future plans for return amongst Albanian immigrants in a Greek-Albanian border town. *Southeast European and Black Sea Studies* 9, no. 4: 539–54.

Michail, D. 2010a. Boundary crossing and boundary maintenance among the Albanian immigrants and the Greek community in Argos Orestiko – Kastoria. In *Boundaries and folk culture in the Balkans*, ed. E. Avdikos, 347–70. Athens: Pedio [in Greek].

Michail, D. 2010b. Language maintenance/shift among second generation Albanian immigrants in Greece: Social integration and mobility. *Ethnologia* 14: 207–24.

Mintz, W.S. 1998. The localization of anthropological practice: From area studies to transnationalism. *Critique of Anthropology* 18, no. 1: 117–33.

National Centre for Social Research. 2003. Greece-Europe: Society-politics-values. Unpublished report.

Nitsiakos, B. 2003. Albanian immigrants in Greece: Identity and religious otherness. *Ethnologia* 10: 161–73.

Portes, A., and M. Zhou. 1993. The new second generation: Segmented assimilation and its variants. *Annals of the American Academy of Political and Social Science* 530: 74–96.

Pratsinakis, E. 2005. Aspirations and strategies of Albanian immigrants in Thessaloniki. *Journal of Southern Europe and the Balkans* 7, no. 2: 195–212.

Smith, E. 2009. 'Gap-fillers' or 'clan-destroyers': Transnational female solidarity towards kin in the region of Fier. *Southeast European and Black Sea Studies* 9, no. 4: 555–73.

Triandafyllidou, A. 2012. Albanian migrant livelihoods during the Greek crisis. Paper presented at the conference 'Albania's 100th anniversary as an independent state' organized by the Albanian Institute of International Studies, March 27, in Tirana, Albania.

Triandafyllidou, A., and M. Veikou. 2002. The hierarchy of Greekness: Ethnic and national identity considerations in Greek immigration policy. *Ethnicities* 2, no. 2: 189–208.

Tseng, Y.F. 2002. From 'us' to 'them': Diasporic linkages and identity politics. *Identities: Global Studies in Culture and Power* 9, no. 3: 383–404.

Varoufakis, Y. 2012. *The global minotaur*. Athens: Livanis [in Greek].

Vathi, Z. 2011. The children of Albanian migrants in Europe: Ethnic identity, transnational ties, and pathways of integration. PhD diss., University of Sussex.

Vertovec, S. 2010. Introduction: New directions in the anthropology of migration and multiculturalism. In *Anthropology of migration and multiculturalism*, ed. S. Vertovec, 1–17. New York, NY: Routledge.

Vullnetari, J. 2007. Albanian migration and development: State of the art review. IMISCOE Working Paper 18. Amsterdam: International Migration, Integration and Social Cohesion in Europe (IMISCOE).

Vullnetari, J., and R. King. 2011. *Remittances, gender and development*. London: I.B. Tauris.

Zachou C., and E. Kalerante. 2009. Intergenerational representations of the self of the Albanian female immigrants: A phenomenological approach. In *Minority and migrant experiences: Experiencing the 'culture of the state'*, ed. F. Tsimpiridou, 193–225. Athens: Kritiki [in Greek].

Transnational actors in national contexts: migrant organizations in Greece in comparative perspective

Jennifer Clarke

School of Social Policy, Sociology and Social Research, University of Kent, Canterbury, UK

As migrant organizations are increasingly viewed as transnational actors, there is a risk of overlooking the ongoing relevance of national contexts in shaping their role. The singular context for migrant incorporation in Greece, a country which experienced the largest proportional increase in immigration in the EU between 1990 and 2005, makes a salient case study for an exploration of this issue. This paper aims to examine how national contexts affect migrant organizations as transnational actors. It does this by reviewing the growth of migrant organizations in Greece and then comparing them and their opportunity structures in this country with those in the contrasting environments of the UK and the Netherlands.

Migrant organizations as transnational actors: issues and challenges

Migrant organizations[1] have been the subject of sustained interest for social scientists for almost a century (Gold 1992). They are widely considered to play an important role in migrants' lives, despite their limitations such as problems of representation, and divisions both within and between organizations (Griffiths, Sigona, and Zetter 2005; Temple and Moran 2006). With the advent of the 'transnational turn' in migration studies (Glick Schiller, Basch, and Szanton Blanc 1995; Portes, Guarnizo, and Landolt 1999; Vertovec 1999), migrant organizations have increasingly been categorized as 'transnational actors'. In fact, the role of migrant organizations in 'maintaining and strengthening links with the society of the homeland' has long been acknowledged (Rex and Josephides 1987, 19), but this role has come more sharply into focus as a result of two factors: an increased emphasis on migrant transnationalism and the renewed emphasis on the importance of 'grassroots' participation in development (Faist 2008; Morales and Jorba 2010; Portes, Escobar, and Radford 2007). Drawing on the earlier insights of Faist (1998, 214), Morales and Jorba (2010, 269) have argued that:

> Civil society actors – and, in particular, migrants' organisations – should [...] be privileged agents in transnational practices because they provide the networks and infrastructure to facilitate and sustain various forms of transnational engagement by individuals and communities.

These forms of transnational engagement are diverse. Most fundamentally, they provide 'transnational social spaces' (Faist 2008) for the development and maintenance of a transnational identity amongst migrants. For example, Vertovec argues that 'diaspora consciousness' is especially witnessed in 'the ever more effective and organized expressions of group concerns' (1997, 283), and Sardinha similarly describes how 'double identity worlds' are promoted by migrant organizations, *inter alia* through social and cultural activities (2009, 276). Linked to this, migrant organizations also mobilize a range of transnational resources, including 'financial capital such as money in the form of remittances and/or investments; knowledge and professional experience; and political ideas, such as ideas on forms of government, rights and responsibilities, and democracy' (Faist 2008, 27). Recognition of their ability to mobilize such resources has also resulted in migrant organizations being cast as 'transnational development agents' (Faist 2008).

One of the issues that has emerged from these analyses is that too narrow a focus on transnationalism runs the risk of overlooking the role of national contexts in shaping the development of migrant organizations (Faist 2008, 36). As Faist (2008, 36) argues: 'More attention needs to be paid to how states structure transnational social spaces'. The rich extant literature on migrant organizations in various parts of the globe (Moya 2005), offers relatively few insights in this respect because – with some important exceptions detailed later in this paper – the majority of this scholarship comprises single-country studies. As Wimmer and Glick Schiller note (2002), such a narrow one-country focus makes it difficult to avoid taking national context discourses for granted. Therefore, in order to understand how migrant organizations are affected by the different national contexts in which they are located, a broader lens is required. In other words, rather than treat migrant organizations 'as a naturally occurring part of the policy landscape', it is necessary to contextualize their role and function, by using a comparative framework (Griffiths, Sigona, and Zetter 2005, 205). The present paper does just that by drawing on my doctoral research on migrant organizations in three contrasting national contexts – Greece, the UK and the Netherlands.

Though relatively few in number, the studies that take a comparative approach to the analysis of migrant organizations offer many valuable insights into these issues (e.g. Jenkins 1988; Koopmans et al. 2005; Rex 1987). In particular, Koopmans et al. (2005) contribute to a growing body of literature which demonstrates the relevance of the 'opportunity structures' approach, initially developed in social movements theory, to research on migrant organizations. Although this literature has mainly focused on comparing the political role of migrant organizations, the approach can be adapted, bearing in mind that 'opportunity structures can vary enormously from one issue field to another' (Koopmans et al. 2005, 19). Adapting the five 'levels' of opportunities conceptualized by Koopmans et al. (2005) to the subject in question, I propose that migrant organizations might be particularly affected by the following inter-related dimensions of the national context in which they are situated:

- *national cleavage structure*: fundamental ideas relating to nationality and citizenship;
- *institutional structures*: the nature of institutions relating to immigration and integration, and the nature of the wider third sector and its infrastructure;
- *policy*: approaches to immigrant incorporation, civil society development, and local and international development;

- *political alliances*: the dynamics between parties with a positive, neutral, or negative stance towards immigration and immigrants;
- *discursive opportunities*: the way in which migrants and their organizations are presented in public discourse and in the media.

These dimensions will be used to structure the comparison of the three national contexts below.

Methodology

The paper draws on a total of 48 semi-structured interviews (comprising part of my doctoral research) with representatives of a purposive sample of individual and umbrella migrant organizations and other key informants, carried out in Greece, the UK and the Netherlands between February 2011 and September 2012. The sample was selected in order to include refugee/asylum seeker and more general migrant organizations representing different communities, old and new organizations, and organizations with varying resource levels in each of the countries, and to offer insights into the respective opportunity structures. To gain the widest insights possible within the scope of the project, an emphasis was placed on interviewing representatives of umbrella organizations and second-tier agencies with knowledge of many migrant organizations. In Greece, the 15 respondents comprised: four representatives of two umbrella migrant organizations representing over 40 member organizations, the directors of four individual migrant organizations in Athens, representatives of an NGO working with refugees, an international organization working with migrants, an NGO network, a donor foundation, a local authority, a state school and an academic expert, Mary Leontsini. In the Netherlands, 10 respondents were interviewed, including representatives of two umbrella migrants' organizations representing over 90 members, representatives of four individual migrant organizations, representatives of an agency working with refugees, a second-tier agency with links with over one thousand migrant organizations, an official migrant representative body and an academic expert, Sander Kramer. In the UK, interviews were conducted with a representative of an umbrella migrant organization representing 25 member organizations, 19 representatives of 14 individual migrant organizations, representatives of two second-tier agencies with links with at least 200 migrant organizations, a large agency working with migrants, and a state school.

The interview questions explored migrant organizations' history, institutional nature, resources, sources of funding and other forms of support, activities, institutional links, future priorities, needs and problems and challenges faced. All interviews were conducted in English and/or Greek, in which latter case the transcriptions were translated into English by the author; it is recognized that this may have affected expression and comprehension (Temple and Edwards 2002), although no significant communication barriers were perceived. The interpretation was facilitated by the use of qualitative data analysis software. My previous practitioner experience working with migrant organizations was advantageous in terms of promoting the credibility of the research with potential respondents, but also brought a risk of preconceptions about the issues to be researched; this is a limitation I aimed to manage through reflexivity and triangulation throughout the research process.

The analysis is further informed by secondary data. I drew in particular on the most comprehensive surveys of migrant organizations available in each of the three countries to date: Harokopio University's (2009) survey of over 150 organizations working with immigrants, identified in a field study across all of Greece's major cities; Van Heelsum's (2004) analysis of around 4000 migrant organizations in the Netherlands, as well as Nijenhuis and Zoomer's smaller but more in-depth survey of 60 migrant organizations in the Netherlands (2012); and the nationwide survey of over 300 refugee organizations in England conducted by Refugee Council and Refugee Action (2007). All participating individuals and organizations remain anonymous; their consent to participate was secured on that basis. Due to logistical reasons, this research does not provide the cross-national data required for a full-scale comparative study. Nonetheless, its qualitative focus enables the emergence of a number of key insights.

The growth of the migrant organization sector in Greece

Compared to both the UK and the Netherlands, Greece has a relatively short history as an immigration country. Flows of immigrants grew sharply in the 1990s, with Greece experiencing the largest proportional increase in immigration in the EU between 1990 and 2005 (IOM 2008). Although they have been growing rapidly, migrant organizations in Greece have received relatively little attention to date (see Gropas and Triandafyllidou 2005; 2009; Leontsini 2010).[2] In the most comprehensive survey to date, Athens' Harokopio University (2009) identifies over 150 organizations working with migrants, including Greek NGOs. For the comparative purposes of my study and in line with the definition provided at the start of this paper, I classify 128 of these as migrant organizations.[3] Using their year of registration as an indicator, a tenfold increase in the number of migrant organizations during the period 1995–2009 can be observed (Figure 1). Although there is some variation in organizational proliferation between different ethnic and national groups (an issue which is beyond the scope of this paper), the pattern observed broadly supports the findings of others who have identified size of immigrant population as a factor influencing the number of migrant organizations (Hein 1997).

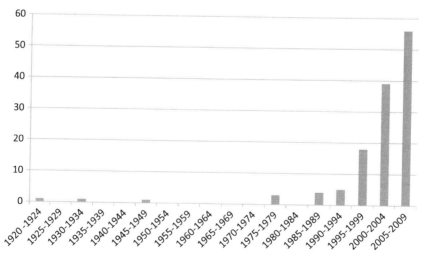

Figure 1. Year of establishment of migrant organizations in Greece.
Source: My analysis of data from Harokopio University (2009) study.

By 2009, these organizations represented migrants from at least 40 countries, as well as from other ethnic groups including Assyrians and Kurds. Most organizations are active in a number of different areas, with practical support and cultural activities being the most important (Figure 2).

A further significant development in recent years has been the establishment or consolidation of several umbrella migrant organizations, which are playing an increasing role in supporting and building the capacity of individual organizations. Migrant organizations are thus now seen as constituting a significant part of a 'rich, active, and increasingly vocal civil society' in Greece (Gropas and Triandafyllidou 2009, 4).

Comparing migrant organizations in Greece, the UK and the Netherlands
Patterns of proliferation

It would be inaccurate to try to draw a precise comparison of the proliferation of migrant organizations across different countries, because of incomplete information, and the different ways of defining migrants and organizations – problems which become more complex over time (Schrover and Vermeulen 2005). It is safe, however, to suggest that by 2012 there are still far fewer migrant organizations in Greece than in either the UK or the Netherlands. Migrant organizations in Greece are also more densely concentrated around the capital than in either the UK or the Netherlands, with approximately 75% of organizations registered in the greater Athens area (Harokopio University 2009). Whilst it is true that the Greek population is more highly clustered (to the tune of about 40%) around the capital city than is the case for the UK or the Netherlands, the degree of concentration of migrant organizations in and around Athens is still disproportionate. In the Netherlands, the Union of Refugee Organizations (VON) records 400 member organizations across the country by 2012, whilst Van Heelsum identified around 4000 broadly defined

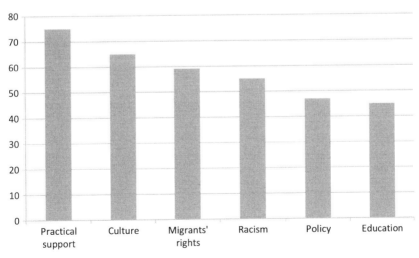

Figure 2. Areas of activity of migrant organizations in Greece (% organizations active in each area of activity).
Source: My analysis of data from Harokopio University (2009) study.

migrant organizations in 2004. In the UK, there are estimated to be around 1000 first-generation 'refugee and migrant community organizations', of which approximately half are thought to be in the London region (Evelyn Oldfield Unit 2010; Refugee Council and Refugee Action 2007), and between 5000 and 11,000 'Black and Minority Ethnic (BME) organizations'[4] more broadly defined (Voice4Change 2007). However, the current proliferation pattern in Greece may not be so dissimilar to the situation in the UK just two decades ago, when Rutter (1994) was able to identify only 47 refugee organizations across the UK, over 90% of which were London-based.

Resources and institutional development

Across all three countries in the study, the majority of migrant organizations are volunteer-based and have typically low levels of income. In both the UK and the Netherlands, existing data indicate that migrant organizations have a lower level of income compared to other voluntary sector organizations (de Bruyn 2008; National Equality Partnership 2008). The same pattern appears to be the case in Greece as well, given that less than 5% of migrant organizations surveyed by Harokopio University (2009) reported having staff, whilst only a small minority had their own premises (either rented or owned). There is, however, a significant difference in terms of the sources of funding between organizations in the three countries. In Greece, more than half of the organizations (59%) rely exclusively on their members for income, either through fees or donations, whilst less than 5% of organizations had received any funding from a governmental or other public body (my analysis of Harokopio University 2009 data). Respondents in my own research sample referred to only one migrant organization which had received external grant funding. Other sources of funding mentioned included donations from private individuals and income generating activities such as bazaars, advertising within community newspapers and renting out hall space.

By contrast, migrant organizations in the UK tend to have multiple sources of funding, with grants from charitable trusts and local government bodies often constituting a larger proportion of an organization's income than membership fees (MODA 2010). Similarly, in the Netherlands, Nijenhuis and Zoomer's survey of 60 migrant organizations found that a quarter of them had received support from local government and nearly half from foundations or NGOs (2012, 13).

This difference in funding patterns has implications for the forms of institutional development of migrant organizations. Thus, organizations that rely primarily on their own community for resources tend to be 'grassroots' entities that operate according to downwards accountability, i.e. from their management to their general members. Their activities correspond to the priorities of the community only and are often informal, ad hoc and volunteer-run. In contrast, organizations that receive external funding tend to become 'professionalized', necessarily operating according to principles of 'upwards accountability', meaning that activities must correspond with the priorities of the external funders. Moreover, in order to meet external funding criteria, such as compliance with insurance and health and safety regulations, activities are likely to be formally organized and may be run by paid, qualified staff. The high levels of external funding suggest that both in the UK and in the Netherlands, a significant proportion of organizations are 'professionalized'; in

Greece, by contrast, the vast majority of organizations would be characterized as 'grassroots' organizations:

> We have tried [to fund migrant organizations]. But it's very difficult to find immigrant organizations that have the capacity to write a proposal, that know how to manage a project. (Representative of a Greek donor foundation, Athens)

Areas of activity

Social and cultural activities

Social and cultural activities constitute important areas of activity for migrant organizations in all three countries (Refugee Council and Refugee Action 2007; Van Heelsum 2004). They include the celebration of national days, religious festivals and other special dates; mother-tongue classes; and musical or literary events. These activities are broadly considered as helping migrants to support a 'dual identification' with both country of origin and country of settlement (Sardinha 2009, 276). The following quotes are quite illustrative in this case:

> We always join in the African Cultural Festival – with food, and with music. (Representative of migrant organization, Athens)

> Last month there was a dinner for Women's Day. The women they all prepare some food, and they all get together in a large apartment near here. (Representative of umbrella migrant organization, Athens)

> Every year we have a party to cut the New Year cake – it's a Greek tradition. (Representative of umbrella migrant organization, Athens)

Practical support

Whilst there is a broad similarity between organizations across the three countries in the fact that many provide practical support and services for migrants such as translation and signposting, there are also some significant differences in this area to highlight. In Greece, many migrant organizations play an important role in meeting fundamental needs such as food and accommodation. The following quote from a representative of a refugee organization in Athens is an example of this:

> We have around 20 [migrants] staying here now. We give first to people with greater needs, many children, or [those with] some kind of psychological problems. It's a struggle – to pay the rent, to feed everyone.

Refugee organizations in particular also devote much of their capacity to physically accompanying and assisting individuals with their efforts to go through the asylum process, in which some individuals had been waiting for up to seven years (see also Cabot 2012). For example:

> Most of our time is taken up dealing with individual cases [...] Yesterday I had to go to [the police department dealing with asylum applications] because the police had confiscated the pink [temporary permit] cards of seven people. When I turned up speaking Greek and English, the cards were returned. (Representative of refugee organization, Athens)

In the UK, direct involvement in meeting fundamental needs or assistance with the asylum process is rarer. Although cuts in provision to asylum seekers were made throughout the 2000s, most basic needs are met by the state, and as the director of one migrant organization in Leeds stated, since the introduction of the 'New Asylum Model'[5] in 2007:

> people are getting (asylum) decisions really quickly – asylum seekers don't have chance to get to organizations like us anymore.

Those organizations that still help new arrivals tend to play an advisory role, sign-posting rather than actually providing settlement services. In the Netherlands, by contrast, migrant organizations rarely come into contact with asylum seekers, because, as the policy officer of a large refugee NGO pointed out, 'they [organizations] don't go to reception centres' where asylum seekers are held; their activities are, therefore, aimed at settled migrants only.

Education and training

There is also a notable distinction regarding the involvement of migrant organizations in education and training activities. In the survey of Harokopio University (2009), a significant proportion of migrant organizations in Greece indicate that they are involved in education activities of some kind (Figure 2). My interviews indicate that educational activities are mainly restricted to informal, volunteer-taught mother-tongue and Greek language classes, illustrated by the two speakers below:

> Last year an NGO sent us volunteer teachers. We last had 2 classes of 20, each 3 times per week. (Chair of migrant organization, Athens)

> Many volunteers are willing to help teach Greek, students are always willing to help. (Chair of umbrella migrant organization, Athens)

In the UK, migrant organization involvement in education and training is more wide-ranging, including both informal and accredited English language classes, schooling support, and training in a range of vocational skills. In the Netherlands, however, the involvement of individual migrant organizations in providing any education and training activities is very rare. When asked about education and training activities, the only example that representatives of two separate umbrella organizations were able to cite was training related to community awareness-raising on the issue of female genital mutilation (FGM).

Campaigning and lobbying

Data from the survey by Harokopio University (2009) indicate that a large proportion of migrant organizations in Greece consider themselves to be involved with campaigning and lobbying related to immigrants' rights and policymaking (Figure 2). The more detailed data from the semi-structured interviews in this study with representatives of umbrella and individual migrant organizations who had knowledge of a significant proportion of migrant organizations in Greece, suggests that only a minority of the better-established organizations are actively involved in these areas, often in partnership with a small core of sympathetic NGOs, academics and political figures; a large number of other organizations are involved more passively, for example as signatories of declarations. Amongst the key themes of concern are immigrant official representation vis-à-vis authorities, immigrant workers' rights, asylum seekers' rights and citizenship for the second generation:

> Our main aim is to communicate with the government, and second to provide social support. We have met with the Minister of Interior and other high officials. We lobbied the UNHCR and the EU to suspend the Dublin convention. I feel we have made progress in that respect now and several countries have stopped returning [asylum seekers] to Greece. (Chair of umbrella migrant organization, Athens)

> The key aim of the organization is to be officially recognized [as a representative body]. At the moment migrants have no official representative body. (Chair of umbrella migrant organization, Athens)

Although the scale of campaigning and lobbying activity of migrant organizations is inevitably constricted by limited resources, it is notable that their work is seen by Gropas and Triandafyllidou (2009, 5) to be influencing wider Greek civil society active in these areas:

> This growth and increased activity among the migrant population has developed in parallel to a phase of maturation of Greek civil society as well and these two parallel processes have fed into one another and in many cases strengthened one another too – particularly in the human rights and anti-discrimination field.

By contrast, both in the UK and in the Netherlands, migrant organizations are considered to be lagging behind other areas of civil society in terms of campaigning and policy influence (de Bruyn 2008; Phillimore and Goodson 2010).

Links with countries of origin

In Greece, as in the UK and the Netherlands, many migrant organizations maintain close contact with countries of origin. Although their aims have since broadened, some organizations had originally been established in order to help individuals to migrate, for example being founded as students' or workers' associations which *inter alia* facilitated access to information about available opportunities to potential migrants:

> I came over as a student. I wanted to help my compatriots to come to have the same opportunities that I had here. (Chair of migrant organization, Athens)

Organizations also help individuals to return:

> Now I am asking the community to help me with the cost of returning home. I have money for the fare, but I need help with shipping all my books and belongings after fifteen years here. I have helped others all these years, now it is my turn. (Board member of migrant organization, Athens)

One organization had originally been established to help to repatriate deceased bodies from Greece to the country of origin, Pakistan. Many migrant organizations in Greece function as a focal point for the sharing of information between countries of origin and the country of settlement, with this role being facilitated by blogs, social networking sites and the ability to post online videos, for example of organization meetings, as well as printed newsletters and newspapers. Many organizations also help collect and send remittances, for example:

> Just last week we sent €1500 to help a member's mother who has cancer, to help pay for treatment expenses. (Chair of migrant organization, Athens)

However, none of the migrant organizations I spoke with in Greece referred to any involvement in formal development projects in countries of origin. This is also reflected in the survey by Harokopio University (2009), in which less than 5% of migrant organizations declared that they work internationally. This was in marked contrast to the situation in the other two countries. In the UK, a specialist migrant organization development officer estimated that approximately half of the organizations she was working with had recent, current or planned involvement in international development projects. Likewise in the Netherlands, the representative of a second-tier organization with links with many migrant organizations stated that:

> I can't think of a single one [migrant organization] that doesn't have a project or some link in their homeland country, even if is only remittances.

A comparative analysis of the opportunity structures for migrant organizations

The comparison of migrant organizations across the three countries reveals similarities as well as differences. A comparative analysis of the levels of the respective opportunity structures as set out by Koopmans et al. (2005) will help to cast light on the role of the national contexts in producing these patterns.

National 'cleavage structure'

National identity and ideas of citizenship in Greece are linked to its short and turbulent history as a modern state. This legacy is reflected in ideas of citizenship that, although gradually shifting, are closely linked with Greek Orthodoxy (Triandafyllidou and Veikou 2002), and a national identity in which ethnic and cultural minority issues are associated with insecurities about territorial integrity (Kyriakou 2009). The predominantly *jus sanguinis* citizenship regime is one of the most restrictive in the EU (Howard 2010), and non-EU immigrants face an 'exclusionary' or 'guest-worker' approach to incorporation (Entzinger 2000, 100; Soysal 1994, 17–22). This exclusionary approach appears to have a direct impact on the activities of migrant organizations, in terms of the relatively higher levels of involvement in immigrants' and human rights issues and policy activism than in either the UK or the Netherlands. Both these countries have comparatively liberal citizenship regimes (Howard 2010), though in the UK the multicultural model has been a predominant influence on ideas of citizenship over the past half century, whereas in the Netherlands there has been a greater emphasis on cultural integration (Bruquetas-Calleho et al. 2007).

Institutional structures

The exclusionary context in Greece can be seen as influencing the various other levels of the opportunity structure for migrant organizations there. For example, at the level of institutional structures there is no formal national representative or consultative body for immigrants in Greece. This has, therefore, been a focus of campaigning by migrant organizations. In contrast, such representation issues were not mentioned as a priority by organizations either in the Netherlands or the UK, both of which have developed distinct – although not unproblematic – approaches towards immigrant and minority representation (Soysal 1994). As a strategy for dealing with the lack of formal inclusion in policymaking, however, it has been noted that in Greece an 'informal network and affiliation facilitates a flow of information between the immigrant communities and the political elites' (Gropas and Triandafyllidou 2005, 17).

Illustrating this point, the director of a long-established organization took a call from a former minister during the interview. He later explained that the minister had been his university supervisor and that 'he is proud of me and I am proud of him'. Another organization representative described how in their organization they were able to renew members' work permits very quickly because 'we know all the people, we've done it so many times'. This reliance on informal contacts, which has been identified as a characteristic of the wider Greek civil society (Sotiropoulos 2004), puts new migrant communities, including recent refugee arrivals from Africa and the Middle East, at a considerable disadvantage.

A further significant factor at this level of opportunities is that Greece's institutions for managing immigration have not yet adapted to the increased migration flows. In particular, the asylum system is currently near to non-functional (Council of Europe 2010). It is in this context that many migrant organizations in Greece devote most of their resources to meeting basic needs of newcomers, a context which represents the extreme version of what Watters and Hossain (2008) identify as a 'Southern' approach to asylum in which the third sector plays a key role. By contrast, third-sector organizations bear less of the burden of meeting basic needs in the UK, where there is a decentralized 'Western' approach to asylum, and are barely involved in the highly state-centric 'Northern' approach applied in the Netherlands (Watters and Hossain 2008).

Finally on this point, there is the nature of the wider third sector and its corresponding infrastructure. In the UK and, to a lesser extent, the Netherlands, there is a third-sector support structure potentially accessible even for small migrant organizations, including targeted 'grassroots' funding and capacity building support. In Greece, the third sector as a whole is less developed and there are fewer funding opportunities and a lack of infrastructure support (Gropas and Triandafyllidou 2005). As a result, it is very rare for migrant organizations to access external funding. This inevitably limits the range of activities that they are able to undertake, but also affects the form of institutional development of organizations, as they have little incentive to evolve into 'professionalized' organizations.

Policy

Moving now to Koopman et al.'s (2005) third level of opportunities, one factor which appears to have a particularly profound impact on migrant organizations is the approach to immigrant dispersal and settlement. It is indicative that migrant organizations proliferated across the UK following the introduction of a dispersal policy for asylum seekers in 1999 (Griffiths, Sigona, and Zetter 2005). Similarly in the Netherlands, dispersal policies have been noted as one reason for the high number of very small migrant organizations there (Van Heelsum 2004). In Greece, in the absence of a dispersal policy, the relative concentration of immigrants and their organizations in the Athens area is considerably higher than that of the native Greek population. Related to this, many immigrant communities have formed only a single organization, restricting organizational proliferation.

Immigrants are evidently affected not just by migration and integration policies, but by the whole spectrum of policymaking, which may shape migrant organizations in different ways, depending in part on the status granted to organizations by policymakers. In Greece, it has been noted that immigrant integration policy is relatively underdeveloped, thus limiting the potential role for migrant organization involvement in this area (Gropas and Triandafyllidou 2005). The recent establishment of municipal 'Migrant Integration Councils'[6] has, however, been seen by some migrant organizations as a first opportunity to become more actively involved in local-level policymaking. Migrant organizations are rarely involved in wider government initiatives, in contrast to the country's church organizations and NGOs, some of which – at least until recently – received public funding for work related to areas such as public health and poverty. The general lack of involvement of migrant organizations in Greek government policies may be related to the exclusionary approach to immigrant incorporation and/ or may reflect their very limited capacity. Many organizations certainly feel that they are not trusted by authorities, as illustrated by the following comment:

> We are trying to give the main message to the government that we are refugees, not terrorists. (Representative of umbrella migrant organization, Athens)

In the UK, at least until recently, the importance of multicultural principles across a wide range of policymaking opened up opportunities for migrant and other minority organizations to become involved as partners in state service provision across a range of areas. These included, amongst others, the provision of housing, and formal education and training through partnerships with colleges and schools. In the Netherlands, by contrast, since the shift away from a 'Minorities Policy' in the 1990s, integration policy has had a strong emphasis on cultural integration (Bruquetas-Calleho et al. 2007, 20), narrowing the scope of engagement with migrant organizations. The representative of an umbrella organization stated that 'they [the state] mainly only want to fund activities about integration'.

Unlike in both the UK and the Netherlands, there have been no 'co-development' policies to involve migrant organizations in Greece's fledgling international development role. This is consistent with the exclusion of migrant organizations from other policy areas, but also reflects a limited involvement of wider civil society in Greece's international development policies (Gropas 2008).

Political alliances

At the level of political alliances, one significant factor affecting migrant organizations in Greece has been the longstanding presence of anti-immigrant nationalism in national politics, recently exacerbated by the economic crisis and the decline of centrally positioned parties. This has had a tangible impact on migrant organizations, some of which have suffered violent attacks, whilst others have reported losing long-term Greek volunteers and supporters of their work due to fears of becoming targets of far-right violence:

> Volunteers' parents don't let them come anymore – they're afraid they'll get beaten up. (Representative of migrant umbrella organization, Athens)

Anti-immigrant parties have also played a significant role in Dutch politics since the 2000s (Bruquetas-Calleho et al. 2007), but appeared to be perceived differently by the respondents in my sample: they linked this to reduced funding for immigrant organizations, but not reduced volunteer support, perhaps because the non-immigrant population did not feel threatened in the same way as was the case in Greece.

However, a further aspect of political alliances affecting migrant organizations in Greece is the presence of multiple pro-immigrant left-wing parties, trade unions, and anti-racist groups which have mobilized in support of immigrants. These parties and groups are frequently partners in the aforementioned lobbying and campaigning activities for immigrants' rights. It is indicative that on the wall of one migrant organization there is a photograph of its representatives at a trade union event entitled 'The common struggle of Greeks and immigrants against the plutocracy and its parties'. It is difficult to imagine such outspoken political support for immigrants in either the UK or the Netherlands.

Public discourse

Turning finally to the last level of opportunities (Koopmans et al. 2005), the picture is similarly mixed, with migration and integration being a contentious and divisive issue in the Greek public. In European surveys, Greeks have consistently expressed higher levels of resistance to immigrants than either the UK or the Netherlands (Spencer and Cooper 2006). Yet, despite – or perhaps because – of this, posters, rallies and events decrying racism and proclaiming solidarity with immigrants are a more familiar sight in Athens than in either London or Amsterdam (Figure 3). A number of migrant organizations in Greece use such opportunities to participate in the public discourse, as an alternative to the mainstream media, where opportunities for the representation of immigrants' views are limited (Gropas and Triandafyllidou 2005) and reporting is often negative (e.g. Kapllani and Mai 2005). For example:

> Next month there is the Anti-Racism Festival. It's a good event, good to meet people there. (Chair of migrant organization, Athens)

Whilst negative reporting of migrants in the media has also been a longstanding issue in both the Netherlands and the UK (Bennett et al. 2011, 10), there are also opportunities for migrant organizations to engage with the media in these countries, given that Dutch-speaking print media were found to include relatively frequent and neutral quotations from migrant spokespersons and local London media coverage of migrant issues was found to be wide-ranging and frequently sympathetic (Bennett et al. 2011, 16, 20).

Figure 3. Pro-immigrant public discourse: Underneath the signpost for the Municipality of Athens, a poster reads 'Whoever raises a hand against immigrants should have it cut off. We must protect our decency and order!'.

The effects of national contexts on migrant organizations and their transnational engagement

The comparison of the profile of migrant organizations and their respective opportunity structures across three contrasting contexts enables some observations to be made regarding the role of national contexts on migrant organizations and their transnational engagement.

Most fundamentally, it is evident that national contexts affect the degree of proliferation of migrant organizations. As well as the size of immigrant populations, approaches to immigrant dispersal have an important effect on the numbers of migrant organizations established. Given that the global significance of migrant organizations as transnational development actors is partly related to the aggregate quantity of such organizations (Portes, Escobar, and Radford 2007, 276), this is an important area of state influence.

The national context also appears to influence the forms of institutional development of migrant organizations, depending on the incentives offered for organizations to become 'professionalized'. This has important implications, given that the role of self-funded 'grassroots' migrant organizations as transnational actors is far less open to the influence of states and other external actors than that of externally-funded 'professionalized' migrant organizations, as suggested by the following statements:

> The local government likes to keep us at a certain capacity but not more. They don't want us to be too powerful. (Representative of a state-funded migrant organization in the Netherlands)

We haven't received a single cent from the government. We wouldn't want to, we don't want to lose our independence. (Migrant organization director, Athens)

In terms of the effect of national context on the areas of activity of migrant organizations, the picture is more nuanced. There are some types of activities that appear to be conducted by many migrant organizations regardless of the national context. These include social and cultural activities, information sharing both in and between countries, and practical assistance for community members in both country of origin and country of settlement. These 'core' activities correspond remarkably closely to the key functions of migrant organizations originally identified by Rex almost 40 years ago (quoted in Rex and Josephides 1987, 19). The comparative analysis indicates that migrant organizations are flexible and innovative in identifying a range of resources available within the given opportunity structure in order to conduct these core activities, drawing on community resources, volunteers, and informal contacts, where external resources and formal support mechanisms are not available. This suggests that, relatively independently from the national context in which they are located, migrant organizations are characterized by two aspects. Firstly, they are able to function as transnational social spaces, in which 'diaspora consciousness' (Vertovec 1997) is shaped and maintained. Secondly, they are active in mobilizing a range of transnational resources, including linguistic and cultural knowledge, news and other information, and remittances, albeit usually on a small-scale, ad hoc basis.

At the same time, the comparative analysis draws attention to a number of differences between the activities of the organizations in the three countries. Beyond their 'core' activities, it appears that the areas of activity of migrant organizations are affected by the inter-related levels of the opportunity structure presented by the national context. Four patterns can be distinguished analytically, although these may co-exist in practice (Figure 4).

Firstly, when a state fails to meet the most fundamental needs of immigrants, it appears that migrant organizations undertake a *compensatory role*, attempting to fill in for inadequate state provision. It is evident from the above analysis that, because of the dysfunctional asylum system, migrant organizations and in particular refugee organizations in Greece play a more important role in meeting basic needs than their counterparts in the UK and the Netherlands. It was similarly observed that when benefits for asylum seekers were reduced in the UK over the previous decade, migrant organizations became increasingly involved in providing basic support (Griffiths, Sigona, and Zetter 2005). The long-term lobbying and campaigning by migrant organizations in Greece for a consultative body can also be seen as a response to addressing fundamentally inadequate provision for immigrant representation.

Secondly, where migrant organizations are incentivized by the state or other actors to conduct activities which do not otherwise correspond with their interests or priorities, they undertake a *co-opted role*. In the UK, a concern was expressed that migrant organizations were being co-opted when they were formally incorporated into unpopular dispersal arrangements (Griffiths, Sigona, and Zetter 2005). In the Netherlands the director of an umbrella organization felt that some migrant organizations were being co-opted into activities that reflected governmental and public prejudices about immigrants, such as the training about FGM.

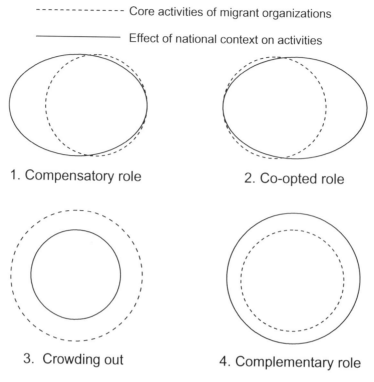

Figure 4. Effect of national context on the activities of migrant organizations.

Thirdly, if a state or other actors are very active in providing the services or activities that would otherwise be conducted by migrant organizations, then migrant organizations may become '*crowded out*', and their activities may decrease. The idea that the state can 'crowd out' civil society is longstanding in American scholarship (see Bloemraad 2005). One possible example of this is that migrant organizations in the Netherlands appeared to be less involved with language teaching than their counterparts in the UK and Greece, perhaps because they have been crowded out by the private organizations contracted to manage compulsory integration courses (Joppke 2007, 7).

Fourthly, when the existing interests or priorities of migrant organizations are supported by state actors, they play a *complementary role*. Examples of this are the support of initiatives of migrant organizations to help their families and communities in countries of origin through co-development programmes such as those developed in the UK and the Netherlands (de Haas 2006); and the support provided in the UK for 'supplementary schools' run by many migrant organizations, to support mainstream education. Such partnerships have the potential to build on the strengths of migrant organizations, including community knowledge, commitment and the ability to access 'hard to reach' groups, and to mitigate some of their frequent weaknesses, including limited resources and narrow perspectives (de Haas 2006). However, such complementarity requires shared goals and a basic level of trust between the migrant organization and the state or other sponsors as well as a minimum level of capacity on the part of migrant organizations. At present these conditions do not appear to exist in Greece and the current economic and political contexts are not likely to facilitate their development in the immediate future. Within this study, it is notable that, although both the UK and the Netherlands have recognized migrant organizations as complementary partners in their international development work, it is only in the context of the multicultural approach to migrant incorporation in the UK that migrant organizations have been involved on a wide scale in complementary initiatives in the country of settlement.

Of the four patterns identified, it is the complementary role which appears to have the most significant effect on the transnational engagement of migrant organizations, in terms of increasing the level of resources they are able to mobilize. The most obvious examples of this are the state-sponsored co-development programmes, which have enabled even very small migrant organizations to undertake moderate-sized development projects in countries of origin. Illustrative of this is the case of a Sudanese organization interviewed for this study, which was based in a Dutch city in which only four Sudanese families had been dispersed (and only two remained) and which had succeeded in building a school, library and training centre in Sudan through involvement in the Dutch co-development programme. Other research has documented an amplifying effect of sending states' development programmes, such as the Mexican *tres-por-uno* initiative to match emigrants' remittances with state funding (cited in Portes, Escobar, and Radford 2007, 27), but no examples of sending state-instigated complementary initiatives were identified in my study. Although less obvious, I would argue that complementary initiatives targeting migrants in countries of settlement, such as the state support for migrant organizations' educational activities in the UK, also increase the mobilization of transnational resources, since they draw on migrant organizations' understanding of their respective communities, deriving from their links with the country of origin, in order to achieve an impact in the country of settlement.

Conclusions

The comparative perspective of this research offers a number of insights into the ways in which migrant organizations and their transnational engagement are affected by national contexts. The rapid growth of migrant organizations in Greece, despite a lack of state support, complicates the argument that organizational proliferation is due to state sponsorship (Kelly 2003), or that 'too much and too little competition (from governments and others) leads to reduced organisational activity' (Schrover and Vermeulen 2005). A number of basic similarities between migrant organizations in Greece and their counterparts in contrasting national contexts point to the resilience and flexibility of these organizations. Nevertheless, national contexts have been found to affect patterns of proliferation, forms of institutional development, and the type of activities conducted, beyond certain 'core' activities. As a consequence, national contexts also affect the transnational engagement of migrant organizations. Although their ability to create transnational social spaces and mobilize various transnational resources relatively independently of the national context supports their characterization as important transnational actors, the scale of the resources mobilized appears to be greatly increased in contexts in which their activities are supported by states or other actors. This has not happened to date in Greece.

I conclude with an observation for further research in this field. Both literature and policy to date have focused on effects of the transnational resources mobilized by migrant organizations, on countries of origin. But, as this study emphasizes, migrant organizations also bring transnational resources to countries of settlement. As Faist (2008) has argued, a transnational perspective should consider the development role of migrant organizations in the country of settlement as well as in the country of origin. I suggest that the concept of 'human development', developed by Sen (1999), Nussbaum (2011) and others, lends itself to this purpose. The emphasis of this approach on the multi-dimensional nature of human well-being makes it appropriate for assessing the highly diverse activities of migrant organizations. Moreover, its location of development in the individual, rather than in one country or another, fits well with the transnational perspective. An asset – but also a challenge – of this approach is that it calls for an assessment of the transnational role of migrant organizations in the lives of individual migrants, a potentially fruitful avenue for future research.

Acknowledgements

I am grateful to the ESRC for funding the fieldwork on which this research is based, to Charles Watters for his supervisory support, to Sander Kramer and Mary Leontsini for their advice and input, and to Julie Vullnetari, Russell King and workshop participants for their constructive feedback on an earlier version of this paper presented at the IMISCOE Annual Conference in Amsterdam in August 2012.

Notes

1. Here I use this term to refer to formally established organizations that have been registered by, are led by, and primarily serve first- and/or second-generation immigrants, but excluding faith-based organizations and organizations of immigrants from EU countries.
2. In Greece, as in other countries, migrant organizations are as diverse as the individuals involved in them. Whilst keeping this diversity in mind, for analytical purposes it is necessary to look beyond the specificities of individual organizations with the aim of identifying trends at a sectoral level.
3. It should be noted, however, that respondents considered this source not to be entirely comprehensive, and that the number of formal organizations is likely to represent a small proportion of the overall associational activity of migrants in Greece, including informal women's networks, and unofficial Mosques and other religious groups.
4. In the UK this term is often used to refer to a broader category of organization, which includes many migrant organizations, but which is not limited to groups established by first- and/or second-generation immigrants.
5. This is a policy aiming to manage most asylum claims within a month, introduced by the Home Office in 2007.
6. Introduced in local government reforms in 2010, these include representatives of the municipality, migrant communities, and relevant NGOs, and have a consultative role on migrant integration issues.

References

Bennett, S., J. ter Wal, A. Lipiński, M. Fabiszak, and M. Krzyżanowski. 2011. *Migrants and media newsmaking practices*. Thematic report 2011/02: Media content for the 'Media for Diversity and Migrant Integration (MEDIVA)' Project. Florence: European University Institute.

Bloemraad, I. 2005. The limits of de Tocqueville: How government facilitates organizational capacity in newcomer communities. *Journal of Ethnic and Migration Studies* 31, no. 5: 865–87.

Bruquetas-Calleho, M., B. Garcés-Mascareñas, R. Penninx, and P. Scholten. 2007. Policy-making related to immigration and integration: The Dutch Case. IMISCOE Working Paper 15. Amsterdam: International Migration, Integration and Social Cohesion in Europe (IMISCOE).

Cabot, H. 2012. The governance of things: Documenting limbo in the Greek asylum procedure. *Political and Legal Anthropology Review* 35, no. 1: 11–29.

Council of Europe. 2010. Third party intervention by the Council of Europe Commissioner for Human Rights, under Article 36, paragraph 2, of the European Convention on Human Rights: 26494/09 Ahmed Ali v. the Netherlands and Greece. https://wcd.coe.int/wcd/ViewDoc.jsp?id=1595689 (accessed July 28, 2012).

de Bruyn, T. 2008. *Evaluation of Oxfam Novib's capacity building programme for diaspora organizations.* Study Commissioned by Oxfam and Novib. Leuven: Katholieke Universiteit Leuven.

de Haas, H. 2006. *Engaging Diasporas: How governments and development agencies can support diaspora involvement in the development of origin countries.* A study for Oxfam Novib. Oxford: University of Oxford, International Migration Institute.

Entzinger, H. 2000. The dynamics of integration policies: A multi-dimensional model. In *Challenging immigration and ethnic relations politics: Comparative European perspectives*, ed. R. Koopmans and P. Statham, 97–118. Oxford: Oxford University Press.

Evelyn Oldfield Unit. 2010. *Refugee and migrant community organisations in 2009.* London: Evelyn Oldfield Unit.

Faist, T. 1998. Transnational social spaces out of international migration: Evolution, significance and future prospects. *European Journal of Sociology* 39, no. 2: 213–47.

Faist, T. 2008. Migrants as transnational development agents: An inquiry into the newest round of the migration-development nexus. *Population, Space and Place* 14, no. 1: 21–42.

Glick Schiller, N., L. Basch, and C. Szanton Blanc. 1995. From immigrant to transmigrant: Theorizing transnational migration. *Anthropological Quarterly* 68, no. 1: 48–63.

Gold, S.J. 1992. *Refugee communities: A comparative field study.* London: Sage.

Griffiths, D., N. Sigona, and R. Zetter. 2005. *Refugee community organisations and dispersal: Networks, resources and social capital.* Bristol: Policy Press.

Gropas, R. 2008. *Ten years of Greek development co-operation and peace-building: Challenges and recommendations.* Initiative for Peace Building Capacity-Building Cluster, Country Case Study: Greece. Athens: Hellenic Foundation for European and Foreign Policy (ELIAMEP).

Gropas R., and A. Triandafyllidou. 2009. *Immigrants and political life in Greece: Between political patronage and the search for inclusion.* Policy Brief for EMILIE project. Athens: Hellenic Foundation for European and Foreign Policy (ELIAMEP).

Gropas R., and A. Triandafyllidou. 2005. Active civic participation of immigrants in Greece. POLITIS Research project. http://www.uni-oldenburg.de/politis-europe/9812.html.

Harokopio University. 2009. *Guide to NGOs and migrant associations: Profile of organizations in Greece active in migration issues.* Athens: Department of Geography, Harokopio University [in Greek].

Hein, J. 1997. Ethnic organizations and the welfare state: The impact of social welfare programs on the formation of Indochinese refugee associations. *Sociological Forum* 12, no. 2: 279–95.

Howard, M. 2010. The impact of the far right on citizenship policy in Europe: Explaining continuity and change. *Journal of Ethnic and Migration Studies* 36, no. 5: 735–51.

IOM. 2008. *Migration in Greece: A country profile 2008.* Geneva: International Organization for Migration.

Jenkins, S. 1988. *Ethnic associations and the welfare state: Services to immigrants in five countries.* New York, NY: Columbia University Press.

Joppke, C. 2007. Beyond national models: Civic integration policies for immigrants in Western Europe. *West European Politics* 30, no. 1: 1–22.

Kapllani, G., and N. Mai. 2005. Greece belongs to Greeks!: The case of the Greek flag in the hands of an Albanian student. In *The new Albanian migration*, ed. R. King, N. Mai, and S. Schwandner-Sievers, 153–72. Brighton: Sussex Academic Press.

Kelly, L. 2003. Bosnian refugees in Britain: Questioning community. *Sociology* 37, no. 1: 35–49.

Koopmans, R., P. Statham, M. Giugni, and F. Passy. 2005. *Contested citizenship: Immigration and cultural diversity in Europe*. Minneapolis, MN: University of Minnesota Press.

Kyriakou, N. 2009. *Minority participation in public life: The case of Greece*. Florence: European University Institute.

Leontsini, M. 2010. *Migrant women's organizations in Athens and multicultural democracy: Gender, social capital and social cohesion*. Athens: Department for Early Childhood Education.

MODA. 2010. *Migrant and minority community organisations: Funding, sustainability and ways forward*. London: Migrant Organisations' Development Agency (MODA).

Morales, L., and L. Jorba. 2010. The transnational practices of immigrants' associations in Spain. In *Diaspora and transnationalism: Concepts, theories and methods*, ed. R. Baubock and T. Faist, 267–94. Amsterdam: Amsterdam University Press.

Moya, J.C. 2005. Immigrants and associations: A global and historical perspective. *Journal of Ethnic and Migration Studies* 31, no. 5: 833–64.

National Equality Partnership. 2008. *Supporting equality groups: An overview of support to the diverse third sector in England*. London: National Equality Partnership.

Nijenhuis, G., and A. Zoomer. 2012. Transnational activities of immigrant organizations in the Netherlands: Do Ghanaian, Moroccan and Surinamese diaspora organizations enhance development? Paper presented at the Transnational Organizations Network, May 11–12, in Princeton, NJ.

Nussbaum, M. 2011. *Creating capabilities: The human development approach*. Cambridge, MA: Harvard University Press.

Phillimore, J., and L. Goodson. 2010. Failing to adapt: Institutional barriers to RCOs engagement in transformation of social welfare. *Social Policy and Society* 9, no. 2: 181–92.

Portes, A., C. Escobar, and W. Radford. 2007. Immigrant transnational organizations and development: A comparative study. *International Migration Review* 41, no. 1: 242–81.

Portes, A., L. Guarnizo, and P. Landolt. 1999. The study of transnationalism: Pitfalls and promise of an emergent research field. *Ethnic and Racial Studies* 22, no. 2: 217–37.

Refugee Council and Refugee Action. 2007. *Refugee community organizations in England: Realising potential*. London: Refugee Council and Refugee Action.

Rex, J. 1987. Introduction: The scope of a comparative study. In *Immigrant associations in Europe*, ed. J. Rex, D. Joly, and C. Wilpert, 1–10. Aldershot: Gower.

Rex, J., and S. Josephides. 1987. Asian and Greek Cypriot associations and identity. In *Immigrant associations in Europe*, ed. J. Rex, D. Joly, and C. Wilpert, 11–33. Aldershot: Gower.

Rutter, J. 1994. *Refugee children in the classroom*. Stoke-on-Trent: Trentham Books.

Sardinha, J. 2009. *Immigrant associations, integration and identity: Angolan, Brazilian and Eastern European communities in Portugal*. Amsterdam: Amsterdam University Press.

Schrover, M., and F. Vermeulen. 2005. Immigrant organizations: Introduction. *Journal of Ethnic and Migration Studies* 31, no. 5: 823–32.

Sen, A. 1999. *Development as freedom*. Oxford: Oxford University Press.

Sotiropoulos, D. 2004. Formal weakness and informal strength: Civil society in contemporary Greece. Discussion Paper 16. London: London School of Economics, Hellenic Observatory.

Soysal, N.S. 1994. *Limits of citizenship: Migrants and post-national membership in Europe*. Chicago, IL: The University of Chicago Press.

Spencer, S., and B. Cooper. 2006. *Social integration of migrants in Europe: A review of the European literature 2000–2006*. Oxford: COMPAS.

Temple, B., and R. Edwards. 2002. Interpreters/translators and cross-language research: Reflexivity and border crossings. *International Journal of Qualitative Methods* 1, no. 2: 1–12.

Temple, B., and R. Moran. 2006. *Doing research with refugees*. Bristol: The Policy Press.

Triandafyllidou, A., and M. Veikou. 2002. The hierarchy of Greekness: Ethnic and national identity considerations in Greek immigration policy. *Ethnicities* 2, no. 2: 189–208.

Van Heelsum, A. 2004. *Immigrant organizations in the Netherlands*. Utrecht: FORUM [in Dutch].

Vertovec, S. 1997. Three meanings of diaspora, exemplified among South Asian religions. *Diaspora* 6, no. 3: 277–99.

Vertovec, S. 1999. Conceiving and researching transnationalism. *Ethnic and Racial Studies* 22, no. 2: 447–62.

Voice4Change. 2007. *Bridge the gap: What is known about the BME third sector in England*. London: Voice4Change.

Watters, C., and R. Hossain. 2008. From policy to practice: The reception of asylum seekers in Europe. Report to the European Commission. Tenth European Conference on the Reception of Asylum Seekers, March 5–7, in Malta.

Wimmer, A., and N. Glick Schiller. 2002. Methodological nationalism and beyond: Nation-state building, migration and the social sciences. *Global Networks* 2, no. 4: 301–34.

Index

Note: Page numbers in **bold** type refer to figures
Page numbers in *italic* type refer to tables
Page numbers followed by 'n' refer to notes

Aarburg, H.P. von 107; and Gretler, S. 107
academic hierarchy: transnational 17
Academy of Sciences of Moldova (ASM) 34–6, 46n
activism 3, 108–9
actors 23, 39, 99n, 173; civil society 157; development 89; external 170; international 46, 88, 91, 99n; local 99n; national 46; non-state 90; political 116; state 172; transnational 13, 170
Ad-Astra Network 33
Adriatic Sea 11
Africa 167
African Cultural Festival 163
Age of Migration, The (Castles and Miller) 2
aid: foreign 90; international development initiatives 88; social 57
Albania 1, 8, 12–13, 72, 148–9; Tirana 137n
alliances: political 168–9
Ambrosetti, E.: Cela, E. and Fokkema, T. 4, 10, 71–85
Amelina, A. 4, 9, 17–31
Amsterdam (Netherlands) 169
antagonism 13, 147–8, 152
anthropological epistemology 122
anthropology 143–4; classical 150
anti-discrimination 165
anti-immigrant nationalism 168
anti-immigrant parties 169
areas of activity of migrant organizations in Greece 160–1, **161**
ASM-EPFL research project 46n
asylum seekers 11, 106, 117n, 159, 164–5, 171
Athens (Greece) 159, 163, 168–9
austerity measures 142
Australia 8, 108
Austria 12, 123, 126, 132–5
authority: collective 134; hegemonic patriarchal 133; patriarchal 133, 134

Babić, B. 11, 87–101
Balkans 103–5, 109
Ban, C. 54–5
Barth, F. 150
Baylina, M.: *et al.* 51
behaviour: transnational 75–6, 76–9, *76*
Belarus 18
Belgium 108
Belgrade (Serbia) 108
Berlin Wall (Germany) 7, 72
Bernat, J.S.: and Viruela, R. 67
Bielenin-Lenczowska, K. 136
Binder, S.: and Tošić, J. 150
Bistrita valley 10, 57, **58**
Black and Minority Ethnic (BME) organizations 162
Bleahu, A.: *et al.* 61
Boccagni, P. 3–4
Bojičić-Dželilović, V.: and Wittman, A. 99n
borderland countries 2
Bosnia and Herzegovina (BiH) 8, 11, 87–101, 126; Goražde 92–7; Srebrenica 94–5; Teslić 93–7
Bourdieu, P. 17, 21–3; field theory 17, 21–3
brain circulation 20
brain drain theory 20
Brazil 151
Brettell, B.C. 145, 150–1
Brunnbauer, U. 3
Brusa, M.M. 117n
Brussels (Belgium) 67
Bulgaria 14n, 19, 54
Burawoy, M. 52–3

Calmy-Rey, M. 106
Cape Verde 72
capital: social 38, 146
capitalism 6, 51; Western 52

INDEX

Čapo Žmegač, J. 123
Castello (Italy) 66–7
Castles, S. 141; and Kosack, G. 52
categorical power 17–31
categorization: class-related 26–7; gendered 23; social 24, 29
Catholics 77, 80–1
Cela, E.: Fokkema, T. and Ambrosetti, E. 4, 10, 71–85
Center for Local Development and Diaspora (CLDD) 11
Chile 72
China 37
Christians: Orthodox 77, 80–1
Christou, A. 150–1; and King, R. 144
Cingolani, P. 82
circular mobility 19
citizenship 2, 12, 66, 106, 123, 158, 165–6; dual 3
civil society 89–91, 161; actors 157; Greek 165–7
civilization 131
Clarke, J. 13, 157–77
class 54; hierarchy 21; inequality 24
class-related categorizations 26–7
classic migration model (Hirschman) 52
classical anthropology 150
classical assimilation theory 73
Coe, N.: *et al.* 51
Cola, M. 117n
collective authority 134
collectivization 55
Colombia 34
Combinatul de fire si fibre sintetice Savinesti (CFS) 57–9
Commonwealth of Independent States (CIS) 40
community: ethnic 124; immigrant 105, 116, 168; international 99n; knowledge 38; local 93, 122, 127–37; migrant 105, 116, 146, 174n; religious 124; transnational 146
Constantin, D.L.: *et al.* 66
consumerism 150
consumption 142
control variables 77–8
cooperation actions: of skilled Moldovans abroad *43*, 44
credibility 159
Croatia 2, 8, 97
cross-border mobility 9, 17–23, 29
cross-border science 17–31
cultural activities 163
cultural identity 3
cultural minority 166
cultural modernity 115
Czechoslovakia 19

Dahinden, J. 103, 107
Danciu, A.R.: *et al.* 66

Dannecker, P. 5
Dayton Peace Agreement (1995) 87
de-industrializing urban space: self-employment in 60–1, **60**
democracy 158
Democratic Union of the Centre 118n
democratization 88
departures: from northeast Romania 61–2, **62**
destination countries: Romanian immigrants 62–4, **63**
developing countries 33, 75
development impact 42–4
Di-LoK (Dani lokalnog razvoja i dijaspore) 91–2, 97
diaspora 45, 97, 104, 111, 115–17; consciousness 171; emerging 41; Kosovar 105; scientific 4, 9
discrimination 74, 81, 82n, 110–11, 115, 125; anti- 165
diversity 174n
dual citizenship 3

Easyjet 113
École Polytechnique Fédérale de Lausanne (EPFL) 46n
economic crisis 141–55, 169
economic development 9, 27, 89–90, 94, 142–3, 146–50
economic growth 5, 20, 45, 66
economic integration 82n
economic liberalization 89
economic marginalization 111
economic power 136
economic/financial support 107–8
economy: knowledge-based 37; market-oriented 126; Marxist political 6; post-socialist 64
educational attainment 82n
educational background 147, *147*
emerging diaspora 41
emigration 1–2, 6–12, 14n, 19–26, 33–4, 71, 124–7, 143; mass 34, 41
employment: of Albanians in Greece 147–8, *148*
empowerment 91–2
engagement: transnational 170–3
England 133, 160
entrepreneurs: ethnic 148
equality: gender 27
ethnic Albanian identity 115
ethnic categorizations 23
ethnic communities 124
ethnic entrepreneurs 148
ethnic groups 106, 121, 161
ethnic identification 151
ethnic labelling 25, 151
ethnic minority 166
ethnic rivalry 147

INDEX

ethnic tensions 138n
ethnicity 3, 12, 17, 23–4, 79–81, 150; Albanian 124
ethnicization 24–6; paradoxical 9; self- 24–6
Europe 17–20, 43, 51, 66, 74–5, 131, 142–4; Eastern 73; Western 40–1, 60–2, 92, 99n, 108, 121, 126
European Commission 66
European Common Market (ECM) 6
European Neighbourhood Policy (ENP) 36
European Research Area (ERA) 36
European Stability Initiative (ESI) 108
European Union (EU) 1, 7, 17–18, 36, 64, 137, 165–6, 174n; FP7 Programme 45; Moldova Mobility Partnership 36
external actors 170

Facebook 114
Faist, T. 73, 81, 157–8, 174
faith-based organizations 174n
family: development projects 141; formation 127
Favell, A.: and Hansen, R. 66
FDI (foreign direct investment) 56, 66
female genital mutilation (FGM) 164, 171
feminism: socialist 27, 28
Ferguson, J.: and Gupta, A. 150
Fibrex Nylon 59
field theory (Bourdieu) 17, 21–3
financial remittances 121, 129
Fokkema, T.: Ambrosetti, E. and Cela, E. 4, 10, 71–85; and de Haas, H. 38, 132
foreign aid 90
France 6, 42–4, 62–4, 126
Freeman, G.P. 52
friendship ties 127
Frykman, M.J.: Vullnetari, J. and King, R. 1–16

Gaugas, P. 36
gender: equality 27; inequality 14n
gendered categorizations 23
geographic mobility 17, 20
geopolitics 2; global 6
Germany 6–9, 35, 62–4, 93–4, 107–8, 118n, 126, 133–5; Berlin Wall 7, 72
Giorguli Saucedo, S.: and Itzigsohn, J. 74, 81
Giugni, M.: et al. 158, 166–7
Glick Schiller, N.: and Levitt, P. 21, 123; and Wimmer, A. 158
global geopolitics 6
globalization 72
Goražde (BiH) 92–7
Goschin, Z.: et al. 66
governability 46
grassroots organizations 163
Greece 1, 7–10, 13, 14n, 51, 62, 72; Labour Force Survey 147; National Centre for Social Research (EKKE) 141; National Welfare Institute (IKA) 147

Greek identity 142
Greek Orthodoxy 166
Gretler, S.: and von Aarburg, H.P. 107
Grigoras, V.: et al. 61
Gropas, R.: and Triandafyllidou, A. 165
gross domestic product (GDP) 4, 8, 35–6, 90, 107
Guarnizo, L.E.: Portes, A. and Haller, W. 81; and Smith, M.P. 52
Gupta, A.: and Ferguson, J. 150

Haas, H. de 6, 39, 98, 122, 129; and Fokkema, T. 38, 132
Haller, W.: Guarnizo, L.E. and Portes, A. 81
Hansen, R.: and Favell, A. 66
ul Haq, M. 5
Harokopio University (Greece) 160–6
hegemonic patriarchal authority 133
Hemming, A. 136, 149
heterogeneity 122
hierarchization 28–9
hierarchy 17–31; class 21; transnational academic 17
Hirschman, A. 52–4; classic migration model 52
Hoffmann, B. 52
Hossain, R.: and Watters, C. 167
host countries 40–2
human capital 33–4, 37–8, 41, 46, 129
human development 99n, 174
Human Development Index (HDI, UNDP) 5, 8, 14n, 35
human rights 165
Hungary 19, 61
hybrid mobility 3

identification: self- 150–1
identity: Albanian 132, 142; cultural 3; Greek 142; national 166; self- 144; transnational 158
IMF (International Monetary Fund) 54–5, 59, 66–7
IMISCOE (International Migration Integration and Social Cohesion in Europe) 2
immigrant community 105, 116, 168
immigrant organizations 169
immigration 1, 13, 20–6, 57, 71–2, 141, 157–9, 167; mass 71; probationary 41
income: personal 82n
India 37
individualization 137
industrialization 125; socialist 57
industrialized countries 33
inequality 21–8, 98; class 24; gender 14n; social 18–24, 28
initial migratory phase (mid 1960s to mid 1980s) 131
instability: political 111

INDEX

integration: social 2, 145
Integrometro survey (2008–9) 10, 71–7, 81
inter-state translocality 123
interlinkages 73–5
internally displaced persons (IDP) 87, 93–5
international actors 46, 88, 91, 99n
international community 99n
international development aid initiatives 88
international migration 20, 37, 82; of scientists 18–21
International Organization for Migration (IOM) 35, 110
international organizations 89
internationalization 109
Internet 115
interpersonal networks 22
Iran 72
Ireland 64, 67
Iron Curtain 17–20
irregular migration 72
Iseni, B. 11–12, 103–19
Israel 35, 61–2
Italy 10, 51, 59–62, 134, 146; Castello 66–7
Itzigsohn, J.: and Giorguli Saucedo, S. 74, 81
Ivanova, M.N. 53–4

Janeska, V. 138n
Japan 95
Jorba, L.: and Morales, L. 157

Kcarney, M. 146
Kiev (Ukraine) 19, 25–8
King, R. 72; and Christou, A. 144; Frykman, M.P. and Vullnetari, J. 1–16; and Vullnetari, J. 149
kinship ties 126–7, 131
knowledge communities 38
knowledge-based economy 37
Koopmans, R.: et al. 158, 166–7
Kosack, G.: and Castles, S. 52
Kosovar diaspora 105
Kosovo 9–12, 103–15, 118n, 125–6
Kosovo Liberation Army (KLA) 11, 109
Kramer, S. 159

labelling: ethnic 25, 151
labour: migration 37, 41, 52, 71; mobility 121, 124; mobilization 54
Labour Force Survey (Greece) 147
Labrianidis, L.: et al. 51
Latin American dependency theory 6
Leeds (UK) 164
legalization 56
legitimacy 54
Leontsini, M. 159
Levitt, P. 3, 146; and Glick Schiller, N. 21, 123
liberalization: economic 89; wage 54
liberty 133

life-course 64–5
Likert scale 144
links: transnational 42–4
local actors 99n
local community 93, 122, 127–37
local municipality 92–8
local society 46
London (UK) 162, 169
low-skilled service sector 72

Macedonia 4, 8, 11–12, 103–10, 113; Struga **128**, 129, **130**, 136; Tetovo 110, 124, 129
Maghreb states 6
Mandel, R. 151
marginalization: economic 111
market-oriented economy 126
Markov, I. 4, 12, 121–40
marriage 136
Marxist political economy 6
mass emigration 34, 41
mass immigration 71
material remittances 152
materialism 51
Mediterranean countries 7; non-EEC 6
Meeus, B. 1, 51–70
membership: transnational 22
Mexican New York (Smith) 3
Michail, D. 12–13, 14n
micro-states 8
Middle East 167
migrant community 105, 116, 146, 174n
Migrant Integration Councils 168
migrants: transnational ties 106–9
migration: determinants 40–2
Migration and Remittances Factbook (World Bank) 8
migration-development interactions 122
migration-development nexus 6, 11, 87–101
Mihai, A.: et al. 61
minority: ethnic 166; groups 35
mixed marriages 136
mobility 6–7, 18, 28, 37, 51, 62–6, 142; circular 19; cross-border 9, 17–23, 29; geographic 17, 20; hybrid 3; labour 121, 124; scientific 9, 29n; short-term 17–19; social 18, 23, 65, 116, 147; transnational 9
mobilization 34, 67, 110, 115, 173; labour 54; political 52, 107–9; transnational political 52; working-class 54
modernity: cultural 115
modernization 125; theory 150
Moldova 1, 8–10, 18, 72
Moldovan Diaspora Congress 47n
Montenegro 11, 103, 106
Mora, M. 67
Morales, L.: and Jorba, L. 157
morality 133
Morocco 72

INDEX

Moscow (Russia) 137n
Mosques 174n
motivation 141–55
MSN 115
multi-locality of professional commitments 21–2
municipalities 92–5, 98, 129, 174n; local 92–8; rural 92
Muslims 77, 80–1, 125, 137n

nation-building 26
nation-state 18–20, 26–8, 53, 123, 151
national actors 46
National Centre for Social Research (EKKE, Greece) 141
national cleavage structure 166
national context effect: on activities of migrant organizations 171, **172**
National Human Development Report 35
national identity 166
National Institute of Statistics 72
National Welfare Institute (IKA, Greece) 147
nationalism 3, 52, 123; anti-immigrant 168
nationalities 12, 71–2, 114, 123, 158
NATO (North Atlantic Treaty Organization) 110
naturalization 106, 110
neo-Marxism 6
neoliberal era 10
neoliberal ideologies 90
neoliberal principles 51
neoliberalism 55–7; Romanian 51–4
Netherlands 13, 157–68, 171–3; Amsterdam 169; Union of Refugee Organizations (VON) 161
networks: social 12, 21, 39, 52, 114, 122, 123, 131; transnational 53; transterritorial 137
New Asylum Model (2007) 164
NGO (non-governmental organization) 13, 91, 159–64, 168, 174n
Nieswand, B. 135–6
Nijenuis, G.: and Zoomer, A. 160–2
non-corporeal communication 4
non-migrants 121
non-state actors 90
North America 8, 40–1, 108
nostalgia 112
Nussbaum, M. 174

OECD (Organization for Economic Co-operation and Development) 36
Ohrid Agreement (2001) 138n
organizations: faith-based 174n; grassroots 163; immigrant 169; international 35, 89, 110; migrant (Greece) 160–73, **160**; non-governmental (NGOs) 13, 91, 159–64, 168, 174n; refugee 163, 171; umbrella 168, 171
Orthodox Christians 77, 80–1

Pakistan 165
paradoxical ethnicization 9

PARE 1+1 programme 47n
Passy, F.: *et al.* 158, 166–7
patriarchal authority 133, 134
patriarchal society 133
patriarchy 12
patriotism 3, 112
peace-building 88
permanent migration 17–18
personal income 82n
Philippines 72
Piatra-Neamt (Romania) 57–61
Pichler, R. 12, 123
Piore, M.J. 52
pluralism 10
plutocracy 169
Poland 19, 72, 80
Polanyi, K. 52
political activism 3, 108–9
political actors 116
political alliances 168–9
political instability 111
political mobilization 52, 107–9
political stability 33, 46
populations: transnational Albanian-speaking 103–19
Porcescu, S.: Tejada, G. and Varzari, V. 4, 9, 33–49
Portes, A.: Haller, W. and Guarnizo, L.E. 81
Portugal 6–7, 10, 51
post-socialist economy 64
post-socialist era 9
post-Yugoslav decade 126–7
post-Yugoslavia 1
poverty 6, 14n, 35, 107–8, 168
power: categorical 17–31; economic 136; relations 29n; symbolic 26; of unions 54–5
Presevo Valley (Serbia) 106–10, 113
prestige 135–6, 145
Principal Components Analysis (PCA) 75–7
private organizations 172
private sector 147
privatization 56–60, 89
pro-immigrant public discourse 169, **170**
probationary immigration 41
productivity 129
public discourse: pro-immigrant 169, **170**
public services 55

Radu, C.: *et al.* 61
realization: self- 152
Refugee Action 160
Refugee Council 160
refugees 11, 106, 159; organizations 163, 171
relations: transnational 104
religious communities 124
religious groups 174n
remittances 5, 13, 148; material 152; social 5, 12, 152

183

INDEX

Republika Srpska 11, 91–4
research and development (R&D) 36
residence 71–85; duration 80
resilience 141–55
rivalry: ethnic 147
Romania 10, 14n, 19, 33, 51–7, **58**, 72
Romanian neoliberalism 51–4; Third Way 56
Rugova, I. 109
rural areas 107, 125
rural municipality 92
Russia 18–19, 35; Moscow 137n
Rutter, J. 162

salaried workers: in Romanian northwest 57, **58**
Samers, M. 52
Sandu, D.: *et al.* 61
Sardinha, J. 158
Savinesti platform 57–60
Saxenian, A. 38
Schengen countries 62
scientific diasporas 4, 9
scientific mobility 9, 29n
seasonal sector 72
second-generation migrants 141, 150–2
segmented assimilation theory 73
segregation: spatial 53
self-employment: in de-industrializing urban
    space 60–1, **60**
self-ethnicization 24–6
self-identification 150–1
self-identity 144
self-realization 152
Sen, A. 5, 174
Senegal 72
Serban, M.: *et al.* 61
Serbia 8, 11, 103–6, 125; Belgrade 108;
    Presevo Valley 106–10, 113
service sector: low-skilled 72
services: public 55
Shaqiri, X. 118n
short-term mobility 17–19
skilled Moldovans 33–49, *43*
Skype 115
Slovenia 2, 8, 124
Smith, A.: *et al.* 51
Smith, M.P.: and Guarnizo, L.E. 52
Smith, R.C. 3
social activities 163
social aid 57
social capital 38, 146
social categorization 24, 29
social development 9
social fields: transnational 123
social groups 146
social inequality 18–24, 28
social integration 2, 145
social mobility 18, 23, 65, 116, 147
social movements theory 158

social networks 12, 21, 39, 52, 114; theory 12
social order 18
social relations 22–4, 123, 135
social remittances 5, 12, 121–2, 152
social spaces: transnational 171–3
social status 121, 135–6, 145, 152
social welfare 56–7
socialism 25, 55, 61, 65; state 53
socialist feminism 27
socialist feminist ideology 28
socialist ideals 125
socialist industrialization 57
socialist period 125–6
socialization 113
society: civil 89–91, 157, 161, 165–7; local 46;
    patriarchal 133
socio-cultural and economic integration 76–7, *77*
socio-economic development 44
Soviet ideology 27
Soviet Union 7–8, 25–6
Spain 7, 10, 51, 62–7
spatial segregation 53
Srebrenica (BiH) 94–5
stability: political 33, 46
stabilization 110
Stalin, J. 137n
state actors 172
state socialism 53
Statham, P.: *et al.* 158, 166–7
Statistical Package for Social Sciences (SPSS)
    145
status: social 145, 152
stigmatization 99n
Stockholm (Sweden) 87–8, 91–2
Struga (Macedonia) **128**, 129, **130**, 136
Sudan 173
super-tenants 67n
sustainability 38
Sweden 11, 91–3, 96–7, 99n, 126; Stockholm
    87–8, 91–2
Switzerland 6, 11–12, 123, 126, 135
symbolic power 26

technocrats 55–6
Tejada, G.: Varzari, V. and Porcescu, S. 4, 9,
    33–49
tensions: ethnic 138n
tertiary sector 72
Teslić (BiH) 93–7
Tetovo (Macedonia) 110, 124, 129
Third Way neoliberalism (Romania) 56
Tilly, C. 24
Tirana (Albania) 137n
Tito, J.B. 137n
Torche, D. 110
Tošić, J.: and Binder, S. 150
Toth, A.: *et al.* 61
trade unions 169

INDEX

transition countries 33
translocality 4; inter-state 123
transmigrants 123
Transnational Villagers, The (Levitt) 3
transnationalism 122–3, 143–4, 158
transnationality changes 104
transnationalization 21–2
transterritorial networks 137
transterritoriality 4
Treaty of Rome (1957) 6
Triandafyllidou, A.: and Gropas, R. 165
Tseng, Y.F. 151
Tunisia 72
Turkey 6, 61, 95, 137n
typology 73–4, 81, 145

Ukraine 1, 8–9, 72, 80
umbrella organizations 168, 171
Union of Refugee Organizations (VON, Netherlands) 161
United Kingdom (UK) 13, 64, 67, 157–68, 171–3, 174n; Leeds 164; London 162, 169
United Nations Development Programme (UNDP) 5–6, 89; Human Development Index (HDI) 5, 8, 14n, 35
United Nations High Commissioner for Refugees (UNHCR) 89, 99n, 165
United Nations Mission in Kosovo (UNMIK) 117n
United Nations (UN) 2, 6, 14n
United States of America (USA) 3, 34–5, 64, 74, 81, 108, 135, 137n, 144
University of Lugano (Switzerland) 104, 111
unproductive sectors 55
urbanization 57
USSR 27

Van Heelsum, A. 160–1
Varzari, V.: Porcescu, S. and Tejada, G. 4, 9, 33–49
Vathi, Z. 151
Verdery, K. 67n
Vertovec, S. 143, 158
Vietnam 72
Viruela, R.: and Bernat, J.S. 67
Vullnetari, J.: and King, R. 149; King, R. and Frykman, M.P. 1–16

wage liberalization 54
Watters, C.: and Hossain, R. 167
welfare 51–70; regimes 18; social 56–7; system 57
well-being 4–5, 129, 135 6, 142 3, 147, 174
West 25, 43, 52, 64–5, 126
Western capitalism 52
Western Europe 40–1, 60–2, 92, 99n, 108, 121, 126
Wimmer, A.: and Glick Schiller, N. 158
Wittman, A.: and Bojičić-Dželilović, V. 99n
Women's Day 163
work: migrants 51–79
work migration: motivations over life course 64–5, **65**
working-class mobilization 54
World Bank 6, 55, 66, 89–91, 107; *Migration and Remittances Factbook* 8
World War II (1939–45) 125
world-systems theory 20

Yugoslavia 1–2, 6–7, 11, 72, 99n, 103–6, 121, 125–6; post- 1

Zoomer, A.: and Nijenhuis, G. 160–2